MODELING & VISUALIZING
INTERIORS

AutoCAD Release 13 & 13c4

KINGSLEY K. WU
Purdue University
West Lafayette, Indiana

Prentice Hall
Upper Saddle River, New Jersey 07458

Library of Congress Cataloging-in-Publication Data

Wu, Kingsley K.
    Modeling and visualizing interiors : AutoCAD Release 13 and 13c4 /
Kingsley K. Wu
      p.   cm.
    Includes index.
    ISBN 0-13-530932-8
    1. AutoCAD (Computer file).   2. Architectural drawing—Data
processing—Programmed instruction.   3. Computer-aided design—
Programmed instruction.   I. Title.
NA2728.W8
720'.2855369—dc21   97-13768
                                                        CIP

Acquisitions Editor: Elizabeth Sugg
Editorial Production Services: WordCrafters Editorial Services, Inc.
Managing Editor: Mary Carnis
Director of Production and Manufacturing: Bruce Johnson
Prepress Manufacturing Buyer: Ed O'Dougherty
Marketing Manager: Danny Hoyt
Editorial Assistant: Emily Jones
Cover Designer: Miguel Ortiz
Cover Illustration: Kingsley K. Wu
Printer/Binder: Banta, Menasha, WI

©1998 by Prentice-Hall, Inc.
Simon & Schuster/a Viacom Company
Upper Saddle River, NJ 07458

Printed in the United States of America

10 9 8 7 6 5 4 3 2 1

ISBN 0-13-530932-8

Prentice-Hall International (UK) Limited, *London*
Prentice-Hall of Australia Pty. Limited, *Sydney*
Prentice-Hall Canada, Inc., *Toronto*
Prentice-Hall Hispanoamericana, *Mexico*
Prentice-Hall of India Private Limited, *New Delhi*
Prentice-Hall of Japan, *Tokyo*
Simon & Schuster Asia Pte. Ltd., *Singapore*
Editora Prentice-Hall do Brasil, Ltda., *Rio de Janeiro*

For Susan and her father, Mr. Tai Hing Au.

PREFACE

For people who are in architecture, interior design, and other constructive professions, there exists an innate curiosity to find out how things are built and a desire to examine building details close up. For these people, it is most exasperating if they cannot look under furniture or behind walls to see how materials come together. Besides overall spatial qualities, and beyond the look of surface finishes, it is how an opening in a wall is trimmed or how a corner is turned on a table top that gives satisfaction to the practiced eye of the professional designer.

The same frustration arises from reading books about design and its components. Many show how to create simple, basic shapes, but do not go beyond to deal with realistic forms. Many books show pictures of sophisticated projects that are already built. You, the reader, are left to wonder: "Well, how did they DO that? " I tried to address this problem in my first book, *Freehand Sketching in the Architectural Environment* (VNR, 1990). In it, I had many of the sketches reproduced in full size relative to the original drawings. Readers can see the marker pen strokes in full scale, so they can replicate the way the hand has to move, and the amount of pressure to put on the nib, in order to achieve the resultant texture and feeling of the individual strokes that make up a finished drawing. So with this book, I am carrying on the intention to show how realistic architectural interiors are built from simple, basic entities.

However, design is ultimately a creative process, ever evolving and never satisfying all requirements for all times. Similar to those other basic elements—atoms, genes, and molecules—that make up our life form, there is an infinite variety of possibilities and combinations in the way the elements come together to form a whole building.

Having infinite possibilities is not necessarily an asset when it comes to design; it is really an excess. There can simply be too many open possibilities and that leads to confusion. For one of the most difficult aspects of the design process is the coming together of concept and technique: what to do and how to do it. Now, designing through the computer adds to, and lessens, the difficulty, for the computer provides both limitations and promises. The computer is, after all, a machine. It does what it is told to do and it can only do what it is told to do. However, beyond its limitations, it can give you fantastic views of your design from any angle and virtually in all colors. It does this instantly, tirelessly, and unerringly. It can show you obvious mistakes and bring out aspects of your design you have never even considered.

So the computer is a tool with which you can look closely at details. In examining details and techniques, one can gain a better understanding of the whole.

The architectural examples in this book are meant to be demonstrative environments. They show a sequence of steps in using the computer to design, but they are not meant to be the final word on either design or the use of the computer. Read the book and work through the tutorials. You will understand an important tool and refine your design sensitivity as well.

This book is not an endorsement of, nor do I receive any financial support from, the manufacturers of any of the computer hardware or software mentioned. These products are used primarily because of my familiarity with them through more than a decade of teaching their use in the classroom.

Prentice Hall, the publisher, and I, the author, cannot guarantee that the hardware and software will always work as detailed in this book.

ACKNOWLEDGMENTS

I must first thank my dean, David Caputo, now president of Hunter College, for asking the initial question: "Why don't you do a book on CAD?" That was five years ago.

Special thanks also to our expert reviewers: John Eric Peaslee, University of Alabama; William Kobrynich, Art Institute of Fort Lauderdale; and Patricia Viard, Western Michigan University.

Many thanks to Mary and John McGrath for their support; to Jim Motonaga of Philpotts and Associates for helping out; to my colleagues: Gary Bertoline, Alan Mehringer, Dennis Short for good technical advice and support; to Jeff Carr of Aidex Corporation for answers to my many questions about AutoCAD: to my students: Heather Carter, Natasha Eaker, Alicia Kline, and Jennifer Schnabel for the initial reading and going through some of the tutorials in bits and pieces.

I must thank all the good folks at Prentice Hall: Marianne Frasco, Emily Jones, Lisa Nash, and Charles Viola; to Miguel Ortiz for the cover design; to Elizabeth Sugg, Acquisitions Editor, for accepting and managing this project. Special thanks go to Laura Cleveland of WordCrafters for thoughtful copyediting and thorough production management. I hope it has been as enjoyable for you as it has been for me.

And my appreciation goes to my family: Susan and Chauncey for their patience and moral support.

NOTICE TO THE READER

TRADEMARKS

CONTENTS

Chapter 4   EXERCISES AND TUTORIALS   87

ABOUT THE BOOK

PREMISE

In the fast-changing world of computer technology, there is a myriad of enhanced programs, specialized applications, and add-on modules as soon as a software program or a piece of hardware becomes popular. Amidst all the hype and hyperboles, it is very difficult to decide on what you should acquire, if anything, to allow you to do your job. It is the premise of this book that, if you really know how to use the capabilities of a standard set of software, you can better select enhancements, specialized features, and third-party developments.

Most people use computers by learning just what they need to know to get started and then picking up additional skills as they go along. There is no need for a thorough knowledge of all the capabilities of a set of software to begin. Using a set of software for computer-aided design (CAD) is not any different.

Design, however, is a generic term encompassing numerous disciplines that have their own subcultures. Design is also a creative process that is infinitely variable. There is, after all, no perfect design and no one way to arrive at design solutions. There are also a number of methods and innumerable angles from which to view a design. This book will concentrate on those aspects of architecture concerning the creation and visualization of interior spaces.

The typical user's manual or instructional book shows abstract, simple examples that are disjointed, leaving you to piece together disparate information spread over several volumes. Even publications that deal with a specific discipline, such as architecture, typically cover a wide range of subjects from hardware configuration to project management. For the actual designer who wants to ideate through the computer, there is not a lot of training material for learning how to create realistic objects for visualization.

This book shows the creation of specific three-dimensional objects and interior spaces within the building. It takes you through the building of a design project by a sequence of steps from two-dimensional floor plan to three-dimensional visualization, from simple to complex detailing, from basic colors to textured surfaces, and from wireframe block plane viewing to fully rendered pictures. The tutorials advance sequentially in complexity, but can be used separately, depending on your familiarity with the software and your need for refreshing skills in CAD.

This book goes beyond mere drafting. It delves into the use of CAD as a design tool for checking three-dimensional design characteristics, proportions, the interaction of solids and voids, and into full photorealistic renderings.

It is assumed that you have the appropriate hardware and software running properly. It also assumes you have knowledge of the basic form of the software. See the discussion of AutoCAD-related matters in the section on mannerisms and the chapter on essentials (Chapter 3).

RATIONALE

There are several major computer-aided design (CAD) software programs for general drafting and design purposes. Historically, they developed from such professions as mechanical engineering. For each of these programs, many publications deal with their installation, configuration, and basic application. Since sophisticated CAD programs, such as the one used in this book, tend to be flexible, they can be used in many design disciplines. Publications about the programs, to varying degrees, are broad, general manuals covering application in several professional fields. The result is that they cite rather basic, generic examples. For those who are looking for applied solutions in their professions, far fewer references are available.

In the architectural professions—city planning, landscape architecture, interior design, and others—there is widespread acceptance of CAD. This is especially so for complex, contract, commercial projects, where the volume of drawings and other documents tends to be large. Rapid development of powerful hardware allows the use of increasingly sophisticated CAD software. AutoCAD is a general computer-aided drafting and design program based on the desktop microcomputer that has been widely adopted by those in architecture.

A number of software programs have been developed to serve the architectural design market. Some of the programs are highly specialized for specific applications such as mechanical systems planning and engineering. Others make the layout of kitchens and baths readily accessible. There are also numerous third-party-developed add-on or enhancement programs to the basic version of AutoCAD, because AutoCAD is so widely used in the field and in so many applications.

Even in architecture, aside from the major areas of design, there are many subareas: planning, managing materials databases, project scheduling, and so on. Since it can handle many of these areas, most publications about AutoCAD try to cover all the areas, resulting in books that may be comprehensive, but not very thorough beyond giving simple and general examples.

The vast number of software enhancements and publications provide a picture so confusing that there is a need for detailed instructions on how to realize specific examples of architectural models created from using the standard version of AutoCAD Release 13.

Therefore, this book is not a comprehensive manual covering every aspect of AutoCAD. It is restricted to the areas of designing, detailing, and rendering interior architectural spaces and components.

The book contains a selective review of necessary steps, with detailed examples of applied tasks to create solid models. It shows the criteria for selecting certain variables to set up naturalistic perspective viewpoints. And it demonstrates the use of the software's capabilities for photorealistic renderings. This book shows the use of the three-dimensional database for viewing and checking on design concepts and ideas for the interiors of a medium-sized commercial building.

As design and, to a lesser extent, detailing are creative endeavors, there is usually a reluctance on the part of book writers or instructors to be specific about how to create an item, be it a space or a piece of furniture. A general deficit exists, therefore, in the way of applied instructions about how to go about creating something, because too many variables are involved.

Now, this book is not an attempt to tell you how to create; the examples given are not meant to be end products in themselves. They are meant to be guideposts. The tutorials give specific methods and approaches that you can use to apply to your own designs.

Manufacturers tend to push high-end, sophisticated software and hardware. Often it is difficult to continuously upgrade equipment every few months. This book shows how to use the resources already in the software so that you can better decide on whether or not to acquire other enhancements.

ORGANIZATION

This book reviews selected AutoCAD R13 functions and commands, particularly those pertaining to 3D modeling and visualization that are used in the tutorials. The text goes beyond standard manuals provided by the manufacturer. It offers in-depth discussion, practical tips, and caveats. It is followed by a discussion and explanation on the use of the AutoVision R2 rendering software.

A series of exercises and tutorials demonstrates the use of AutoCAD and AutoVision software.

AutoCAD R13 solid modeling is different from R12 and its companion, AME (Advanced Modeling Extension). Many of the capabilities of AME have been incorporated into R13, but R13 regards solid objects differently. Some of the very fundamental commands of AME are not present in R13. If you are used to working with AME, you will have to change the way you think about building and editing 3D objects with R13.

The exercises and tutorials in Chapter 5 demonstrate the use of 3D modeling techniques. The tutorials use the first floor of a hypothetical bank. They show step-by-step buildup of a building interior beyond a two-dimensional floor plan drawn on the computer. The tutorials show some of the ways simple and complex spaces are constructed in solid geometry. They demonstrate various ways of viewing the interior spaces.

Tutorial 1 is of a customer seating and lounge area near the conference room used for the next tutorial. It is in an area at the end of a two-story lobby. Although the furnishings are quite simple, the space is rather complex and dramatic.

To visualize the space realistically on the computer, you need to draw a good deal of the rest of the building. Hence, Tutorial 1 is not the easiest of the tutorials. It is, however, the most comprehensive, as it involves the creation of most of the bank building and, thus, should be at the beginning of the design process.

Tutorial 1 completes much of what can be used in later tutorials, although you can do the other tutorials without completing the first one.

Tutorial 2 is of a conference room. It shows the process of building solid models by creating ceiling surfaces, built-in lighting, doors, cabinetry, and furniture pieces in 3D.

Tutorial 3 is of an open office environment and teller counters next to the main entrance. The teller counters present another opportunity to create in 3D. A set of component and individual furniture pieces will be created for insertion into this space.

These tutorials illustrate the idea that design is an open-ended process. Although the tutorials take you to a stage where you can generate realistic views, still much more can be done. More details can be added, surface materials or textures can be refined, and lighting can be adjusted.

The tutorials are not meant to be ends in themselves, but parts of an exploratory process in thinking through computer-aided design, whether it is with AutoCAD or some other software. As you become familiar with the software, you will transcend the computer and make it a part of your creative process. CAD is a tool, not an end product.

After the tutorials are completed, the next chapters of the book show how the drawings can be used to create perspective views and fully detailed renderings.

A description of output at the end of the book is kept brief in keeping with the premise that this is a book about using standard CAD software in a basic computing environment. Color plotters, printers, and multimedia equipment demand much higher computing power.

This is also why the DOS/Windows 3.x version of R13 is stressed. As AutoCAD goes to the next release, there will undoubtedly be more need for faster CPUs, RAM capacities, and disk storage space. Still, what you will learn from this book will be relevant as you advance in the world of CAD.

HOW TO USE THIS BOOK

This book is aimed at two groups of CAD users. Among the first group are students in organized classes. The second is comprised of designers and drafters in interior space planning and architectural firms. Either group is assumed to have some knowledge of CAD, but may vary in familiarity with AutoCAD R13 from basic to intermediate to advanced.

Chapter 3, Essentials of AutoCAD R13, reviews many of the commands and features of the software. This chapter is a reference where you will find elaboration and demonstration of AutoCAD functions beyond those given in user's manuals. If you are an instructor, have your students try out the commands and features by replicating the illustrations accompanying the text in this chapter.

In Chapter 4, there are exercises and tutorials. The exercises use general strategies rather than specific instructions to demonstrate the use of solid modeling techniques.

The tutorials use step-by-step instructions and a limited number of commands repeatedly so that you can become thoroughly versed on their use. In some cases, different series of steps or commands are used to accomplish the same or similar objectives as a means to demonstrate alternative methods. At times, steps are taken in a certain sequence mainly because it is an established habit. In other instances, it may be because a certain command is more easily accessible through one menu than another.

Although the tutorials are based on areas within one building, you may do them separately. Within each tutorial, some later sections may be simpler than the beginning part of that tutorial. This is especially true of Tutorial 1, which starts with creating most of the bank building, first in 2D grid and guide lines, then as a 3D database. Once the structure is completed, the furnishings and accessories are a lot simpler to create. The rationale is that the tutorials reflect the process of designing architectural interiors: that interior design is space planning and not just furniture stuffing. Hence, each tutorial starts with the creation of the spatial volume, then it goes into structural and architectural details, to built-in equipment, and finally to furnishings. Rendering under AutoVision then covers surface materials and colors.

If you are an instructor using this book as a text, you may follow the tutorials all the way through. Alternately, you can pick and choose from among the tutorials. Try to match a tutorial with your students' skill level. If you want your students to start with very basic models, start with the sections that deal with building simple furniture forms. If your students are already familiar with drawing floor plans, you may opt to skip that part of the tutorial by using the building shell drawing that is on the diskette in the Instructor's Manual.

As a user of this book, or a teacher making assignments, you may select from not only the tutorials, but from parts of each as well. For example, there are five types of chairs detailed in this book. They all use different approaches in their creation. Following only these tutorials provides a means of learning five ways to create 3D models.

If you have had at least a semester-long, college-level course using AutoCAD, particularly in R12, you should not have any difficulties in following the tutorials in this book. If your knowledge of AutoCAD or CAD in general is quite dated, you may find it easier if you review some of the basic steps in the AutoCAD *User's Guide* and *Reference Manual*. There was quite a jump between R12 and previous versions.

Term	*Meaning, action, or response*
Click on Pick Select	Make a selection by placing the cursor on an item, in the drawing field, or an on-screen menu, then press the LMB.
LMB	Left mouse button. Usually the button to use in selecting objects.
RMB	Right mouse button. Usually used to end a command.
RMB+*X* LMB+*X* Crtl+*X* Shift+*X or* 'X	Hold down the RMB, LMB, Control, or Shift key and press *X* at the same time. This method is used for overrides or for accessing additional functions.
Enter	Press the Enter key.
Pulldown menu	The AutoCAD pulldown menu is accessible by placing the mouse cursor on the Status Bar across the top of the monitor screen. Slide the cursor to any command category; it (and the last command use in that category) will be highlighted. Select that category or command by clicking the LMB.
Side menu	The vertically laid out AutoCAD menu categories on the right-hand side of the monitor screen. Highlight a category by placing the cursor on it.
Category > Choice	The syntax for highlighting Category and the Choice through the pulldown menu.
CATEGORY/ Choice	The syntax for highlighting CATEGORY on the side menu, then picking Choice.
@0,0,0	Data to be entered verbatim are shown in *italics*.

A typical sequence of instructions in the exercises and tutorials might read:

> **Draw> Circle> Center, Radius**
> Center point: *'From*
> From: Pick P1
> Offset: *@–18'6",4*
> Radius: *18*

The sequence means:

> Draw a circle using the **Center, Radius** option.
> Locate the center: –18'6" (negative x direction) and 4" (positive y direction) from the object or point marked P1 in the accompanying illustration.
> The radius of the circle is 18".

Pick the command from the pulldown menu bar at the top of the monitor screen. Highlight and click on **Draw**. Scroll down to **Circle**, then slide over and click the LMB on the **Center, Radius** option. If you are in the Windows version, use the Draw Toolbar, click on the Draw icon, and the Center, Radius flyout button.

'*From* means use the **From** Object Snap filter. A list of filters is invoked by clicking the ******** under **AutoCAD** on the side menu bar, or by pressing SHIFT+RMB.

Generally speaking, distances of 24″ or shorter are listed in inches only; and the inch mark (″) is usually omitted, unless there may be some confusion.

You are assumed to know that at the end of a line of instructions, you have to press the RMB or the Enter key; you are usually not reminded to do that in the instructions.

When you enter a command, AutoCAD may respond with a list of options, or you may be presented with a number of choices. You pick an option by typing in the capitalized letter(s) of the option, or accept the <default> by pressing Enter or the RMB.

In the exercises and tutorials, those options not used at that stage of the command are not listed for the sake of brevity. Similarly omitted are the ones in which you simply press Enter or the RMB to accept defaults to cycle to the next prompt. For example, in **Construct> 3D Array**, after you have selected rectangular array and picked objects, the first prompt is: Number of columns <1>. If you are arraying only one column, you simply press Enter or the RMB. In this book, you will not be instructed to press Enter or the RMB, as that would restate the obvious.

HARDWARE, SOFTWARE, AND CAD

The purpose of this book is to show how you can create sophisticated, professional-looking graphic pictures using a rather basic set of equipment and an off-the-shelf set of software. The equipment list reflects this philosophy. Although the software manufacturer notes that slower computers may be used, the one used in the preparation of this book is more realistic, even if it is generally considered to be slow and outdated.

A better computer may make the software run better, but it does not negate the premise that one should learn the basics of the software first.

HARDWARE

Minimal Hardware Requirements

The tutorials and renderings prepared for this book were all done on a computer with:

Intel 486DX2-66 Central Processing Unit
20 MB Random Access Memory (RAM)

Two 210 MB hard disks

3.5″ 1.44 MB diskette drive

SVGA color monitor, displaying 256 colors at 1078 x 768 resolution

Two-button mouse

Double speed CD-ROM drive

Some Possible Enhancements

Of course, you may be equipped with better, more sophisticated equipment.

AutoCAD R13, the software used for this book, is written for processing data in 32-bit chunks. To make full use of it, you should have a computer with the Pentium microprocessor that operates in 32-bit mode. Select one with the fastest clock-speed above 100 MHz that you can. Another step up would be RISC computers.

According to the software installation guide, a RAM capacity of 8 MB is all you need to run in the DOS platform. It will, however, be slow, especially when your 3D database becomes large, or when you want to edit complex 3D shapes. A RAM of 12 MB is better, but 16 MB to 20 MB would be much better for the DOS/Windows 3.x version. To run AutoCAD R13 in Windows 95 or Windows NT, you should have 32 MB of RAM.

Using a high-performance computer operating in one of the higher Windows operating systems makes the software run faster and smoother. It does not negate the basic idea of this book: to learn the use of the standard set of software. Most of the commands and certainly all the functions have their equivalents in the higher Windows environments, so this book is useful even if you are working in those areas.

Getting a hard disk with adequate capacity will be necessary for storing large drawings. Many so-called entry-level computers are now equipped with at least 1 GB of hard disk storage. If you are doing your work in an office, you may want to have a backup tape storage device where your files can be saved to prevent contamination by others. Alternately, you may want to be networked because of the large storage capacity.

If you wish to have copies made of your work, you must have access to plotting and/or other output devices, depending on the end purpose of your work. It is now rather easy to have your work digitized and stored on compact discs. You can then make presentations wherever there are suitable computers with CD-ROM devices. Speaking of which, you will also need stereo speakers if you want to get into multimedia presentations.

Other enhancements include high-resolution graphics cards and monitors, digitizers, and tablets. There are also numerous enhancements to tweak a computer. But then, we digress from the basic tenet of this book: that it be a tutorial for working in a run-of-the-mill computing environment.

SOFTWARE

The software under discussion is made by Autodesk, Inc. of San Rafael, California. It is AutoCAD Release 13 (often referred to as Release 13, or simply, R13) installed in the DOS/Windows 3.x environment.

Of all the CAD software, AutoCAD is probably the most widely used in schools and in the professions. Since the early 1980s, Autodesk has steadfastly retained the basic structure of AutoCAD. Although there has been rapid development in hardware and increased sophistication in computer users, AutoCAD has kept pace. It has also encouraged the development of third-party software and specialized applications through widespread distribution of its AutoLISP programming language. Together with the ready availability of the PC/DOS computing environment, AutoCAD is often viewed as the standard of the industry.

This release of AutoCAD may also be loaded in a Windows 95, Windows NT, or UNIX operating system. The higher Windows versions require much more RAM capacity than would be within the premise of this book. Similarly, the UNIX environment presupposes a powerful work-station-type, or RISC, computing platform.

During the preparation of this book, AutoCAD Release 13 was updated to R13c4. At the same time, AutoVision R2 was also updated to R2c4. The updated versions contain some changes that affect solid modeling. These will be mentioned in specific sections in the text. Other information regarding R13c4 is in the .TXT files: INSTALL, README, READPC, READDOC, READDEV and READHIST that came with the product upgrade material.

There are strong adherents of AutoCAD in the Windows environment. However, unless you have Windows 95 or Windows NT, you are not really using R13 to its fullest extent because you are not processing data in a 32-bit mode. AutoCAD will likely discontinue support for DOS in the future but the graphic screen, menu structure, command logic, and so on will remain. Hence, this book strongly recommends that you use the on-screen menus rather than working in the old DOS habit of entering data by typing in the keyboard. At the least, you will be used to interfacing with the screen if AutoCAD does go on to a more graphical mode.

For more comments about other software options, see the summary section of Chapter 7.

WORKING IN CAD

It is important to establish good working habits and manners early. In most CAD software, there is more than one way to execute a command, input data, or manipulate entities on the screen. The objective of good working habits is to achieve a continuous, natural flow between the brain, the eyes, the hands, and, of course, the computer.

Posture and Ambient Light

Sit up straight and tall. Adjust the monitor so that the screen is straight ahead or slightly lower than your eye level. To lessen fatigue, turn the brightness and contrast levels of the monitor down. The ambient lighting level of the room where you are working also should not be very bright or too contrasting, nor should it reflect on the monitor screen or on the keys of the keyboard.

Monitor Color

Avoid the use of dark, hard-to-see colors, such as blue, for basic line color unless you have turned the Contrast knob of the monitor so that the background color of the screen appears to be a light gray.

Keyboard

Position yourself so that the keyboard is slightly on the left-hand side and the mouse is on the right. Both devices should be within easy, natural reach without your having to stretch for them.

Mouse

Keep your pointing hand on the digitizing device. Place your right hand on the mouse—if you are right handed and using a mouse—and use your other hand to type in data entries. Guide the cursor around the screen while you keep your eyes on the screen. Make use of the various menus accessible through the screen and the mouse. Do not rely on typing in commands. If you keep taking your hand away from the mouse to type in commands or enter data, the eye-hand coordination is disrupted and you frequently have to refocus your attention on the screen after you have finished typing. The result is a disruptive manner of working. With so much busy hand work, you can easily become fatigued, not to mention developing the dreaded Flying Fingers Syndrome!

Software Structure

Most interactive computer software is structured so that its functions are laid out in logical categories and accessible through menus and prompts. When you select a category, features associated with it become evident on the monitor screen in a cascading or descending order. Then, when you select a task, you are prompted for the next step. You work with the computer by telling it what to do in sequential steps.

In AutoCAD, think of **Draw** and **Construct** if you want to create an object. Think of **Modify** if you want to change a drawing. And click on the **View** button when you wish to reset your display. The other categories are support functions and not used as often as the three main categories.

Thinking in categories keeps an overview of the software in the forefront of your mind. You do not have to memorize the location of each command. Invoking commands solely by entering on the keyboard means you are memorizing the commands individually. Your understanding of the overall software structure is restricted, and so you tend to use only the commands and capabilities familiar to you. Or you give up trying to find something unfamiliar. Group the functions in categories and you will not have to hunt for a command.

Ultimate Challenge

The challenge is to do very little drawing per se, but to devise ways to edit, modify, and transform objects. Let the computer do repetitious tasks; you do the thinking.

WORKING WITH AUTOCAD R13

AutoCAD R13 is a very powerful set of software straight out of the box. There are many more capabilities than you will need to use. Detailing all the capabilities or all the ways to use the software would be contrary to the premise of this book: that it be a concise, applied tutorial based on certain, but not all, approaches to a solution. As there are many ways to achieve the same or similar results, what is covered in this book is not necessarily the best nor, by any means, the only way.

Nonetheless, there is some general advice and some rather specific points about working with R13 with which you should be familiar.

AutoCAD Commands

You work with AutoCAD by issuing commands to tell it what to do. A command can be issued in three ways. One way is by typing it in on the Command Prompt Line. The other ways are through either of the on-screen menus: the pulldown menu and the side menu. Select an item you want by highlighting and clicking the pick button (LMB) of your mouse. If you are using a tablet, that is another way to issue AutoCAD commands, but here you are assumed to be using a mouse as the pointing device.

Menu Structure

The commands of AutoCAD are structured in the form of a multibranched tree. At the root is a collection of the **categories** of functions, tools, and capabilities. When you select a category, you move from the root along the trunk to one of the branches representing various submenus belonging to that category. Further options can be likened to branchlets and leaves.

The section on menus in Chapter 3 details the R13 menus.

Use On-Screen Menus

While working in AutoCAD, think of the category of task, move the cursor to that category on screen, click to highlight it, and scroll down to the specific item you want. For example, if you want to draw a line, pick **Draw**, then **Line**, and you will be prompted for inputs *From* point *To* point. In the syntax of this book, the sequence is expressed as **Draw> Line**. As suggested earlier, learn to talk to yourself mentally in the cadence in which the hardware and the software "thinks."

Working with categories of tasks through on-screen menus will become a habit; you will be scrolling down the menus time and again. As you do so, they become imprinted on your mind, and you will be most familiar with the capabilities available in AutoCAD. If you only type in commands directly, they are just disparate entities in your mind. You will not have much of a holistic picture of AutoCAD and its range of options.

The pulldown menu and the side menu generally echo each other, but some of the subsequent options available appear differently and some commands are more directly accessed through one or the other menu. You will also find yourself favoring one or the other. For this book, commands will be listed as if they are from the pulldown menu in most cases, and some of the differences will be pointed out.

Many AutoCAD commands respond with dialog boxes in which there are options you can select. You can access some of these dialog boxes directly by typing in the name of a dialog command, which is usually in the form of *DDcommand*. For the reasons already given, it is preferred that you enter commands through either of the on-screen menus.

Keyboard Input

Of course, there are times when it may be necessary or more advantageous to input data from the keyboard, such as when you have to enter coordinates. Learn to be ambidextrous. Use your left hand (if you are right-handed) to work the keyboard. At times this may be somewhat awkward, such as when you have to use the relative sign: @ (Shift +2). This is an exceptional case requiring a slightly unnatural twisting of the hand to accomplish. But such options are sometimes also available on the side menu on screen.

Save Your Eyes: Zoom

Working with precision graphics such as AutoCAD means a great deal of focusing on fine lines, picking tightly packed intersections, or selecting from a host of closely spaced objects, especially if your monitor is set at a high resolution. Zoom in on the picture so that you do not have to squint to select objects. You may also need to adjust the size of the pickbox (do this through the dialog box in **Options>Selection...**).

Repeating a Command

You may recall the immediate last command by simply pressing the RMB, or enter a Null Return, that is, press Enter on the keyboard, and the very last command is reissued.

Once you have issued a command from the pulldown menu, you can repeat that command by double clicking the category box at the top of the screen. For example, if you have used **Construct> Offset**, you can cause Offset to be issued again just by double clicking the Construct box. The last command used in a category is considered the default and highlighted, so you can reissue that command by default even if you have since used commands from other categories.

You do not actually have to remember which command you last used. When you highlight and click on a category box, the last command used in that category is displayed in a cascading list and is highlighted. So just click the LMB once more to issue the command again.

Develop the habit of momentarily checking to see which selection is already highlighted when you click on a category box. If the selection happens to be the one you want, then simply click the LMB again to select. You would not have to scroll down the menu to pick the selection again.

Use Grips and Preselects

If **Options> Grips** is enabled, and you select an object before you issue a command, that object becomes active and is highlighted by little blue boxes. AutoCAD calls these boxes *grips*, which can be used as handles for grabbing onto for editing purposes such as, move, rotate, scale, and stretch.

Click the LMB on one of the grips and a list of options appears on the Command Prompt Line. You can use the current editing function, or click the RMB to cycle to other editing options. Note that landscape objects have slightly different functions assigned to their grips.

When an object is displayed with its grips on, the object has been preselected. If you proceed to click on Erase, for example, the object will be erased without the usual selection and confirmation queries.

Use **Undo** to backtrack, if necessary. To remove the active grips, enter Ctrl+C twice.

Windowing

Normally, you open an on-screen window from left to right. Objects that lie completely within the window are selected and highlighted. This gives you better control over object selection.

A window that is opened from right to left is known as a *crossing window*. Any object that the window crosses, even if it is partially within the window, becomes selected. Oftentimes, a crossing window includes more objects than you want, making it necessary to use the R (for Remove) option to remove the unintentionally selected objects from the selection set.

Make it a habit to open normal windows by first picking the lower left-hand corner, then drag the cursor to the upper right-hand corner. There are no real reasons for this rule, other than that, if AutoCAD asks for corner inputs, it usually asks for the lower left-hand corner first. In the case of the Text command, AutoCAD expects the starting point of a line of text to be the lower left corner of the first letter. If there are no other criteria, select the lower left corner of an object as the insertion point when you are defining a block. If you do this consistently, there is less guessing when time comes to insert a block. The left to right convention, once gotten used to, becomes the standard for other incidents and lessens confusion.

Use Osnap

There are several filter tools collectively under Object Snap (Osnap, for short) that should be used to pick out definite points or parts of objects. They are very useful in precision drawing.

The Osnap filters, or overrides, allow you to specify Center, Endpoint, Intersection, Midpoint, Perpendicular, or Tangent. New to R13 are Implied Intersection and From.

You can set your selection mode to automatically pick certain Osnap filters, and/or you can choose one to use as the need arises. Select **Tools> Object Snap Modes** to call up the dialog box where you can specify or remove Osnap filters. Once set, they remain in effect as the default pick mode until you remove them from the dialog box.

The easiest way to access Osnap is by holding down the Shift key while pressing the RMB (Shift+RMB). A list of filters appears in a box on screen. You can scroll to the Osnap filter you want, then select it by a click of the LMB. Osnap responds by allowing you to transparently specify, for example, *Intersection of*:

Alternately, you can call up the list by clicking on the * * * * line under the AutoCAD logo at the top of the side menu on screen. Scroll down to highlight and pick the one you want. However, under this method, Osnap returns with the noun only, e.g., *Midpoint*. To get it to ask *of:* (meaning *Midpoint of:*), press the RMB.

Osnap filters should be used whenever you need to be precise. (And you need to be in most instances.) For example, you can Move an object by an *Intersection* as the base point and Osnap to the *Midpoint* of another line as displacement point. Do not rely on visually picking such points as intersections. Use the appropriate Osnap filter at all times. This is especially true if you are working in 3D view and/or with 3D objects.

Direct Distance Entry

A point may be specified by first moving the cursor in the desired direction then entering a value for the distance. This feature works with commands where distance or length can be specified relative to a first point. For example, after you have specified the starting point of a line, you can move the cursor in the direction where the line is to go, then type in a value for the length of the line. This is particularly useful when drawing rectilinear figures with ORTHO turned *On*.

Command Prompt Line

The Command Prompt is the line on the bottom of the screen where AutoCAD expects the next input or information. Always keep an eye on it. When you see **Command:** *blank*, it means AutoCAD is waiting for you to tell it what to do. Once you have entered a command, the Command Prompt Line scrolls up and the bottom line is replaced by the next prompt or a response to your command. The prompt waits for you to supply the appropriate information.

Always be very aware of what is on the Command Prompt Line so you know what stage in a command you are currently in, or supply what AutoCAD is expecting from you. Also, be aware of what you have typed so you can correct any mistakes before you press *Enter;* this will save time and consternation.

AutoCAD often responds to command inputs with a list of options and some variable in angular brackets: < xxx >, which is the default. If you supply any information, it will be assumed that you mean it for the default variable.

The default AutoCAD configuration sets up a command prompt area to accommodate three lines of text. The lines scroll upwards so that the current line is always at the bottom of the prompt area. If you need to check on lines that have scrolled out of sight, press the **F1** key to toggle between the graphics screen and the text screen.

The list of options contains words, some of which are capitalized, sometimes seemingly oddly. If you type in just the capitalized letter(s) at that stage, AutoCAD considers it equivalent to typing in the entire word and will respond accordingly. It saves typing time. Since you are not encouraged to type in responses, this feature does not matter, but you should be aware that AutoCAD will accept options entered only with the capitalized letters to save you time from having to type in entire words.

AutoCAD does accept a number of abbreviated commands known as Command Aliases. They are usually entered through the keyboard. Some examples are *pline*, for Polyline and *mledit*, for Multiline Edit. You can even set up your own. But I will not tell you about them, because I do not want you to type in commands.

Although we are concerned here with the DOS/Windows 3.x version of R13, most of the commands and features are present in the Windows 95 and Windows NT versions.

ESSENTIALS OF AUTOCAD R13

INTRODUCTION

From the user's point of view, the Drawing Editor, menu layout, and data input methods of AutoCAD R13 are not substantially different from those of the last release. There are a lot of enhancements and more powerful capabilities in the software. Many of them are in the Windows platform, so they are not of any real concern to you, the DOS user. The graphic interface is about the same as the one in the previous release.

If you are not conversant with AutoCAD through R12, you should review basic skills and techniques dealing with CAD. You will also find it useful to go through the *AutoCAD User's Manual* supplied with the R13 software. If you have been working with R12, you should have no difficulty in making the transition.

As AME (Advanced Modeling Extension) software was often installed along with R12, many people got used to working in 3D. However, R13 handles solid modeling in a fundamentally different way than AME does. Many convenient functions of AME, such as SOLCHP, where multiple capabilities are available under one command, no longer exist in R13. Once you get used to the new surfaces and solids functions, the new graphic driver for 3D objects (ACIS) is very easy to use. The tutorials in this book show how solid models are built with R13 only.

R13 is powerful, nevertheless, and there are a number of subtle changes that affect the way you need to think in order to use R13 effectively and intelligently.

The functions and capabilities of AutoCAD are arranged along certain categories in menu groups. You can invoke a command by typing it on the keyboard at the Command Prompt. But it is preferred that you call up a command by selecting from the screen menus: either the on-screen menu across the top of the monitor or the side menu along the side. When you use these menus, your hand stays on the mouse, guiding the cursor around the screen. There is no disrupting the flow from your mind to the mouse and screen, which is what happens if you rely on typing in commands. If you do have to use the keyboard to, say, enter coordinates, use your other, nonpointing hand. Develop a mental cadence of a step-by-step sequence in the same way the on-screen menus are laid out.

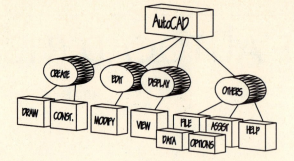

This chapter begins with a section on setting up a new drawing environment. After setting up a drawing, you will find that the majority of functions you use in a drawing session are located in only three areas that are in line with the natural process of design. The first area contains categories of commands that have to do with *creating*. The next area deals with *editing*, while *displaying* is the third area where there are various ways to better see what you are creating and modifying. Other functions lie mostly in management and technique enhancement.

To work with AutoCAD efficiently, think in terms of these areas and you will readily find the commands. For example, if you want to create a circle, click on the **Draw** menu and the **Circle** option. After you have created an object and you wish to edit it, go to the menus under **Modify**.

The commands and features discussed here are not inclusive of all the features of R13. Rather, those pertinent to the tutorials of this book, those that differ from R12, and those that students often find confusing are included.

THE AUTOCAD DRAWING EDITOR GRAPHIC SCREENS: DOS AND WINDOWS VERSIONS

AutoCAD begins with the Drawing Editor screen. You can access most of the functions and commands through on-screen menus.

Pulldown menus lie across the upper part of the screen in both DOS and Windows versions.

File Assist View Draw Const Modify Data Options Tools Help

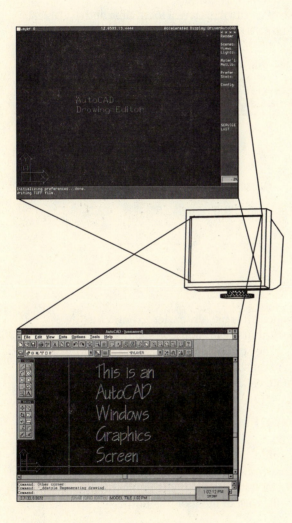

The DOS Drawing Editor

In the DOS version, display the pulldown menus by clicking on the status bar.

Side menus are located along the edge of the screen.

The Windows Drawing Editor

In the Windows version, the pulldown menus, standard toolbar, and the status bar are displayed one above the other.

Toolbars can be docked or float anywhere on the graphic area.

Setting Up a New Drawing

Drawing Units

Data
Units ...

When you start up a new drawing using the default *acad.dwg* prototype, the drawing units are set at the decimal style, where 1 inch is the basic measurement.

Typically, architectural measurements in the United States are expressed in the English system of feet (′) and inches (″). You can change the drawing units to this style by the **Data> Units> Architectural** sequence of menu selections.

The basic unit is an inch, expressed as 1″, or simply, 1. Even though it may not seem like much to type in a (″) mark, not having to do that over the course of a drawing saves a lot of time and is just another way to use AutoCAD efficiently.

Distances can be expressed as shown in the following chart:

Measurements	*In AutoCAD, enter as:*			
1 inch			1″	**1**
10 inches			10″	**10**
1 foot	**1′**		12″	**12**
1′-4″	**1′4**	**1.3′**	16″	**16**
3′-6½″	3′6-1/2	**3′6.5**	42.5″	**42.5**
36′-0″		**36′**		

Boldface indicates the more convenient input style.

Notice that if the distance is short, it is usually easier to enter the measurement in inches and without the (″) mark. When they are large, enter measurements in feet rather than converting them into inches. Note also that you must include the (′) mark or AutoCAD will interpret the distances as inches.

View

Modelspace/Paperspace

**Floating
    Modelspace
Paperspace**

In AutoCAD, you draw or build up a design in modelspace, which is three dimensional, and you plot in paperspace, which is flat and two dimensional. The default drawing puts you in modelspace. That is where you will work in most of this book.

Setting up the two types of spaces is described in the section on display later in this chapter. For a full discussion on these types of spaces, see the *AutoCAD User's Guide* and the *Command Reference*.

The default prototype AutoCAD drawing *Acad.dwg* uses the Cartesian coordinate system and starts in the plan view of the I Quadrant. That is to say, the x and y coordinates are expressed in positive values. (The + sign is usually omitted in value expressions.) The origin (or x,y,z = *0,0,0*) is located in the lower left corner of the graphics area. The default view is set as the plan view of the WCS (World Coordinate System) and can always be recalled as such. The I Quadrant is the most convenient quadrant in which to input graphic data as absolute coordinates can be expressed in + values.

In plan view, drawings are drawn on the x-y plane, that is, z = 0. In working with 3D models, the z coordinate will no longer be set to 0. While you can work above or below the x-y plane, or have your model penetrate the x-y-plane, it is more convenient to work above the x-y plane, so that the coordinates will be expressed as + values.

The 3D Coordinate System

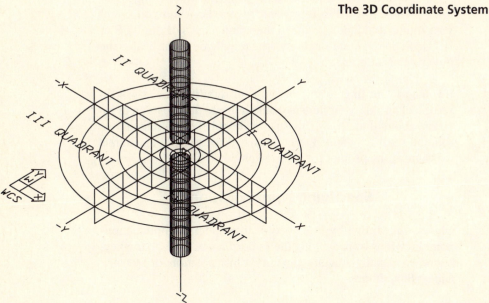

In this book, as in most architectural applications, the default x-y plane in WCS at the I Quadrant is used as the basic floor plane. Walls can be drawn in 2D plan views on this plane before extruding in the +z direction into the third dimension. Solid objects can also be constructed directly in 3D, usually also in the positive x, y, z quadrant. Since it is easier to input coordinates as + values and to draw as if in plan view, you can set a UCS (User Coordinate System) on to, say, the lower left-hand corner of a wall. Call up the plan view of the UCS, which sets the surface of the wall on the screen as if it is horizontally in plan view. You can then draw on the wall or attach objects just as you would if you were working on the floor plan.

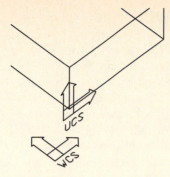

Set UCS

With **View> Set UCS**, you can set a coordinate system by rotating the existing x, y, or z axis. You can also place the origin and set a UCS by defining three points (origin, + direction of x axis, and + direction of y axis).

Right Hand Rule

AutoCAD uses the Right Hand Rule as an aid for showing the orientation of the x, y, and z axes in either the WCS or any UCS. The rule is also used for seeing how objects rotate about an axis.

To use this rule, open your right hand and fold the third and little fingers toward the heel of your hand. The extended thumb represents the x axis, the index finger forms a right angle with the thumb and represents the y axis, while the middle finger naturally bends upward to represent the z axis. When you orient your thumb and index finger to the x and y axes of the WCS or UCS icon on the monitor screen, the middle finger indicates the direction of the z axis.

If you curl your fingers and extend your right thumb in the + direction of an axis, your fingers would indicate the direction of rotation about that axis. This is the default counterclockwise rotation setting. To specify a clockwise direction, put in a minus (–) value at the prompt for rotation angle.

Specifying Point Locations

Objects are drawn by line vectors from point to point. Input point locations by specifying their coordinates through the keyboard, by visually dragging the cursor into position, or by using Object Snap filters.

You can also specify the next point relative to the last referenced point by placing the @ sign in front of the displacement distance. For example, if you enter @4′6,5′ when you are prompted for the next point of a line segment, a line will be drawn that is 4′6″ in the +x direction and 5′ in the +y direction from the current location. If you enter @-3′6,-14′, the point will be located at those distances in the *negative* direction from the current position.

Data
Drawing Limits

Drawing Limits

DATA
Limits:

Typically, you work in AutoCAD by drawing in full size, then plot in scale. How large a drawing field should you set? The general rule of thumb is to define the drawing field about 50% larger than the sides of the building in plan view. When you invoke Drawing Limits, the lower left corner is set at *0,0*. Leave it at that. If your building measures 80′ × 50′, set the next prompt, the upper right corner, at *120′,75′*. This will allow ample space for notes and dimensions usually found on plan drawings. You can, of course, always reset the drawing limits during the course of a drawing.

There are other drawing limits considerations when working in paperspace, but it is still a good rule to place your building comfortably within a field.

Assist
Grid

Options
Drawing Aids...

Grid (F7)

ASSIST
Grid:

OPTIONS
DDrmode:

You can toggle a grid *On* or *Off* through the Assist button on the screen menus or by pressing the **F7** function key.

The nonplotting grid can be set as a guide to give you a sense of the relative sizes of objects you are drawing.

Do not space the grid too closely. A dense grid is more confusing than helpful. For a floor plan, set the grid at *4′* or *5′*, which approximates the standard size of many architectural materials. For close-up work and detailing, grid spacing of *1″* or *4″* is often useful as material comes in 2×4 modules.

Assist
Ortho

Ortho (F8)

ASSIST
Ortho:

Toggle the Ortho(graphic) switch by pressing the **F8** key or through the Assist button, and you can only draw lines that are oriented to the x and y axes of the current coordinate system.

While this feature is useful as you draw floor plans, remember to toggle Ortho to *Off* when you work in 3D views or with 3D objects. The reason is that Ortho *On* also forces the z coordinate to be set at 0. You may not be specifying an endpoint in space even if it looks like you have grabbed it visually.

Create Area: Draw Commands

Among the pulldown menus of R13, there are the Draw and Construct category buttons which you can highlight and click on to reveal commands that you can use to create objects. You can find the same commands, sometimes with additional or different optional choices, in the side menus under DRAW, DRAW2, and CONSTRUCT.

Pulldown menu and options in the **Draw** category:

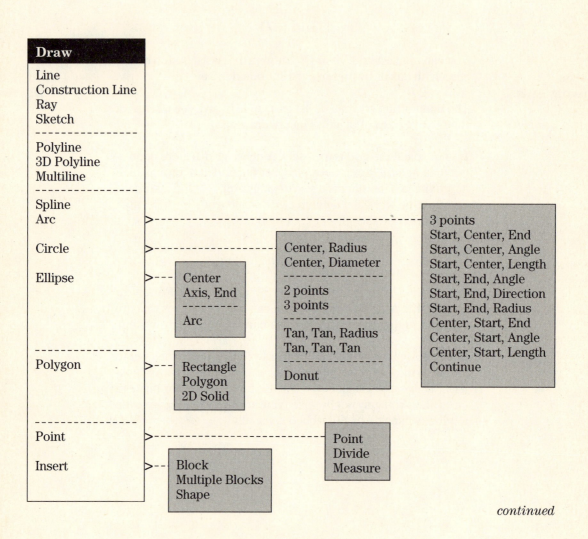

continued

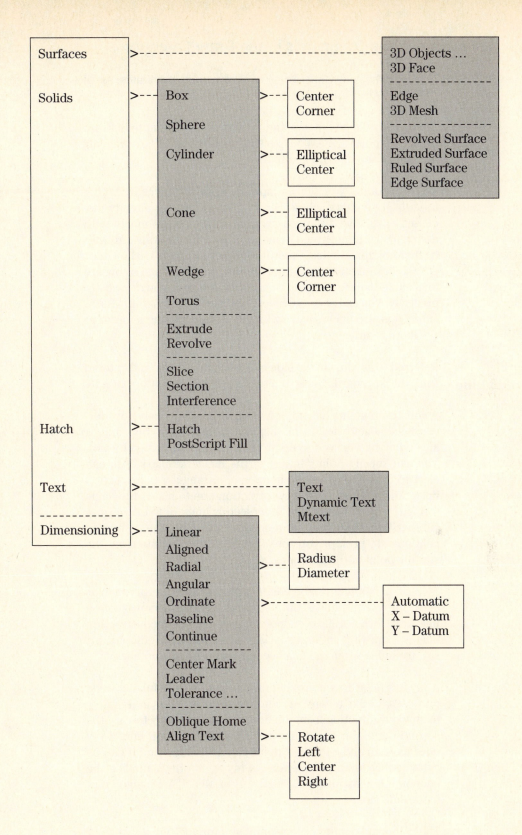

Surfaces >- -

3D Objects ...
3D Face
- - - - - - - - - - - - - -
Edge
3D Mesh
- - - - - - - - - - - - - -
Revolved Surface
Extruded Surface
Ruled Surface
Edge Surface

Solids >- - -

Box >- - - Center / Corner

Sphere

Cylinder >- - - Elliptical / Center

Cone >- - - Elliptical / Center

Wedge >- - - Center / Corner

Torus
- - - - - - - - - - - - -
Extrude
Revolve
- - - - - - - - - - - - -
Slice
Section
Interference
- - - - - - - - - - - - -

Hatch >- - - Hatch / PostScript Fill

Text >- - - - - - - - - - - - - - - - - - -

Text
Dynamic Text
Mtext

- - - - - - - - - - - - -
Dimensioning >- - -

Linear
Aligned
Radial
Angular
Ordinate
Baseline
Continue
- - - - - - - - - - - - -
Center Mark
Leader
Tolerance ...
- - - - - - - - - - - - -
Oblique Home
Align Text

Radius
Diameter

Automatic
X – Datum
Y – Datum

Rotate
Left
Center
Right

The Commands in the Draw Category

Draw
Line

Line is perhaps the most basic of all drawing commands, as all objects in AutoCAD are expressed in line segments.

As you invoke the command, you will be prompted: From point... To point..., etc. You can enter points visually by dragging the mouse and clicking the LMB.

To be accurate, you should input definite distances by typing them in. Use aids such as Direct Distance Entry already discussed or relative distances (by preceding a measurement with a @ sign). Turning Ortho *On* makes it possible to draw only vertical or horizontal lines. Press the **F8** key to toggle Ortho *On* or *Off*. Object Snaps, such as Intersection, Endpoint, and so on, are invaluable tools for making certain that the lines you draw meet precisely. You can access Object Snap by the action Shift+RMB. Often, it is also necessary to zoom in on the drawing in order to see more clearly.

Draw
Construction Line

Referred to as Xline in the side menu and as a command entered from the keyboard, Construction Line is a new feature in R13.

A construction line has no definite length. It infinitely goes forward and backward from the first point you define and is aligned along the second point, which is also specified by you. You can specify points in any of the usual manners. You can elect to draw only vertical, horizontal, or angular construction lines. And you can draw a construction line to bisect the angle formed by an existing pair of intersecting lines, or to offset from another line. Once you set a construction line, the command continues to prompt you for other lines that radiate from the starting point of the first line.

A construction line can be edited with the normal tools such as copy, mirror, and move, but you cannot extend a construction line as it does not have endpoints. You can use a construction line as a drawing entity, especially after you have edited it by, say, trimming when the line becomes an edge of an object.

Draw
Ray

A ray is similar to a construction line and is used for the same purposes. Unlike a construction line, a ray radiates indefinitely in only one direction from the first point you specify toward the second definition point. And unlike a construction line, a ray does have an end—the first point you specified—and it can be extended. Extending the end of a ray is, in effect, moving the endpoint. Use **Modify> Lengthen**, or MODIFY/Change/Point in the side menu.

The command continues to prompt you for additional rays until you press Enter to terminate it.

Draw
Sketch

The Sketch feature allows you to draw polylines (set the system variable: *Skpoly = 1*) or regular lines (*Skpoly = 0*) in a freehand sketching manner.

DRAW
Line:

DRAW
Xline:

DRAW
Ray:

DRAW
Sketch:

28   CHAPTER 3   ESSENTIALS OF AUTOCAD R13

Upon invoking the Sketch command, you are prompted for a record increment. The smaller the increment, the smoother the sketched lines will be. You should set the line increment as large as possible so that you will still have a reasonably realistic sketch. Otherwise, you may be building up a very large drawing file that takes up storage space and requires extra time to regenerate.

When you are in the Sketch command, you use the given subset of options to erase, connect, and so on. Use the Pen option to toggle between pen up and pen down. Keep an eye on the <default value> of the Command Prompt line. It tells you the current pen position.

When you have finished drawing, you must use the Record option to "set" the lines you have drawn. Otherwise your drawing will not be saved when you exit to go back to the regular drawing editor.

The Sketch Command

1. In 2D and z-x plane, draw leaf shapes with **Draw> Sketch**, starting and ending each shape at the upper end of vertical line.
2. In plan view, WCS, polar array leaf shapes a full circle. Erase some lines to make it less mechanical looking.

Draw
Polyline

A polyline is a 2D object typically consisting of line segments and/or arcs which are linked together to form a single entity.

DRAW
Pline:

You can have a polyline consisting of only one segment; you can break a polyline apart at its vertices; and you can join other line segments to form one polyline. The default polyline has a theoretical width of 0. You can reset the width of a polyline, but if you extrude a polyline that has width, only its center spine will be extruded. A polyline can, however, have a height in the z direction, which is how you would make a 2D polyline into a solid object. If the polyline has a line type other than continuous, such as dashed, and if it is given a height, each dashed segment of the line will become a polygonal solid.

Draw		DRAW
3D Polyline	A 3D polyline cannot be set to any width other than the default (0) width. You cannot give height to a 3D polyline, nor can you extrude it.	**3D Poly:**

You can use a 3D polyline as an axis of revolution or as a reference object for slicing. If the 3D polyline has multiple vertices, AutoCAD will use the endpoints of the line as the reference object for such functions as rotation and slicing.

In addition to regular editing tools, 2D and 3D polylines can be edited with a special set of options in *Pedit* or under **Modify > Edit Polyline**.

Draw		DRAW
Multiline	Multiline, a new feature in R13, is used to draw segments of parallel lines. It is called *Mline* in the side menu and also can be invoked as such on the Command Prompt.	**Mline:**

Upon entering the command, you can change the defaults, as **Mline** first displays an options list that includes:

Justification = *Top* (Meaning your input line lies at the top, when you draw from left to right. The other elements of the multiline are offset below your input line.)

Zero (Centers your input line. The other elements of the multiline are offset to either side— + offset to the top, and – offset to the bottom, when you draw from left to right.)

Bottom (Your input line lies on the bottom, as you draw from left to right. The other elements of the multiline are offset above your input.)

Scale = Sets width between elements of the multiline. The default width is set in the style definition of the Mline.

Style = Enter an already defined style name. See **Data> Multiline Style** for information on setting up multiline styles.

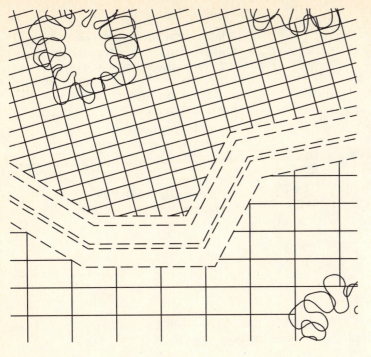

The Multiline Command

A multiline is defined through **Data> Multiline Style**. An individual line in a multiline is an element, and elements are spaced to make up a multiline.

In this example, the multiline is shown dashed for emphasis.

Draw
Spline
Arc
Circle >
Circle > **Donut**
Ellipse

This is a group of commands that generates AutoCAD nonrectilinear 2D objects.

Follow the requests at the bottom of the screen, where the Command Prompt asks for starting point, center, or the next point. Remember that the value or variable within the < > is the default.

In Spline, you can draw a curved line by specifying points much like you would with a polyline or with the Sketch command. As you input points, the curve is shown dynamically on the screen. When you are done with adding points, you are prompted to set the tangential direction of the endpoints. If you accept the default and simply press Enter, you will complete the line and exit Spline.

Upon entering Spline, you may choose the Object option to pick an existing polyline object, which will then be turned into a spline object.

The spline is a much smoother curve than a polyline, and you can edit it with **Modify > Edit Spline**. You cannot give a spline thickness nor can you extrude it. However, you can treat it like a path curve and perform such Surfaces functions as Tabsurf and Rulsurf.

DRAW
Spline:
Arc:
Circle:
Donut:
Ellipse:

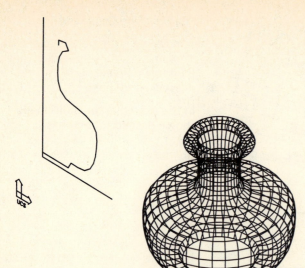

The Spline Command

1. A line is drawn along the x-axis, then a vertical line is drawn along the z-axis. Use the first line as the x-axis, the second line as the y-axis, and the intersection of the lines as the origin of a UCS.

2. A profile is drawn with **Draw>Spline** in the plan view of the UCS.

3. The spline is swept around the vertical line using **Draw> Surfaces> Revolved Surface**.

Donut objects can be filled in or not, depending on toggling in the *Fill* command in the *Ddfillmode* dialog box, or in the system variable *Fillmode*.

Ellipses in R13 are true elliptical objects, rather than the polyline representations of ellipses of previous releases. You can still draw polyline representations of ellipses by setting the system variable: *Pellipse = 1*. The default setting for *Pellipse* is 0 for drawing true ellipses. Specify an ellipse by the endpoints of the two major axes. Instead of a full ellipse, you can create an elliptical arc or an isometric circle.

Draw Polygon > **Rectangle** **Polygon**	These two commands are similar in that they both generate 2D polygons, except that Rectangle obviously draws only rectangles, while you can specify from 3 to 1,024 sides of a polygon. A rectangle is defined by the specification of its diagonal corners. A polygon can be defined by inscribing or circumscribing a circle, or by specifying the endpoints of one edge. Polygons are closed polyline objects and thus can be edited or turned into 3D objects by height or by extrusion.	DRAW **Rectang:** **Polygon:**
Draw Polygon > **2D Solid**	2D Solid (Enter as *Solid* on the Command Prompt) generates closed polygons by specifying diagonal corners that must be on a plane parallel to the current UCS. The Solid command continues to prompt for more third and fourth points until you press Enter to end the command. To see the figures filled in, **Display>Solid Fill** (system variable: *Fillmode*, or *Fill* command) must be *On* and you must be in plan view. Best suited to rectilinear figures, solids are hard to draw unless you know the exact locations of all the corners. It is easier if	DRAW **Solid**

you can first identify the corners by using such aids as grid, construction lines, or rays to make visible intersections, etc. that can be grabbed onto by Object Snaps.

Solids can be extruded to possess heights, making them useful in 3D modeling, if the corners are easily identifiable.

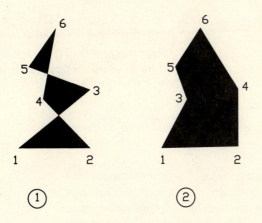

The 2D Solid Command

1. If you use **Draw> 2D Solid** by specifying points 1, 2, 3, 4 sequentially in either clockwise or counterclockwise direction, you will be drawing an intersecting polygon much like a bow tie.

2. Given four vertices of a polygon, draw a nonintersecting shape such as a rectangle by specifying points 1, 2, 4, 3. Point 5 would be linked to Point 3.

Draw
Point >
  Point
  Divide
  Measure

The Point command puts a point object at the specified location. The default style is a dot, which makes a point hard to see. You can change the style of a point by picking a style in **Options> Display> Point Style ...**

DRAW2
Point:
Divide:
Measure:

The Point Style Dialog Box

Note that a point with a style other than a dot (the default) is view-dependent; that is, it enlarges if you zoom in.

The Divide command puts evenly spaced nodes along the length of an object. The object is not actually separated into segments; it is merely marked by the nodes. The nodes are points, so you may need to change the point style to a more visible one. You may use the Osnap Node option to locate the nodes created by the Divide command.

The Measure command is similar to the Divide command except that in Measure you specify the distance between nodes and Measure inserts nodes along the length of the object, starting from the endpoint nearest to the point you pick in selecting the object.

The Point Style and Measure Commands

1. Draw a curved bar in plan view. Set **Options> Display> Point Style** to X.

2. Offset the front outline of the bar a distance that passes through the center of the bar stools. Use **Construct> Offset**.

3. Use **Draw> Point> Measure** to mark the line with points.

4. Select the Multiple Copy option under **Construct> Copy** to insert a circle centered at each point node.

Draw
Insert >
   Block
   Multiple Blocks
   - - - - - - - - - - - - - - -
   Shape
	Use this command to insert previously defined blocks or a separate drawing file into the current drawing.
	
	When using the **Insert> Block** command, you are prompted for the name of a block within the current drawing. Or you can name an external drawing file by checking the appropriate area in the dialog box, where you have to scroll down the list of drives, directories, and/or files until you can highlight the correct drawing to insert.
	
	A block can be inserted one copy at a time. It may be scaled and/or rotated as it is inserted. At insertion, a block may also be exploded into its component entities by the inclusion of an asterisk (*) in front of the name of the block.
	
	Use the Multiple Blocks option to insert a number of copies of a block in a rectangular array. You cannot explode multiple blocks. Each block will have to be exploded individually. But you can insert multiple blocks scaled and rotated in the array.
	
	Compiled and previously loaded shape files (with a *.shx* extension) can be put into the current drawing by the **Insert** command.
		DRAW2
		DDinsert:
		Insert:
		Minsert:
		
		Shape:

Draw
Surfaces >
   3D Objects ...
   3D Face
   3D Mesh
	In the Surfaces group, there are commands that produce 3D faces and mesh objects. These objects are not solid inside, only their faces and surfaces are. Normally shown as wire frames, they can be shown as solid with the Hide, Shade, and Render commands. You need to toggle between wire frame and mesh for the display representations to work.
	
	Under 3D Objects, there are primitive objects that look like those found in the Solids category, except that these are surface meshes and not solid objects. In addition to meshes, there are dishes, domes, and pyramids. The files for mesh objects are much smaller than those for solids. Therefore, use mesh objects if you do not need such solid properties as mass.
	
	A mesh is created by specifying the corners of a polygon and designating the M and N sizes. The corners of a mesh can be in
		DRAW2
		SURFACES:
		Box:
		Cone:
		Dish:
		Dome:
		Mesh:
		Pyramid:
		Sphere:
		Torus
		Wedge:
		
		3Dface:
		3Dpoly:
		
		3dmesh:
		Pface:

3D and, therefore, a mesh can exist in 3D space. However, all the vertices have to be known and entered in the proper sequence before 3dmesh can generate a mesh figure.

Any complex 3dmesh is difficult to draw when you have to enter each and every vertex. So 3dmesh is better suited to be used by programming under AutoLISP.

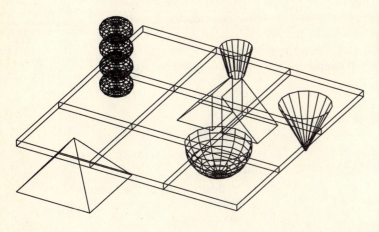

3D Surface Objects

Box, Cone, Dish, Dome, Mesh, Pyramid, Sphere, Torus, Wedge

Draw Surfaces > **Edge**	Edge is really more of a display command than a drawing one, even though you enter it through the Draw category of menus.	DRAW2 SURFACES: **Edge:**

Edge is used to set the visibility of the edges of 3D faces so that you can hide, display, or edit the edges individually.

Upon entering Edge, the command responds with *Display<Select edge>*. You have two choices of action:

1. If you accept the default *<Select edge>* and pick an edge, all the edges of that 3D face are highlighted in dotted lines. Pick any of the dotted lines, press Enter, and that edge will become invisible. If you simply click the RMB or press Enter, the edge by which you selected the object will become invisible.

2. If you pick *Display*, the command responds with *Select/ <All>:*

   If you accept the default *<All>*, the edges of all 3D faces will be shown in dotted lines and the command returns to the *Display/<Select Edge>:* prompt. You can then choose any of the edges to be hidden or displayed.

Draw Surfaces > **Revolved Surface Extruded Surface Ruled Surface Edge Surface**	This is a group of related commands used to generate 3D meshed objects from 2D profiles, sections, regions, or splines. Edge Surface (*Edgsurf*) is a 3D mesh patch covering the area bounded by four adjoining edges. These edges may be polylines, straight lines, or arcs.	DRAW2 SURFACES: **Revsurf: Tabsurf: Rulsurf: Edgsurf:**

Revolved Surface (*Revsurf*) sweeps an object around an axis to form a curved solid mesh. You can sweep an object completely around or set an inclusive angle between 0 and 360. If your object is a multisegment line, make it into a polyline by using the Join option under *Pedit*, before attempting to Revsurf.

Ruled Surface (*Rulsurf*) creates a one-directional mesh between two edges. The edges may be joined at one end or set apart in 3D space. They may be points, polylines, or arcs. If one object is closed, as in a circle, then the other must also be closed (though they do not have to be the same shape or size.) Selecting a closed polyline and a point results in a conic object. Selecting opposite ends of each edge results in a crossed polygon mesh.

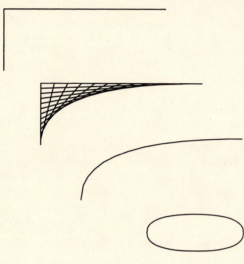

The Edge Surface Command

1. With Ortho *On*, draw two lines at right angles.
2. Pick opposite ends of the lines at the Object Selection prompt of the *Edgsurf* command.
3. Draw a spline or polyline using intersections as nodes.
4. The resultant parabolic curve can be mirrored to form a profile of an oval cushion or pillow.

Tabsurf creates a one-directional tabulated mesh between an object curve and a directional path. The two objects do not have to touch or be coplanar. *Tabsurf* makes a copy of the object curve, positions it at the distance and direction of the path, and fills in the space in between with a preset number of parallel polygons. Notice that *Tabsurf* is called Extruded Surface in the pulldown menu.

The surface character of the mesh is determined by the shape of the object curve. That is, if the object curve is a circle, then the resultant object will be cylindrical. If the object curve is an open polyline with multiple curves, *Tabsurf* will generate an undulating mesh. The path may be three dimensional, but if it is curved, *Tabsurf* will use only the endpoints for distance and direction, ignoring the intermediate vertices.

You can control the number of polygons in the solid surfaces. Set *Surftab1* and *Surftab2* system variables to the number of polygons desired on the surfaces. The denser they are the smoother the object surface, but your drawings are larger in size and slower in regeneration time.

Use 3D Surfaces commands:
Rulsurf 1 and 2.
Revsurf 3, 360° around 4.
Edgsurf 5, 6, 7, and 8.
Revsurf 9, –180° around 10.
Tabsurf 11 and 12.

Draw
Solids >
  Box
  Sphere
  Cylinder >
  Cone >
  Wedge >
  Torus >

This group of commands generates figures known as primitives. Primitives are simple 3D figures used to create composites that can be quite complex. ACIS, the R13 graphics driver, is fundamentally different from AME, the solid modeler of R12. In AME, one can recall and edit the primitive shapes from which a complex form is made. In R13, once a primitive is transformed by such action as Subtract or Union, the database of the figure is changed permanently. Unless you can undo a change immediately or soon thereafter, you cannot recall the original primitive figures by backtracking.

To lessen the impact of this limitation, save a copy of the primitives on a separate layer for later recall. To do this, first copy the object in place, or set it aside (at a defined displacement, if you want the copy back at the same location). Change the layer property of the copy. If you set the copy aside, move it back to the location of the original by using the reverse of the displacement used to move it. Turn off or freeze the new layer before attempting to edit the original.

DRAW2
SOLIDS:
  Box:
  Sphere:
  Cylindr:
  Sphere:

Objects in this category are true solid objects. Although they are displayed as wire frames, you can show them as solids using the Hide, Shade, and Render commands.

To edit a solid object, primitive or composite, you may have to first explode it. See the section on modifying objects.

For more information about using and fine-tuning ACIS objects, see the README.TXT file included in the R13c4 update material.

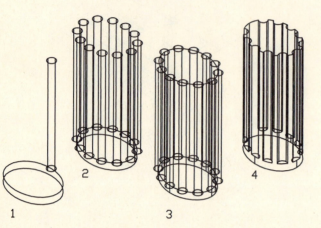

Solid Object: Elliptical Cylinder

1. Under **Options> Display**, set Point Style to X.
   Draw> Ellipse with top at base height.
   Construct> Copy ellipse to bottom of base.

2. **Modify> Divide** upper ellipse into 12 segments. Each point node is marked by an X.
   Draw> Circle> Center, Radius, centered at each node.
   Draw> Solids> Extrude circle to desired height.
   Construct> Copy> Multiple, copy extruded circle to centered at each node point.

3. **Extrude** bottom circle to total height of column.
   Use **Construct> Subtract** to delete tubes from column.

Draw
Solids >
Extrude
Revolve

These two commands allow you to create solid objects from closed 2D figures.

You can use closed polylines, circles, ellipses, polygons, and regions, but not objects in a block (explode them first then join the appropriate lines with *Pedit* into closed figures) or polylines that cross or intersect.

Extrude gives thickness or height to an object that is on the x-y plane of the current UCS. Even though you cannot extrude a 3D object, you can extrude a 2D object along a 3D path, which is new in R13 and very useful for our purposes.

Revolve generates a solid object by taking a sectional profile and revolving it around the x axis, y axis, a path, or a line defined by two points. You can also specify the angle of revolution to create a cut-off view of the object.

DRAW2
SOLIDS:
Extrude:
Revolve:

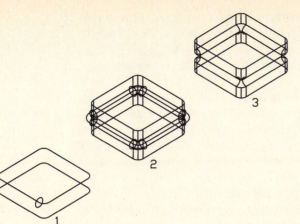

The Extrude Command

1. A polyline loop is created and copied to a higher position. A circle is drawn with its center perpendicular to the copied loop.

2. The circle is extruded with the loop as the path. The circle is now a solid tube. The lower loop is extruded to height to become a solid box.

3. The tube is subtracted from the box to leave a rounded indent around the middle of the box.

Draw
Solids >
   Slice
   Section
   Interference

Slice is used to separate primitive or composite solid objects by slicing with a plane (x-y, y-z, or z-x plane, or by a plane defined by three points) or by the plane of another object, such as a circle, ellipse, arc, 2D spline or polyline. Other slicing options include using a plane perpendicular to the current view. If you pick two points to define a z-axis (you are actually using the z-axis option), the slicing plane will be perpendicular to it.

Objects to be sliced and the slicing plane do not have to be joined or touching as long as the slicing plane can intersect the objects in space.

DRAW2
SOLIDS:
   Slice:
   Section:
   Intrfer:

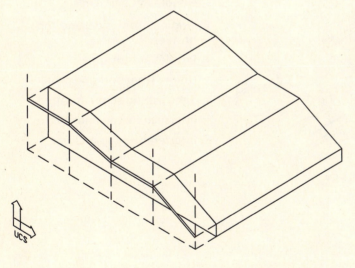

The Slice Command

This is one way to create a nonuniform slicing plane.

1. The solid is first sliced vertically into long sections using the y-z plane of the WCS.

2. Then each section is sliced horizontally using the endpoints of a profile line at their junctures with the vertical slicing line. The top parts are discarded.

3. The remaining bottom parts are merged back into a solid object. If the original slices were spaced closer, the resultant slice profile would be smoother.

Slice prompts you to retain one or both parts after slicing an object. If you want to retain only one of the parts, click on the side of the slicing plane where lies the part you want to keep. If you want to retain both parts, enter b (for Both) on the keyboard.

Specify a sectioning plane in the same manner as you would a cutting plane in the Slice command. The difference is that the objects are not cut into parts. Instead, a new object (the section) is created at the cutting plane. If you have selected separate solids, the section will be separate regions all lying on the cutting plane.

A section is considered to be a region object. It has no thickness but it is a solid planar object. You can treat it as a separate object by moving, extruding, editing it, and so on. The original object remains intact.

When you ask for an interference, a distinct object that occupies the common space between objects (the interference) is created. The original objects remain, and you can treat the interference object as a separate entity. Put it on another layer before you do any editing.

Interference is similar to Intersection, except that in Intersection (found in the Construct category), the original objects disappear and only the object representing the intersection remains. So, if you have a need for the original object, be sure to make a copy of it and store it on another layer.

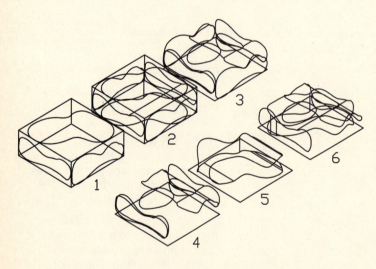

The Boolean Commands

1. Original front, side, and top profiles.
2. Profiles are extruded.
3. **Union:** front and side profiles.
4. **Subtract:** side from front.
5. **Intersection:** top and front.
6. **Interference:** top and side.

Draw
Solids >
   AME Convert

If you have regions and solids drawn in AME R2 or 2.1, AME Convert will change them to the form recognizable by AutoCAD R13. Other drawings are updated to R13 automatically upon opening.

DRAW2
SOLIDS:
AMEconv:

Draw
Hatch >
  Hatch
  PostScript Fill

CONSTRCT
Bhatch:

Generally speaking, Hatch is used to fill an area with a 2D pattern, which may be a customized pattern or a standard Auto-CAD hatch pattern. See the *AutoCAD Command Reference* for a listing and graphic samples of available patterns. You can select the manner in which a hatch pattern fills an area.

Selecting the Hatch command from the pulldown menu is equivalent to entering *Bhatch* (Boundary Hatch) from the keyboard, or from the side menu under CONSTRCT/Bhatch. When a hatch pattern is inserted using *Bhatch*, the pattern fill is adjusted to conform with any modifications to the boundaries of the area. For example, if the boundaries of an area are expanded, *Bhatch* causes the pattern to fill to the new boundaries.

However, if you simply enter *Hatch* on the keyboard, the fill pattern will not be amended when the boundaries of the hatch area are changed.

It is always prudent to check the scale of a hatch pattern, that is, check the size of a single unit of the hatch pattern you want to use. Test it out on a small enclosed area such as a rectangle. Some of the standard AutoCAD hatch patterns are scaled down. So if you attempt to fill a large area, say the side of a building, with a pattern whose default size is an inch or less, it will take a long time to fill and result in a huge file. Once started, it is usually possible to terminate hatch generation by Ctrl-C, but you may have to stop a hatch from continuing to fill by rebooting the computer, thus losing any unsaved part of your drawing.

You can also insert PostScript hatch patterns by using the Post-Script Fill option. PostScript files can rapidly become very large. One usually inserts a PostScript pattern only for effect, say, during a formal presentation, but not saving the PostScript hatch in the drawing database.

Draw
Text >
  Text
  Dynamic Text
  Single Line Text

DRAW2
Mtext:
Dtext:

Text can be inserted into drawings for notational purposes. It is mostly used in technical drawings, such as floor plans and other 2D working drawings. For purposes of visualizing interior spaces, there are not many situations where the use of text is required.

One exception may lie in the use of True Type fonts for labeling presentation drawings. In this case, the text would be inserted in paperspace, as titles and other textual information. AutoCAD provides a number of True Type fonts which can be scaled to fit the space specified by the drawing layout. A sheet of True Type fonts can be found in the file *TrueType.dwg* under the ACADR13\Sample directory.

Some PostScript fonts may have to be compiled and loaded as *.shx* files before you can use them. To use True Type and other PostScript fonts after they have been loaded, select **Dtext/Style/Yes** from the side menu. A dialog box comes up in which you can select text fonts that have *.shx*, *.pfb*, *.pfa*, and *.ttf* extensions.

Selecting the Text option in the pulldown menu is equivalent to entering Mtext on the side menu.

Mtext is an option that allows you to fit a block of text into an area. You are first prompted to specify a window where the text will be placed. Text can be either typed in directly or imported from existing text files in *.txt, .psf* formats.

In Dynamic Text (*Dtext*), you first specify the starting point and the size of text, then a cursor square the size of a letter will appear on screen at the starting point. As you type in the letters, they are echoed on the screen. When you press Enter, the cursor square returns to the starting column one line below the starting point. You can enter letters for the second line and continue to the third and so on. Each time you press Enter, the cursor square returns to the starting column. You must press Enter or click the RMB to register the entered text and exit the command.

Draw
Dimensioning >

Dimensioning is used for annotating technical drawings. It is not usually used in drawings for visualization and, therefore, will not be discussed in this book. For a full explanation of dimensioning, see the *AutoCAD Command Reference* and the *User's Guide*.

DRAW DIM

These are new commands added to AutoCAD Release 13c4. You access these commands by entering their names on the keyboard.

**SOLDRAW
SOLPROF
SOLVIEW**

SOLVIEW is used to create paperspace floating viewpoints in which SOLDRAW will generate profiles and sections of solid objects.

SOLPROF is used to generate profiles or silhouettes of solid objects in the current view in modelspace.

For more information about using and fine-tuning ACIS objects, see the README.TXT file included in the R13c4 update material.

Create Area: Construct Commands

In general, the commands in this category are used to create copies and other mutations of objects already created with commands in the **Draw** category.

These commands can be accessed through the **Construct** button on the pull-down menu or by highlighting the **CONSTRUCT** label on the side menu.

Pulldown menu and options in the **Construct** category:

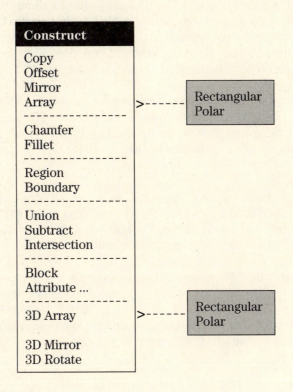

The Commands in the Construct Category

PULLDOWN MENU

Construct
Copy
Offset
Mirror
Array >
   Rectangular
   Polar

SIDE MENU

CONSTRCT
Copy:
Offset:
Mirror:
Array:

This group of construction commands are alike. They use a similar sequence of prompts to make copies of objects.

In most instances, you use these commands to move or copy objects from one location to another. If you want to be precise, you have to be very careful when you select objects and when you specify displacement distances.

You can use a crossing window to select, but be sure that all the objects the window crosses are really the ones you want. This is especially true in plan view, where objects in 3D space may seem to overlap. To aid in selecting, you may be able to see the correct objects better if you switch to a 3D view.

Always use Object Snaps to select such features as intersections and endpoints especially with 3D objects or in 3D space. Never pick them visually with the mouse. Object Snaps are easily and transparently available by holding down the Shift key and clicking the right mouse button (Shift+RMB).

When prompted for a base point, as in the Copy command after object selection, pick an arbitrary point (any point) in the drawing field and use a relative (@) (Shift+2) distance to specify the displacement in units, or distance and angle.

Keep Ortho *Off* or AutoCAD may force your pick points to remain on the x-y plane while you think you are specifying some other points in 3D space. However, in Mirror, having Ortho *On* makes it easier to specify the second point on the mirror line, if that line is parallel to either the x or y axis.

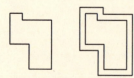

The Offset Command

A closed polyline object may be offset to the inside or outside.

Offset produces a copy of 2D line objects a set distance to either side of and parallel to the original object. If an object is a closed polyline, the offset is a copy to the inside or the outside of the original, spaced by the offset distance.

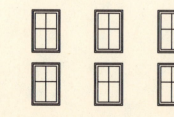

The Array Command

An array of rows and columns may be created by specifying the distance. Distance is measured from center to center, or from edge to corresponding edge from the first column or row to the next.

Array constructs a 2D matrix of rows and columns of selected objects. As in the case of multiple copying, you can think of arraying as using a rubber stamp to make rows and/or columns of one or more objects.

You must remember to include the spacing between objects. To put it another way, think of the distance between rows and columns as the spacing from the center of an object to the center of its copy.

The number of rows and columns to specify is the resultant amount, so be sure to include the original object in your count of rows and columns.

Construct
Chamfer
Fillet

Chamfer transforms a corner between adjoining edges with a predefined straight line in 2D objects, or a bevel in 3D objects. A fillet does the same with a curved line or plane.

The edges do not have to actually meet. They can be implied intersections, but they cannot be divergent.

When you select an edge of a solid to be chamfered, it can be one of two planes that share the edge; only one can be the base plane. One plane will be highlighted to indicate which surface AutoCAD thinks you want as a base plane. If it is not the right one, type *n* (for Next) to cycle to the other plane.

After selecting the base plane, you then select the edges to be chamfered by picking them one at a time or choosing the Loop option to chamfer all edges that are on the base plane.

A similar sequence of steps will take you through the Fillet command. Instead of a Loop, there is an Edge Chain option which allows you to fillet a string of adjoining edges on the base plane.

You may encounter problems when you use Chamfer or Fillet on complex 3D objects. Consult the section on Using Fillet and Chamfer with 3D Solids in the README.TXT file included in the R13c4 update material.

CONSTRCT
Chamfer:
Fillet:

Construct
Region
Bounding Polyline

A region is a solid planar object made by a closed outline, a circle, for example. A region is particularly suited for creating irregular, complex shapes that are composed of curves, including splines, and closed objects such as circles and ellipses. Such a region is considered to be defined by a bounding polyline or a boundary line. You can define a boundary by picking a point inside each area or shape that makes up the region. After selecting such internal points, press Enter and a region will be created.

The region cannot have intersections, nor can it cross over itself. A region can be extruded or combined with solids. Modify regions with the Explode and Edge commands. After exploding, a boundary line will no longer be a polyline. Make it into one by joining all segments under the Edit Polyline command.

CONSTRCT
Boundar:
Region:

**Construct
Union
Subtract
Intersection**

These are the main tools for building 3D shapes.

Composite solids may be built from primitives or other composites. You can use this group of commands with solids and/or regions, but you cannot use them on 3D surfaces, 3D faces, or 3D meshes.

Be aware that in Subtract you first pick the part of the object you wish to remain; then you select the object to take away.

The use of Intersection results in an object that occupies the common space between the objects selected. The original objects are deleted.

As R13 changes the geometry of solids, the previous form of the solids may be unrecoverable, unless you keep making a copy on another, preferably discrete, layer as a backup.

DRAW2
**Union:
Subtrac:
Intersec:**

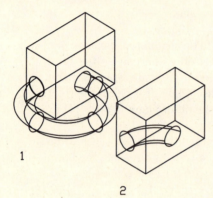

The Union and Subtract Commands

Union and Subtract are Boolean operations used to transform solid objects.

When you use Subtract, first pick the objects you want to retain, then pick the objects to be subtracted from the first ones.

In this example:

1. Box and Torus are unioned.
2. The Torus is subtracted from the box.

**Construct
Block**

Blocking a group of objects is like making a rubber stamp with which you can insert copies of the group into a drawing.

As you insert a block, you can change the x or y scale and its angle of rotation. To edit a block after it has been inserted, use **Modify> Explode**.

A block is a part of the current drawing and stored in the current drawing file.

You can create a copy of the block outside of your drawing by using the Write Block (Wblock) command, which is accessed through **File>Export>Block**.

CONSTRCT
DDatDef:

**Construct
3D Array >
  3D Mirror
  3D Rotate**

Use 3D Array to position copies of one or more objects in a matrix comprised of rows and columns, as well as tiers.

When specifying the number of rows, columns, or tiers, remember to include the first one. That is, the command expects the resultant number of rows and so on, not just the additional ones.

CONSTRCT
**3Darray:
Mirror3D:
Rotat3D:**

It is also important to remember that in specifying spacing, you must provide the distance from the center of a group of objects to the center of the next group.

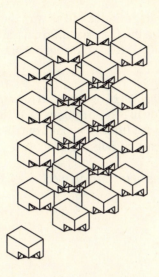

The 3D Array Command

This is an array of two rows, three columns, and four tiers.

Distance is measured from center to center, or edge to corresponding edge between rows, columns, or tiers.

One way you can mirror objects in 3D is by orienting the mirror plane to another object. For example, if you use a circle as a mirror, the mirror is the plane of the circle. You can also define a plane by specifying three points.

3D Rotate allows you to rotate an object by aligning the rotational axis with a straight line, the extrusion axis of a circle or arc, or the vector joining the ends of a polyline.

You can also specify the axis of rotation by selecting two points, or the last object referenced, the current x, y, or z axis. You may use the current viewing direction aligned with the line from a point you pick as the rotational axis.

Remember AutoCAD uses the Right Hand Rule for indicating the direction of rotation.

The 3D Rotate Command

A circle that is tilted in 3D is used as the plane by which the drawing object is rotated in 3D.

Once you have drawn some objects, you invariably have to change them. In AutoCAD, editing commands are grouped under the **Modify** category.

Most of these commands are intuitive in the way they prompt you for additional input. Keep an eye on the Command Prompt area at the bottom of the screen. That is where AutoCAD tells you what it wants to know or what it expects you to input.

At times there is an additional list of options that becomes current after the initial object selection step. You use these options to do the editing. When you are done, exit from the options list first, then exit from the command (by entering x, as in eXit; twice, in the case of Edit Polyline).

Pulldown menu and options in the **Modify** category:

```
Modify
Properties ...
----------------
Move
Rotate
Align
----------------
Stretch
Scale
Lengthen
Point
----------------
Trim
Extend
Break            >------   1 point
----------------          1 point Select
Edit Polyline             ------------
Edit Multiline            2 point
Edit Spline               2 point Select
Edit Text ...
Edit Hatch ...
Attribute        >------   Edit
Explode                    Edit Globally
----------------           ------------
Erase                      Redefine
Oops
```

The Commands in the Modify Category

PULLDOWN MENU

Modify
Properties ...

Under this item, a dialog box appears in which you can modify many of the properties of the object you select. Selecting DDmodify brings on the same dialog box as the one under **Modify > Properties...**, while DDchprp allows you to pick many of the functions by mouse.

You can modify the layer, color, and line type, but the exact properties depend on the type of object selected. If it is a 3D object, such as a 3D Face, certain properties specific to that type of object, including the visibility of edges, may be changed under DDmodify.

The command Change, by which you can change the elevation as well as color, layer, line type, line-type scale, and thickness of objects, can be accessed either through the side menu or by typing it in on the keyboard at the Command Prompt Line.

SIDE MENU

MODIFY
Change:
DDchprp:
DDmodify:

Modify
Move

If you have a copy of an object on another layer, moving that object on the current layer will not affect the copy on the other layer. If the copies are coincidental to one another, that is, if they occupy the same space, but on different layers, make certain that you are selecting the correct copy of the object to edit. A correct copy may be easier to pick out if you put it in a different color or line type or on a layer that you can isolate. You can also move it a set distance aside, edit it, then move it back to the original position.

MODIFY
Move:

You can select objects that are lying on top of, or very close to, one another by cycling through the selection process. For example, if you have more than one object occupying the same space, you can select only one of them at a time by holding down the Ctrl key while placing the cursor on the stacked objects, and clicking the LMB. A copy of the object will be shown in dotted lines, indicating that it has been selected.

Modify
Rotate

Rotate is the command to use for rotating objects on the x-y plane about the z direction of the current UCS. The UCS may be angled and/or tilted relative to the WCS. Rotate will still use the z-axis of the UCS as reference.

MODIFY
Rotate:

The Rotate Command

In this example, two ellipses at different heights are rotated along the z-axis. Then they are joined by **Draw> Surfaces Ruled Surface** into a solid object.

UCS

| Modify
Align | Align allows you to use one, two, or three pairs of points as reference to rotate and relocate objects to be lined up with other objects. | MODIFY
Align: |

Keep an eye on the Command Prompt Line as it alternately asks you for source and destination points. It may help you to visualize if you mark and number the pairs of points on a print of the current view.

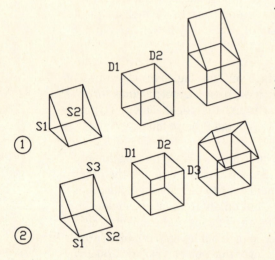

The Align Command

1. Align objects using two pairs of points.
   Align S1 to D2; S2 to D2.

2. Aligning objects using three pairs of points results in objects being aligned and rotated.
   Align S1 to D2; S2 to D2; S3 to D3.

   S = Source point; D = Destination point.

| Modify
Stretch | The default method for selecting an object to stretch is by a crossing window. Stretch transforms an object by the specified distance in the x or y direction. | MODIFY
Stretch: |

The Stretch Command

Select objects with a crossing window.
3D objects may also be stretched along the x-y plane of the UCS.

| Modify
Scale | If a selected object is a 2D object, a 3D face, or a 3D mesh, it will be scaled two-dimensionally in its x-y plane. If an object is a 3D solid, it will be scaled (up or down) by the same distance in its x, y, and z directions. | MODIFY
Scale: |

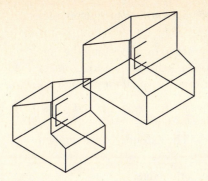

The Scale Command

2D or 3D objects may be scaled by reference to relative size.

Modify **Lengthen**	Lengthen changes the length of open 2D objects in 2D or 3D space. You may opt to change the length by incremental units (Enter: DELta on the options list), by a percentage of the object (Enter: Percent), or by a Total absolute length, with the change extending or retracting from the nearer endpoint. Select Angle to change the included angle of an arc. A + value increases the length or angle, while a – value reduces the same. The DYnamic option allows you to drag an endpoint to another location.	MODIFY **Lengthen:**
Modify **Point**	Invoking this command from the pulldown menu is different from calling the command from the side menu. Either way, you are expected to change the location of the endpoint line object you have selected. In many ways, this command is similar to the **Modify > Lengthen** or **Modify > Properties ...** commands. By changing the location of the endpoint, the line object is lengthened or pivoted to the new position of the endpoint. This is not the command to use for modifying a *point object's* style. For that, you need to use the option under **Options > Point Style ...** to select a different style of point objects.	MODIFY **DDchprp:** **DDmodify:**
Modify **Trim**	Trim first prompts you to select cutting edges, then it asks for the objects to trim. You may use an implied intersection for trimming. Objects do not have to actually intersect in space to be used as a trimming edge or as an object to be trimmed. You can set the mode for edges to project or to extend from the list of options in the command.	MODIFY **Trim:**

The first response of the Trim command is:

> *Select cutting edge (Projmode=0. Edgemode=No extend):*

After you have selected an edge, the second response is:

> *<Select object to trim>/Project/Edge/Undo:*

Of these options,

> *<Select object to trim>* is the default and is obvious.
> /Project/ allows three additional choices: *None/UCS/View.*
>> *0* or *None* means no projection. Only those boundaries that actually intersect will be considered valid selections.

1 or UCS means the selected edges will be projected onto the x-y plane of the current UCS.

2 or View means the mode is set to project along the current view direction, so that objects that appear to intersect in the current view will be trimmed, even if they do not actually intersect.

/Edge/ brings up two options: *Extend/No extend.*

0 or Extend means the edge will be extended to an implied boundary.

1 or No extend will not extend the edge.

/Undo rescinds the last input in the current Trim command and restores the object.

The numbers 0, 1, and 2 are values for the Projmode and Edgemode system variables. And the values in the *Projmode=* and *Edgemode=* equations echo the current setting.

Objects that may be trimmed are 2D objects, including rays, and 3D polylines. Use 3D editing tools for modifying 3D surfaces and solids.

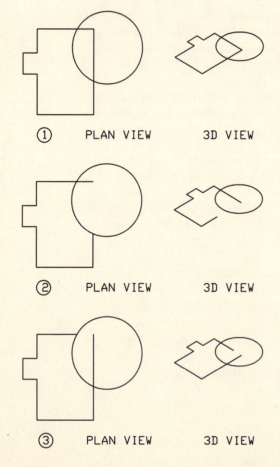

①   PLAN VIEW   3D VIEW

②   PLAN VIEW   3D VIEW

③   PLAN VIEW   3D VIEW

The Trim Command

In the illustration, the circle is drawn at a higher elevation than the rectilinear object.

1. Projmode = None. Edgemode = No extend. The circle cannot be used to trim the object.

2. Projmode = UCS. Edgemode = No extend. In plan view, the circle can be used as a cutting edge to trim off a part of the object.

3. With the same Projmode and Edgemode settings as in number 2, this illustration demonstrates that trimming in 3D view differs from trimming in plan view.

In R13, you are allowed to extend implicitly by implied boundaries rather than having to have actual boundaries to which objects would extend. This can be done in 2D or 3D space and with 2D objects and open 3D polylines, but not objects within blocks or the blocks themselves. You would have to first explode the blocks to be able to extend edges within them.

You can set how surfaces and edges are projected. Extend responds with a list of options similar to those of the Trim command.

The first response of the Extend command is:

> *<Select Boundary edges: (Projmode= UCS, Edgemode: Extend)*

After you have selected an allowable edge, the response is:

> *<Select object to extend>/Project/Edge/Undo:*

Of these options:

> *<Select object to extend>* is the default and is obvious.
>
> */Project/* allows three additional choices: *None/UCS/View.*
>
>> *0* or *None* means no projection. Only those boundaries that actually intersect will be considered valid selections.
>>
>> *1 or UCS* means the selected edges will be projected onto the x-y plane of the current UCS.
>>
>> *2 or View* means the mode is set to project along the current view direction, so that objects that appear to intersect in the current view will be extended, even if they do not actually intersect.
>
> */Edge/* brings up two additional choices: *Extend/No extend.*
>
>> *0* or *Extend* means the edge will be extended to an implied boundary.
>>
>> *1* or *No extend* will not extend the edge.
>
> */Undo* rescinds the last input in the current Extend command and restores the object.

To edit a 2D object by breaking it into two parts, you must specify two points on the object. To be precise, you should use Object Snaps (Osnaps) to specify the points. You may break an object at a point (by entering @ at the prompt for the second point). If you want to break off a specific portion of an object, enter a relative distance from the first point.

```
2 METHODS OF USING
BREAK WITH THE SAME
RESULT.
```

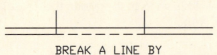

```
BREAK A LINE BY
DEFINING 2 END POINTS.
```

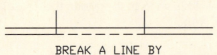

```
BREAK A LINE BY SETTING
FIRST POINT, THEN USE
RELATIVE (@X,Y) TO
DEFINE THE 2ND POINT.
```

The Break Command

Several methods may be used to select an object and points at which to break the selected object.

You can select an object and have it broken into two segments at the point of selection. This is the **1 Point** option.

Picking the 1 Point/Select option allows you to pick an object and a second point to break. The segment between the two points is deleted.

You can select an object, then enter *F* (for First Point), specify the first point, and then specify a second point. These are the **2 Point** and the **2 Points/Select** options.

To be precise, specify points by using Osnaps and Osnap Overrides and relative distances, as shown in the illustration.

Modify **Edit Polyline**	Use this command to edit the attributes. If you select a line that is not a polyline, AutoCAD asks if you want to change it into one. When you have selected a polyline, a special list of options appears. Use these options and not the regular editing commands to edit a polyline. Keep a close watch on the Command Prompt Line. This is one of those incidents where there are submenu options from which you need to exit first, and then exit from the main options list to return to the Command Prompt.	MODIFY **Pedit**
Modify **Edit Multiline ...**	Edit Multiline is called Mledit from the Command Prompt and from the side menu. A Multiline Edit Tools dialog box appears from which you can choose to edit already drawn multilines. There are various kinds of crossings and tees you can use. You can create L-junctions, open or close breaks, and edit vertices of multilines. One caveat is that you should set the multiline style to display joints or you will not be able to see any vertices in the line because they will not be visible. Rather than spending time to figure out which tool to use to achieve the desired result, and depending on the complexity of either the Multiline and/or your drawing, it may be easier to use regular editing tools, such as drawing a Construction Line to use to trim one or more multilines.	MODIFY **Mledit**

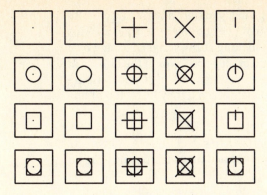

The Edit Multiline Dialog Box

Use **Modify> Explode** to break a multiline down to its components.

Modify **Edit Spline**	As in the case of Edit Polyline, you can choose to create a smooth spline by selecting the Fit Data option, or you can select any of the other options: Open, Close spline, Move vertex, or Refine a curve.	MODIFY **SplinEd:**
Modify **Edit Text**	When you invoke the command, you can select text created by Text or Dtext. In the dialog box that comes up subsequently, edit the text by highlighting it in the text field. You may also edit text attribute definitions such as tags (names), prompt (of the Text command), text height, rotation, and width.	MODIFY **DDedit:**
Modify **Edit Hatch**	Associated hatch pattern types, boundaries, and pattern properties can be edited in this new feature of AutoCAD. A hatch may also inherit the properties of another hatch pattern in the current drawing.	MODIFY **HatchEd:**
Modify **Attribute >** Edit ... Edit Globally	Attributes of text blocks may be changed locally by selected objects or globally. Choose Edit to enable making changes to all text attributes. Select Edit Globally to edit only one text string at a time. Text attributes that can be changed are value, position, angle, style, layer, and color. These attributes of inserted drawings are changed independent of the text block in the original drawing.	MODIFY **AttEd:**
Modify **Explode**	Blocks and polylines may be exploded for editing purposes. You may also explode 3D meshes, solids, polygons, and regions. In R13, you are allowed to explode nonuniformly scaled blocks. If you need to change such items as color, line type, or layer of the component parts of a block, type in *Xplode* (accessible only from Command Prompt), instead of using Explode.	MODIFY **Explode**
Modify **Erase**	After entering the command, select objects to be erased by any of the usual object-picking methods. When you have selected objects, press the RMB. The selected objects will be shown in dotted lines. You can deselect objects by entering *r* (for Remove), then pick the objects you want removed from the selection set. When all the correct objects have been picked, press the RMB again to erase the objects and exit the command.	MODIFY **Erase:**

If a mistake was made in arraying, you may have arrayed multiple copies of an object on top of one another as if in layers. This will not be evident from just looking at the screen. Erasing by a right-opening window will select only one layer of the objects at a time. Selecting by using a left-opening crossing window will result in all the objects being picked, even if they lie on top of one another.

Beware of using crossing windows to select objects. All objects the window crosses will be picked and may include ones you do not want selected. As a general rule, select an object to be erased by a right-opening window that encloses the object or pick the object by clicking LMB on it.

Modify
Oops

You may undo an erasure using the Oops command immediately after exiting from Erase.

You may also undo a Wblock by using Oops immediately after defining a Wblock. The block will still have been written to a file, and the original objects will reappear on the screen as unblocked entities.

MODIFY
Oops:

In R13, a number of commands familiar to users of previous releases are now accessible through the side menu or the Command Prompt. Among them are:

Change (see **Modify> Properties...** above).

Chprop (see **Modify>Properties ...** above).

Elev (see **Modify> Properties ...** above). You can use Move to change the elevation of objects. Remember: Elevation refers to the altitude of the base plane of an object, while Height refers to the thickness of the object.

Display Area: View Commands

To create and modify drawings precisely, you must be able to visualize them from various directions and in fine enough detail especially when you work in 3D space. You need to develop a habit of frequently changing your viewpoint to check on your solid models from different angles and in various powers of magnification. You should make use of AutoCAD's ability to zoom in tightly so you can work on details. Since you have to work on surfaces in 3D, you must set and reset the coordinate systems (WCS and UCS). Therefore, you must be familiar not only with the 3D coordinate systems of AutoCAD, but also with how to manipulate your way in and around these systems. The Display area of menus includes the commands you need to control the visual representation of your creations.

Pulldown menu and options in the **View** category:

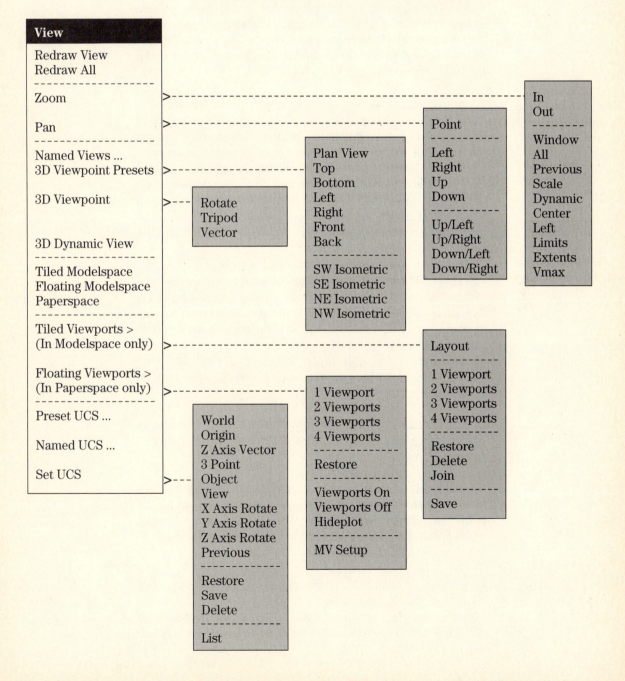

The Commands in the View Category

View
Redraw
Redraw All

As you work in AutoCAD, the screen starts to fill up with blips marking objects that have been transformed by commands such as Erase and Move. These blips clutter up the screen and can become confusing to the eye. To clear up the blips, invoke the Redraw command, which clears up the temporary blip markers. You may also turn the Blip mode to *Off* so that the blips will not appear on the screen, but then you lose the use of a handy reference tool. See the **Options > Drawing aids** dialog box for changing Blip modes.

There are times when, for example, you have moved an object, but there is a copy of the drawing underneath at the original location. The copy may not be visible immediately. Issue a Regen or Regenall command at the keyboard and all the objects on all the active layers will be regenerated. Set the System Variable for Regenauto or type in at the keyboard. Also see the section about the Redo command.

VIEW
Redraw:
RedrawAl:

(Regen)
(Regenall)
(Regenauto)

View
Zoom

Zoom is used extensively in working with drawings and especially in solid modeling. Zoom can be used transparently in most drawing and modifying commands. At the stage when you are prompted for a point specification or object selection, zoom in around a detail of the drawing to avoid any ambiguity. Two of the new features in R13 are: Zoom In and Zoom Out, which incrementally go in or out from the current view. The other useful feature is the ability to zoom by specifying a window around an area for closer examination. Zoom All, Previous, Limits, and Extents are other available features.

VIEW
Zoom:

View
Pan

Pan slides the viewport around the screen much like viewing a Chinese landscape scroll. Pan scrolls around the drawing in any direction vertically, horizontally, and angularly without moving in or out toward the drawing model. It is like moving the view camera while keeping constant the perpendicular distance and tilt angle between the objects and the camera. If Ortho is *On* the panning movement is restricted to only vertical or horizontal movements.

Do not confuse panning with moving the objects. Panning is strictly a viewing function. It does not change the geometry of any part of your design.

You may pan by preset movements such as up, down, to the left, or to the right. Or you may define panning movement by the Point option in which you select two points on the screen, whereupon the viewport will shift in the direction of and by the distance between the points.

VIEW
Pan:

View
Named Views

Save a view by naming it and you can recall the view by selecting it from the dialog box under Named View. If you have not named a view, the current view will be labeled as *No Name* in the dialog box. Type in a name and click on the Rename It button.

VIEW
Ddview:

View
**3D Viewpoint
Presets >**

VIEW
**Plan:
Vpoint:**

Among 3D Viewpoint Presets are standard orthographic views such as Top, Bottom, Left, Right, Front, and Back. There is a plan view option which sets the view to the plan of the current UCS or to that of the WCS.

Other 3D Viewpoint Presets include 45° views from the southwest, southeast, northwest, and northeast quadrants, designated as SW, SE, NW, and NE Isometric, respectively. Selecting a SE Isometric is like specifying a Viewpoint (Vpoint) of 1,–1,1, while a NW Isometric is equivalent to Vpoint –1,1,1.

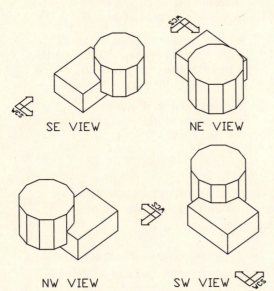

SE VIEW   NE VIEW

NW VIEW   SW VIEW

3D Viewpoint Presets

In addition to orthographic view, you can set 3D isometric views from the SW, SE, NE, and NW by just clicking on the name.

View
3D Viewpoint >
Rotate

VIEW
Vpoint:
Rotate

In the Rotate option, you are allowed to set your viewpoint by selecting a location in the plan view of a compass rose and then by setting an angle from the x-y plane. Place your mouse cursor at the desired position and click the LMB to select. The settings you select are echoed in information boxes as well as by needle indicators.

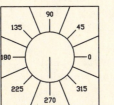
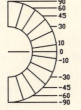

3D Viewpoint Rotate

In this illustration, the Viewpoint is set to look from 270° toward the center and at 0° at the x-y plane. These settings result in an elevation view from the front. Similarly, moving the pointer to look from 180° will result in an elevation view from the left.

| View
3D Viewpoint >
Tripod | There are two icons in this command. One shows the 3D spatial quadrants in plan view, while the other displays a tripod consisting of the x, y, and z axes. The tripod rotates dynamically to reflect the position of the cursor in the plan view icon. | VIEW
Vpoint:
Axes |

The Axes Tripod

The first icon shows a plan view of the 3D space quadrants. The area within the small circle is above the x-y plane (+z direction). The area between the small and large circles is below the x-y plane (–z).

A point on the edge of the small circle is on the x-y plane at 0 height. A point at the center is at 90°, looking straight down the z-axis.

The second icon shows the orientation of the x-y plane as set in the first icon.

```
Z
|
|
|____ Y
/
/
X

AXIS TRIPOD
3D VIEW
ROTATING
X-Y AXES


PLAN VIEW
CURSOR IS A
CROSS
```

| View
3D Viewpoint >
Vector | The Vector option allows you to enter a viewpoint by specifying relative position coordinates, such as VP 1,–1, 1 for approximately a 45° high, SE isometric view. | VIEW
Vpoint:
Vector |

| View
3D Dynamic View | This command allows you to set up camera positions and target points for axonometric and perspective views. You can adjust the focal lengths of the lens and its zoom power. And you can pan, twist, and clip the views. See Chapter 5 for more discussion on using 3D Dynamic View. | VIEW
Dview: |

| View
Tiled Modelspace | When you are creating objects, you are working in 3D space, which is designated as modelspace. When you compose your design on a flat, 2D surface in preparation, say, for a plotted copy, you are working in paperspace. The Tiled Modelspace button toggles a tilemode *On* or *Off* for the purpose of switching between modelspace and paperspace.

Tilemode is set to *On* (Tilemode = 1) when you are in modelspace. Toggle Tilemode *Off* (Tilemode = 0) and you will be working in paperspace. | VIEW
Tilemod: |

| View
Floating Modelspace | In paperspace, you can punch "holes" in your drawing paper to work on your design in modelspace. These "holes" are *viewports* and are created by using **View> Floating Viewports**. Once viewports have been created, you can click on this, the *Floating Modelspace*, command. Then, when you place your mouse cursor in a viewport and click the LMB, that viewport becomes active in modelspace. You can then use any of the modeling commands to work on your design.

After you have switched to modelspace, you can make any viewport current and active by clicking it *On*. | VIEW
Mspace: |

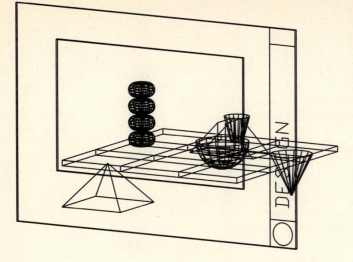

Paperspace and Modelspace

Switch between paperspace and modelspace by clicking on **Paperspace** and **Floating Modelspace**.

See Chapter 7 for more information on working with viewports and plotting in paperspace.

View **Paperspace**	When you select **View > Paperspace**, you are automatically toggling Tilemode = *0* or *Off* and you are placed in paperspace.	VIEW **Pspace:**

You compose a 2D presentation in paperspace on the computer monitor screen. You can make title blocks, insert notes, and draw designs on the "paper," but make extensive use of layers to manage such items and viewports in paperspace. You can have different items and/or viewports on different layers.

If you keep Tilemode *Off* and switch to Floating Modelspace, as described above, you can keep your sheet of paper drawing on so you can edit and model your design.

Turning Tilemode to *On* will switch you back to modelspace. All the layers associated with paperspace will not be visible, so be sure that your current layer is set to one associated with modelspace before you set Tilemode = *1* or *On*.

Whether or not you are plotting a drawing, you can treat the image on the screen as a flat composition in its own right. You can write a script to control the timing and visibility of drawings and objects to make a slide presentation for public display.

Plotting can be from either type of space. You should use the X/XP factor (in **View> Zoom>**) if you want to plot a drawing to scale.

View **Tiled Viewports >**	The display screen can be divided into a number of viewports. Preset patterns of one to four viewports can be selected from the Tiled Viewports menu. Select the desired number of viewports: 1, 2, 3 or 4. Set by specifying opposite corners of the area on the screen that the viewport(s) will occupy.	VIEW **TileVpt:**

Tile Viewports can only be used when you are in paperspace, that is, Tilemode = *0* or *Off*.

View **Floating Viewports >**	If you want to define your own viewports, use the Floating Viewports command. Define viewports in the same manner by which you specify windows. Floating Viewports is available only in paperspace.	VIEW **Vports:** **Mview:**

You can define viewports by selecting the MV Setting option, in which you can set viewports by aligning it to another, or use preset templates such as the one for a title block.

Viewports may be edited—scaled, stretched, moved, and so on—by many of the regular editing commands.

Note: The concepts, usage, and visualization of coordinate systems—the World Coordinate System (WCS), the User Coordinate System (UCS), or Object Coordinate System (OCS)—are of the utmost importance when it comes to working with solid objects in 3D space.

See the beginning of this chapter for a discussion of coordinate systems and the various quadrants in space.

View **Preset UCS ...**	The dialog box under this command allows you to reset the coordinate system back to the WCS, or set the UCS to be aligned with the plane of the top, back, left, front, right, and back of an object.	VIEW **Dducsp:**
View **Named UCS**	Use this option to restore a previously named and saved UCS. If none was named, you can create a new one.	VIEW **Dducs:**
View **Set UCS >**	Set the UCS back to WCS by picking World in the list of options. The rest of the list includes setting a new UCS Origin and setting a CS by defining a z-axis vector.	VIEW

One of the more versatile options is to define a new UCS by three points: the origin, a point in the +x direction, and a point in the +y direction. In this option, use coordinates, axes, and directions relative to the current UCS for defining points.

You also can set UCS by orienting to another object's coordinate system (OCS) or by the current view. You can set a UCS by rotating about the x, y, or z axis. The previous UCS can be recalled.

You can also save, restore, or delete a UCS under, the Set UCS menu. Lastly, you can ask for a list of Named UCSs.

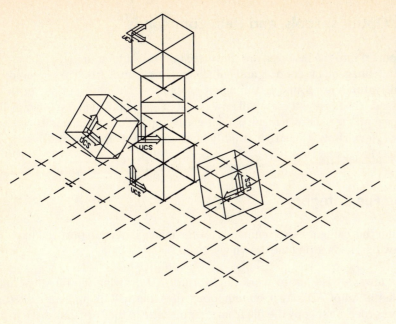

Set UCS

One of the most versatile features is the capability to set a UCS by the **3 Point** option. First, define an origin then specify +x and +y directions by using coordinates relative to the current coordinate system, whether it is the WCS or a UCS.

Other Areas: File, Assist, Data, Options, Tools, and Help Commands

Grouped into the last area are those commands and features that have to do with management, control, and enhancement of AutoCAD. These commands and features are found in the menu categories that have not yet been discussed. The pertinent ones will now be listed and detailed in the order as they appear on the pulldown menu bar across the top of the screen, namely File, Assist (View, Draw, Construct, Modify have already been discussed), Data, Options, Tools, and Help.

The File Category

Under this category are commands for file management, import and export of drawings, and exiting the drawing session.

It is always wise not to work on an AutoCAD drawing file directly from a diskette. AutoCAD may open temporary files that will fill up your diskette in short order. First copy the file from your diskette to the hard disk drive before you begin a drawing session. You can then answer "no" to the startup question that asks if you want to copy a file.

At the end of the drawing session, copy the file back onto your diskette to use it as a backup or as a file to use in the future, when you may be on a different computer.

Pulldown menu and options of the **File** category:

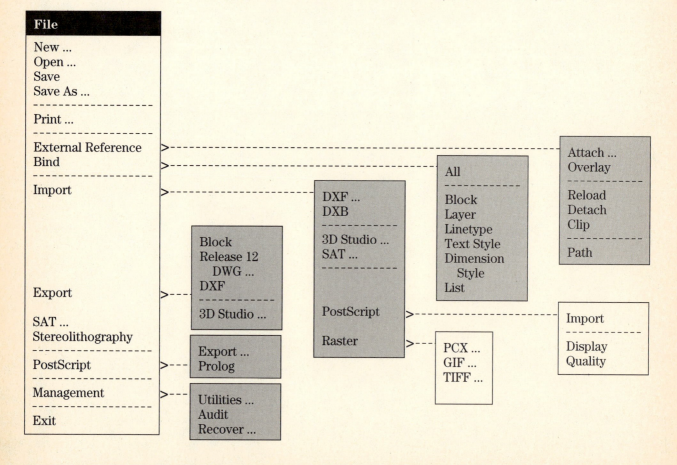

The Assist Category

Commands in this category make object selection easier and more precise.

Pulldown menu and options of the **Assist** category:

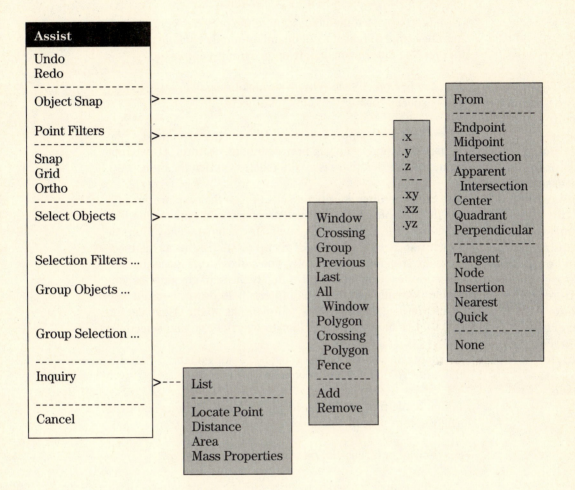

The Commands in the Assist Category

PULLDOWN MENU

Assist
Undo

Under normal conditions, you may backtrack through previous commands in a drawing session by repeated use of the Undo command. You cannot undo back past the current drawing session.

SIDE MENU

ASSIST
Undo:

Assist
Redo

Use Redo to repeat the invocation of the previous command. It may be easier to repeat a command by simply clicking the RMB or pressing Enter immediately upon exiting a command.

ASSIST
Redo:

Assist
Object Snap >
   From
   - - - - - - - - - - - - - -
   Endpoint
   Midpoint
   Intersection
   Apparent
      Intersec.
   Center
   Quadrant
   Perpendicular
   - - - - - - - - - - - - - -
   Tangent
   Node
   Insertion
   Nearest
   Quick
   - - - - - - - - - - - - - -
   None

The use of Object Snap (Osnap) is absolutely necessary to precisely specify the location of point objects.

When lines are supposed to meet, for example, you must make certain that there is no gap between them, or AutoCAD will not acknowledge that there is an intersection at that location.

Use Osnap to filter your point selection so that you are specifying the endpoint, midpoint, and so on exactly, rather than just pointing to the general area visually. If you have set any filters in **Options> Running Object Snap** so such items as intersections are selected automatically, you can override the automatic selection feature manually. Do this is the same manner as you would normally call for Osnap filters: hold down the Shift key while pressing the RMB. This action brings up the Osnap list for you to pick another Osnap filter to override the autoselection.

You may also access the Osnap list by clicking on the **** under the AutoCAD label in the side menu.

In this book, the instruction to use an Osnap is preceded by a single quote ('), as in '*Center* or '*Intersection*.

See the earlier discussion on using Osnap in Chapter 2.

ASSIST
Osnap:

Assist
Point Filters >
   .x
   .y
   .z
   - - - - - - - - - - - - - -
   .xy
   .xz
   .yz

Point filters may be used to identify specific coordinates of parts of objects. Use point filters in conjunction with Osnap.

For example, specify a point by entering .*xy* and '*Int* of a corner of a 3D object; AutoCAD will then ask you to supply a z coordinate. Specifically, the steps are hold down the Shift key and press the RMB once. When the Osnap list comes on, highlight **.xy** and click the LMB. (The command responds with .*xy of*.) Now highlight and pick **Intersection** from the still active Osnap list. (The command then responds with *int of*.) Pick the intersection and you will be asked to supply the distance in the z direction.

In this manner, you tell AutoCAD to use the x and y coordinates of an intersection, while you supply the height in the z direction. Thus, you will be drawing on a non-0 elevation. The process eliminates the need to move an object vertically after you have drawn on the x-y plane.

SERVICE

You can use absolute coordinates, relative directions, or more Osnap filters, such as From, Midpoint, Endpoint, and so on with Point Filters.

Assist
Snap

Usually, the Snap mode is set to *Off*, which allows the cursor to move smoothly as you position it around the screen.

With Snap mode set to *On*, the cursor jumps from one position to the next in increments whose distance is set by Snap Spacing. Depending on the size of the increment and zoom power, the jumpiness of Snap can be disquieting, as well as making specification of intermediate positions more difficult. So, unless you are drawing something that calls for set spacing repeatedly, leave Snap at *Off*.

Toggle Snap *On/Off* with the **F9** function key.

Assist
Grid

Having a grid as a guide to drawing in orthographic views is a valuable tool. In architectural drawings, do not set the grid too tightly. In most plan view drawings, set a square grid of 4 or 5 feet. If you are detailing, say, a cabinet, you should use a smaller grid spacing.

A grid is laid over the x-y plane of the current UCS. So, a grid is also helpful in 3D viewing. As you change viewpoints, the grid shows you the base plane, which you can use as a reference.

Clicking the Grid button in the pulldown menu will bring only toggle Grid *On/Off*, as will pressing the **F7** function key. But picking the Grid command from the side menu will bring up an options list from which you can choose to set grid spacing and so on. To bring up a dialog box to set grid spacing, go through **Options>Drawing Aids ...**

Assist
Ortho

The Ortho mode causes the cursor to snap to positions either horizontally or vertically (orthographically) so you cannot drag the cursor to any other direction. This can be helpful in creating floor plans and other rectilinear figures. You should use the Ortho setting whenever appropriate, but be keenly aware of it when working in 3D, as Ortho also causes the cursor to stay on the x-y plane. So you may not be grabbing on to an intersection, say, even if you have Osnap set to automatically pick intersections. See the discussion on using Ortho in Chapter 2.

An Ortho mode can be set to be the default through the dialog box in **Options>Drawing Aids ...**

You can more easily toggle Ortho *On/Off* by pressing the **F8** function key.

Assist
Select Objects >

You can specify an object-selecting method by using the options in this command; in most cases, these options are directly available in other commands you are using.

Window	A window is opened by picking opposite corners. A good habit to acquire is to open a window by first picking the lower left corner. While holding down the LMB, drag the cursor to the upper right-hand corner, then click the LMB again. In this kind of right-opening window, only objects that lie completely within the window are accepted in the selection set.

See the section below for the difference between a window and a crossing window.

Crossing Window	You can call for a Crossing Window under this menu. You specify a Crossing Window by opening the window from right to left. In a Crossing Window, even objects that are partially within the window are recognized as objects selected.

Also see the discussion under **Options>Selection** later in this chapter and in the *AutoCAD Command Reference*.

Window Polygon	A Window Polygon is a closed figure of more than three sides. As an object selector, Wpolygon selects only objects that lie totally within the polygon.

Crossing Polygon	A Crossing Polygon is a closed figure of more than three sides. Cpolygon recognizes objects that are partially or totally within the confines of the figure.

Fence	A Fence is an open polyline. When you use it as an object-selecting device, any object touching or crossing the fence line is recognized as a selected entity.

Add	The Add option allows you to manually add more objects to be included in the selection set. This feature is the default and is applicable in operations where you are making selections.

Remove	If you have selected some objects by mistake, but do not want to redo the entire selection process, you can invoke the Remove feature to pick out the items you do not want included.

In commands such as **Modify > Erase**, the Remove option is available during the entire selection process, as are the other object selection methods: Wpolygon, Cpolygon, and Fence.

Assist
Selection Filters ...
Group Objects ...
Group Selection ...

This group of tools is mainly used in facilities planning and is thus out of the context of this book.

ASSIST
Filter:
Group:
PickSt:

Assist
Inquiry >
   List

This command lists the type of object, layer, and other properties. In the case of 3D objects, it will also show the bounding box and upper and lower bounding planes within which lie the 3D object(s).

ASSIST
INQUIRY

Locate Point **Distance** **Area**	These are much used tools for checking coordinates of objects. You often need to know precise locations when working with complex objects. You should use Osnap filters to specify exact points about which you wish information. For example, you will receive exact measurements, such as the length of a line, if you ask for the distance from an endpoint to another endpoint using **Assist > Inquiry > Distance** and Osnap filters.
Mass Properties	This area is used in analysis and other material-handling functions. It is not usually used in interior space planning.

Assist
Cancel

You can always cancel a command by pressing the Control and *C* keys at the same time. This is often referred to as Ctrl+C. The *C* does not have to be capitalized.

At most stages of a command, you can cancel by highlighting the AutoCAD label at the top of the side menu and clicking the LMB.

FILE
Cancel:

The Data Category

In this category, there are commands to define the characteristics of object elements, such as the type and style of lines.

Pulldown menu and options of the **Data** category:

```
┌─────────────────────────┐
│ Data                    │
├─────────────────────────┤
│ Object Creation ...     │
│ - - - - - - - - - - -   │
│ Layer ...               │
│ Viewport Layer Control  │
│ (available only in      │
│ paperspace)             │
│ - - - - - - - - - - -   │
│ Color                   │
│ Linetype ...            │
│ Multiline Style ...     │
│ Text Style ...          │
│ Dimension Style ...     │
│ Shape File ...          │
│ - - - - - - - - - - -   │
│ Units ...               │
│ Drawing Limits          │
│ Time                    │
│ Status                  │
│ - - - - - - - - - - -   │
│ Rename ...              │
│ Purge          >- - -   │
└─────────────────────────┘
```

```
┌──────────────────────┐
│ Layers               │
│ Linetypes            │
│ Multiline Styles     │
│ Text Styles          │
│ Dimension Styles     │
│ Shapes               │
│ Blocks               │
│ - - - - - - - - -    │
│ All                  │
└──────────────────────┘
```

The Commands in the Data Category

PULLDOWN MENU		SIDE MENU

PULLDOWN MENU

Data
Object Creation ...

In this dialog box, you can control the properties of new objects by specifying color, layer line type, line type scale, elevations, thickness, and text style. The properties are attached to new objects until they are reset under this command.

SIDE MENU

DATA
DDemode:

Data
Layer ...

This option calls up the Layer Control dialog box in which you can create new layers, set attributes for them, turn them on/off, or freeze/thaw them.

DATA
DDlmode:

Be aware of the idiosyncrasies of this dialog box:

> To create a new layer, first type in a name, then click the *New* button.
>
> To make a layer the current layer, first highlight its name then click on Current.
>
> A layer name must be highlighted before it can be turned on/off, frozen/thawed, or before its other attributes, such as line type and color, can be changed.

Data
Viewport Layer Control

This function is disabled in modelspace. Use this command to control the quantity and locations of viewports on different layers, so that you can have different sheet layouts in a set of drawings.

DATA
VPlayer:

Data
Color

This command loads the sheet of colors from which you can set the default color. However, it is the same color chart that is found in other commands such as Layer and Ddchprop. Normally, you would change the colors of specific items under those commands rather than setting color globally through this command.

DATA
Color:

Data
Linetype ...

You can choose a different line type to be the default, but the line types must have been previously loaded into the line type library before they are available for use.

DATA
DDltype:

In the Linetype ... dialog box, click on the Load... box and select the line type to load from the list.

Data
Multiline Style ...

Before you can use a Multiline Style, it must be loaded in the *Acad.mln* file, which is usually found in the *\ACADR13\COMMON\SUPPORT* directory.

DATA
MLstyle

Once the Multiline Style dialog box comes up, select the name of the style. (You may have to scroll to the above-mentioned directory where the *.mln* file is located.)

After you have highlighted a multiline style, click *Add* and then *OK* to use the multiline right away. If you want to have the style available for use at another time, click *Save* to preserve it.

Each individual line in a multiline is known as an element. A multiline style may be defined by specifying the spacing between elements. If you use 0 as a basis, a spacing with a + value will lie to one side, while an element with a – value will be on the other side of the input line. Exactly which side is considered positive or negative depends on the justification of the multiline. (See **Draw> Multiline** for a discussion on setting justification.)

After specifying a spacing, click *Add* to add a new element to the multiline, which may have as many as 16 elements. *Name* and *Save* the style for future use.

You cannot change the colors and line type once a multiline style has been created. To make changes, replace the multiline style with a new one.

Data **Text Style ...**	Many fonts are loaded with R13 during installation. You will find them under *ACADR13\COMMON\FONTS*. You have to select one of the fonts and enter *Yes* to set that font to be the current text style. You must specify characteristics such as the height and orientation of the text before ending this command.	DATA **Style:**
Data **Dimension Style ...**	Dimensioning drawings is normally done in preparing working documents and finished drawings which are processes outside of the scope of this book and will not be discussed in detail.	DATA **Ddim:**
Data **Shape File ...**	An AutoCAD shape file can be a drawing or a text font with a *.shp* or *.pfb* extension. Such files must first be compiled by the **Tools>Compile ...** feature into a *.shx* file before you can load them. Load a Shape File (*.shx*) through the dialog box much the same way you would import a Text Style. After it has been loaded, you can insert it into a drawing by means of the **Draw> Insert> Shape** command.	DATA **Load:**
Data **Units ...**	*Architectural* is the normal unit used in drawing buildings. You may set other attributes, such as the degree of fractional fineness in which you want AutoCAD to express measurements. You may set fractions to be expressed down to 1/64″. AutoCAD expresses measurements to the nearest fraction. You can enter measurements as fine as the equivalent of eight decimal points regardless of how the default fraction is set. See the section on setting up a new drawing earlier in this chapter.	DATA **Units:**
Data **Drawing Limits**	Set drawing limits to approximately twice the size of the floor plan of your building. Draw the plan so that it "floats" within the drawing limits with one-quarter of its length on either side and that of its depth at the top and bottom of the screen when the drawing is zoomed: *All*.	DATA **Limits:**

Data **Time**	This command reports various time elements connected with the current drawing, such as the last time the drawing was edited. And it reports such elements as the lapse time of the current drawing session.	DATA **Time:**
Data **Status**	This command shows cumulative statistics such as the number of objects in the drawing, its paperspace limits, and other data.	DATA **Status**
Data **Rename ...**	Use this command to rename blocks, dimension style, layer, line type, text style, UCS, view, and viewport. Note that you are only renaming, not resetting, properties under this command.	DATA **Rename:**
Data **Purge >**	Purge can be done at any time during a drawing session. You can purge unused, but named layers, line types, multiline styles, text styles, dimension styles, shapes, and blocks.	DATA **Purge:**

The Options Category

With the exception of setting Running Object Snap and Drawing Aids, most of the commands in the Options category need not be reset from the default in the normal course of using AutoCAD R13.

Pulldown menu and options of the **Options** category:

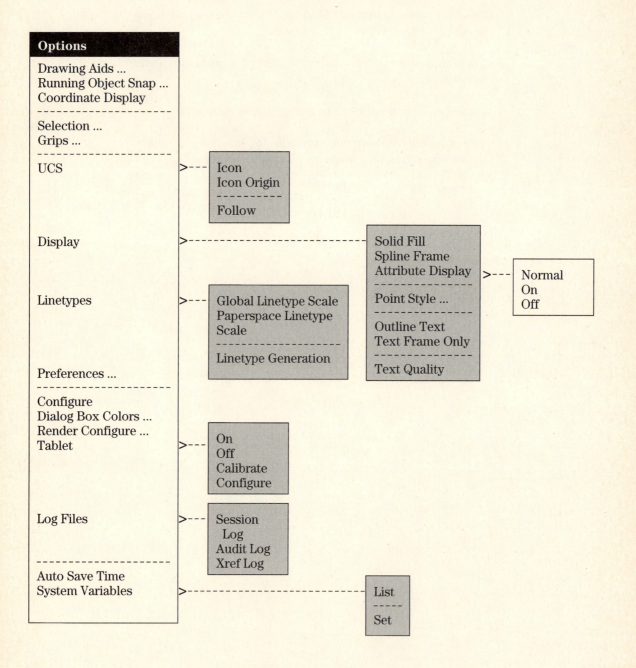

The Commands in the Options Category

PULLDOWN MENU **Options** **Drawing Aids ...**	In the Drawing Aids dialog box, you can toggle *On* and *Off* certain modes: *Ortho*, *Solid Fill*, *Quick test*, *Blips*, *Highlight*, and *Groups*. You can toggle Snap and set Snap spacing or angle. You can also toggle Grid *On* or *Off*, as well as set Grid Spacing. Finally, you can set the *On/Off* mode of Isometric Snap Grid. You can toggle Snap with the **F9** function key, or toggle Isometric Snap Grid with the **F5** function key.	SIDE MENU **OPTIONS** **DDrmode:**
Options **Running Object Snap ...**	Set Osnap filter(s) to be the default. The selected Osnap item, an intersection, for example, will be grabbed onto whenever there is an intersection in the cursor pickbox. You can override a default Running Osnap by manually selecting another Osnap filter. Call up the list of Osnap filters by holding down the Shift key while pressing the RMB (Shift+RMB). See the section on working with AutoCAD R13 in Chapter 2 for more discussion on using Osnap filters.	OPTIONS **DDosnap:**
Options **Coordinate Display**	The current x and y coordinates of the cursor position are reported on the status bar at the top of the monitor screen. You can also toggle the display *On* or *Off* by pressing the **F6** function key.	OPTIONS **Coords:**
Options **Selection ...**	Various modes for picking objects can be set in this dialog box. The default Noun/Verb and Implied Windowing are set so you can select objects before issuing certain Noun or Verb commands. Once these objects are preselected, merely click on a viable command and the action called for will be carried out without the usual queries.	OPTIONS **DDselec:**
Options **Grips ...**	In this dialog box, you can set Grips *On* or *Off*, as well as set their sizes and colors. Using Grips, you can move, rotate, scale, or stretch an object. Note that grips of Landscale Objects have different functions (see Chapter 6). Also, refer to the discussion on using grips in Chapter 2.	OPTIONS **Ddgrips:**
Options **UCS >** **Icon**	You can turn off the UCS icon at the lower left corner of the monitor. The icon is usally not turned *Off* except when showing rendered drawings at client presentations.	OPTIONS **UCSicon:**
Icon Origin	You can move the icon to another position and you can put the icon in different positions from viewport to viewport.	
Follow	This is the system variable UCSFOLLOW. Set it *On* to make the UCS icon display at the origin instead of the lower left corner of the screen. This is useful when working and viewing in 3D. For example, if you have a 3D object with a UCS origin set at a cor-	**UCSfoll:**

ner, the UCS icon will be displayed at that corner and "follow" it around as you change 3D viewpoints.

Options **Display>**	Various options are available to control the way drawings are displayed. They can affect the efficiency of your working session, such as taking less time to regenerate a drawing.	OPTIONS **DISPLAY**
Solid Fill	With solids not filled in, drawing regeneration and screen refresh times are reduced.	**Fill:**
Spline Frame	This system variable, *SPLFRAM*, controls the visibility of edges of 3D faces hidden by **Tools>Hide**. For more information about hiding 3D edges, see the discussion in **Draw>Surfaces>3D Face** and **Modify> Properties ...** in this chapter.	**SplFram:**
Point Style ...	A point is considered an object. You can draw points, but they are hard to see because the default point style is a dot (.). Commands such as Measure and Divide use points as markers, known as nodes, at specified locations. By setting a point style to one other than the dot (.), you can better see the nodes marked by Measure, Divide, and others. For a chart of the available point styles, see **Draw> Point**.	**DRAW2** **Point:** **DDptype:**
Outline Text **Text Frame Only**	If you have many blocks of text in PostScript or Adobe Type 1 fonts, regeneration time can be greatly improved by having the text blocks displayed as outlines, as each change in viewpoint or viewing angle will require less time to regenerate.	**TxtFill:**
Text Quality	The quality or fineness of PostScript and Type 1 fonts can be adjusted to fit the purpose of your drawing. Remember, these types of fonts can greatly increase your drawing's file size.	**TxtQlty:**

Options
Linetypes >
  Global Ltype Scale
  Paperspace Ltype
   Scale
  Linetype
   Generation
	The scale of some linetypes, such as Hidden and Dashed, are set by using these commands. You may set the scale of a line in modelspace or differently in each viewport in paperspace.
	
	2D polylines may be set to have a dash in front of and behind each vertex, by the PLINEGEN system variable.
		OPTIONS
		DISPLAY
		Ltscale:
		PSltscl:
		PlinGen:

	The *Viewres* command, entered at the side menu or at the keyboard, allows Fast Zoom, which speeds up regeneration time at the Zoom, Pan, and View Restore commands.	OPTIONS **Viewres:**
Options **Preferences ...**	You can select English or Metric measurement styles, and you can set an opening drawing other than the default *acad.dwg*.	

A new drawing may be:

> Standard Imperial (the default *acad.dwg*.)
> Metric/ISO Size A
> U.S. Architectural
> U.S. Mechanical
> J.I.S. Architectural
> J.I.S. Mechanical

Options **Configure**	If you need to reconfigure AutoCAD start up, change display devices, or make other hardware changes, follow the list of choices that comes up when you enter this command. See the *AutoCAD Installation Manual* for more details on configuration.	OPTIONS **Config:**
Options **Dialog Box Colors ...**	Use this feature to set the colors of AutoCAD dialog boxes.	OPTIONS **DlgColr:**
Options **Render Configure ...**	See later chapters where specific topics on rendering are discussed.	
Options **Tablet >**	Set up a digitizing tablet in place of using a mouse as the pointing device. Set up the tablet when you install AutoCAD, or invoke **Options> Configure**.	OPTIONS **Tablet:**
Options **Log Files >**	A log is kept of each drawing session. Some features logged are the number of objects drawn and the starting time and duration of a drawing session, as well as features of X-ref files.	
Options **Auto Save Time**	It is a good idea to set a lapse time of about 15 minutes for R13 to automatically save (qsave) your drawing, so that less data may be lost if there is a power outage or systems failure.	OPTIONS **SaveTim:**
Options **System Variables >**	There are a number of system variables. Some are set in the default drawing, *acad.dwg*. You may have to change some settings to fit your drawing needs. Use the Set option in this menu to set a system variable. Use List to see the available variables. The list is quite long. It may be easier to browse through the list under the Help menu or in the *AutoCAD Command Reference* manual.	OPTIONS **Sys Var:**

The Tools Category

Various tools are available to enhance the utility of AutoCAD R13. Among them are rendering options, about which more will be said in Chapter 7.

Pulldown menu and options of the **Tools** category:

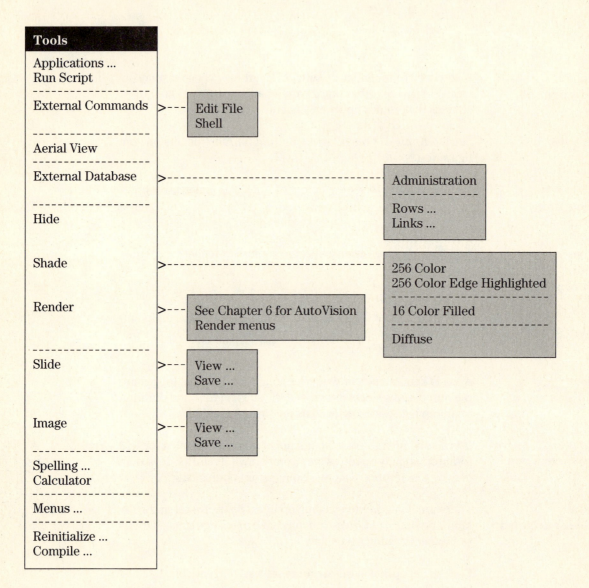

The Commands in the Tools Category

<table>
<tr><td>PULLDOWN MENU</td><td></td><td>SIDE MENU</td></tr>
<tr><td>Tools
Applications ...</td><td>Use this dialog box to load programs in AutoLisp, ADS, and other external applications.</td><td>TOOLS
Appload:</td></tr>
<tr><td>Tools
Run Script</td><td>A script may be written which tells AutoCAD to run or display drawings in a programmed sequence for use as a presentation.</td><td>TOOLS
Script:</td></tr>
<tr><td>Tools
External
   Commands>
Edit Files
Shell</td><td>This feature allows you to edit files by shelling out to DOS. Entering Shell and pressing Enter twice will shell out of Auto-CAD and allow you to use DOS commands. Refer to the Auto-CAD Command Reference for some DOS functions that should not be used while shelled out.

Return to the Drawing Editor by typing Exit.</td><td>TOOLS
Textscr:</td></tr>
<tr><td>Tools
Aerial View</td><td>The Vibrant Display Driver installed by AutoCAD under normal installation includes a feature called Aerial View, which gives you an instant overall view of your drawing limits. The area in which you are currently zoomed is marked by a heavily outlined rectangle to let you know the relationship of the current view area to the overall picture. Click on the button in the upper left-hand corner to turn off Aerial View.</td><td></td></tr>
<tr><td>Tools
External Database ></td><td>This is a database management tool that is not within the scope of this book.</td><td>TOOLS
EXT DBMS</td></tr>
<tr><td>Tools
Hide</td><td>Hide generates an image of your drawing with hidden lines removed in the current screen. Objects must be in Mesh display before they can be shown with hidden lines removed. Objects in wireframe display cannot be shown in hidden line.</td><td>TOOLS
Hide:</td></tr>
<tr><td>Tools
Shade ></td><td>Like the Hide command, Shade displays a hidden-line removed image of solid models, but with the faces shaded. The image, color, and resolution are affected by the systems variables SHADEDGE, and SHADEDIF, as well as by the number of colors your system displays.

Usually, Shade produces a 3D image faster than Hide. You cannot plot a Shade view; however, you can save it to file in Save Image.</td><td>TOOLS
SHADE</td></tr>
<tr><td>Tools
Render ></td><td>A special AutoVision Render selection category appears here in place of the regular AutoCAD Render menu, if you have AutoVision installed.

See Chapter 6 for more details on this menu.</td><td>TOOLS
RENDER</td></tr>
<tr><td>Tools
Slide ></td><td>Creates a "slide" of the current monitor screen for later viewing. Slide does not carry the attributes of your drawing, so a slide is a much smaller file. But you cannot plot a slide.</td><td>TOOLS
Vslide:
Mslide:</td></tr>
</table>

Use VSLIDE to view a slide and MSLIDE to make one.

Tools **Image >**	You can save rendered images to TGA, TIFF, or GIF file formats by using this command. More discussion on handling images follows later in Chapter 7.	TOOLS **SaveImg:** **Replay:**
Tools **Spelling ...**	Use this command to have AutoCAD check the spelling of words entered in Text, Dtext, and Mtext.	TOOLS **Spell:**
Tools **Calculator**	See the *AutoCAD Command Reference* for a detailed discussion on the use of the Geometry Calculator.	TOOLS **GeomCal:**
Tools **Menus ...**	You may use a customized menu instead of the standard one, which is found in *DOS/SUPPORT/ACAD.MNU*.	TOOLS **Menu:**
Tools **Reinitialize ...**	When settings are changed in the plotter or digitizer, it may be necessary to reset the parameters in the initialization files in the **Tools> Reinitialize ...** dialog box.	TOOLS **Reinit:**
Tools **Compile ...**	Uncompiled shape files carry *.shp* extensions, and those of PostScript font files have *.pfb* extensions. These files must be compiled before they can be loaded or used in a drawing. Compiled files have *.shx* extensions.	TOOLS **Compile:**

The Help Category

In this category are standard help commands to help you navigate through AutoCAD Release 13.

Pulldown menu of the **Help** category:

```
┌────────────────────────────────┐
│ Help                           │
├────────────────────────────────┤
│ Help ...                       │
│ ------------------------------ │
│ Search for Help On ...         │
│ How to Use Help                │
│ What's New in Release 13 ...   │
│ ------------------------------ │
│ About AutoCAD ...              │
└────────────────────────────────┘
```

The Commands in the Help Category

PULLDOWN MENU

Help
Help ...

AutoCAD allows you to look for help through this menu button by specifying help items via:

Menu Access (Pulldown menus)

Command Line Access (Keyboard inputs)

Glossary (Definition of terms)

SIDE MENU

HELP
Help:

Help
Search for Help on ...

There is a useful interactive AutoCAD Help section under this button, where a dialog box appears upon activation.

In an upper field, a list of topics or keywords is arranged alphabetically. Scroll down this list, highlight an item, then click on the *Show Topic* button. The selected item will be shown in a lower field. Click on the *Go To* button to display the actual Help comments.

You may also type in a topic. The list in the upper box will scroll to a topic alphabetically nearest to the one you entered.

Help
How to Use Help

This section explains how to use the AutoCAD Help features.

Help
What's New
   in Release 13 ...

In this section, new features of R13 are highlighted. There is also a summary of R13 commands featuring new commands, changed commands, and related commands, such as those of ASE and AME.

Help
About AutoCAD ...

This is a welcome message from Autodesk, including contact addresses and other information.

EXERCISES AND TUTORIALS

ABOUT THE EXERCISES AND TUTORIALS

The exercises and tutorials are intended to be tools for learning to work with AutoCAD. To provide opportunities to use different commands, some of the steps detailed in the lessons may not be the most direct or obvious way to do things. Sometimes, the steps are repetitious and may appear elementary to those who know the software. For the sake of pedagogy and appeal to a wide range of readers, however, such repetitions are unavoidable. So, if you know how to use AutoCAD, you may not have to follow the instructions literally. Examine the illustration to see what is being detailed in the instructions. If you think you can accomplish the results, go ahead and do it your way.

The exercises provide simplified instructions and are generally not as detailed as the tutorials. They are complete individual lessons and can be done in any sequence.

The tutorials are laid out along the line same line as an actual design process. To create a building, a certain amount of basic, background work must be made ready and available. Thus the tutorials begin by laying down much of the overall structural and design parameters before delving into details and, lastly, furnishings.

There are three tutorials: Tutorial 1, Customer Waiting Area; Tutorial 2, Conference Room; and Tutorial 3, Open Office and Teller Section.

You may follow the tutorials serially. That is, you can complete Tutorial 1, then go on to Tutorials 2 and 3. Alternatively, you may pick and choose among the three tutorials. Each of them starts by completing parts of the building as detailed in Tutorial 1, then goes on to detail the design particular to its own area.

The furnishings and accessories are really separate parts of the tutorials. They may be done whether or not you do any part of the building. In other words, you can create the guest chair detailed in Tutorial 3 and insert it into the teller area of Tutorial 4. Since the purpose is to demonstrate a number of approaches, the stylistic details of the building and its furnishings may not be aesthetically correct or wholly unified.

Whether you do the tutorials in series or one at a time, do try to allow enough time to finish the section you are working on before you quit. As the lines of instruction are sometimes similar and as you are often in 3D view, it is more difficult to find the place where you left off if you quit in the middle of a section.

Learning CAD is very much like learning a new language. There are many new terms, certain syntactic conventions, grammar, and, at times, different ways to accomplish similar objectives. Until you become dexterous with any new language, you may have to stay with longer, more tedious methods to achieve an expression. With CAD, there are the additional burdens of learning to think through the computer, understanding its software instructions, and manipulating with fingers and mouse, not to mention having to follow written instructions.

Exercise 1. Banner

This exercise uses **3D Polyline** and **3D Rotate** to create a hanging banner in a slight breeze. The way the banner seems to be fluttering is not drawn with any precise calculations. You may have to experiment with the 3D polylines to create a satisfactory effect.

1. In plan view, WCS, and **Draw> Line**, create two crossing lines, then a third line at the intersection in the +z-axis direction.

Center a circle at the intersection of the lines with **Draw> Circle**.

Under **Construct> 3D Rotate**, select all the objects then pick the x-axis option to rotate. Specify the intersection of the lines as Origin point, then enter 90° to rotate all the objects.

Click on **View> 3D Viewport Presets...** and pick SE Isometric view.

2. Back in plan view, WCS, create four separate wavy 3D polylines by using **Draw> 3D Polyline**. The lines should be separate entities with adjacent endpoints touching.

With **Construct> 3D Rotate**, turn each polyline about its midpoint: on the x-axis, if it is a horizontal line, or y-axis, if it is a vertical line. The rotation angles are arbitrarily selected. These angles are between 15° and 45°, but do not to use 90°.

3. Use **Modify> Edit polyline> Edit Vertex**. Use **Move** to move each endpoint to the endpoint of the adjacent polyline. The 3D polylines remain separate entities but form a closed figure.

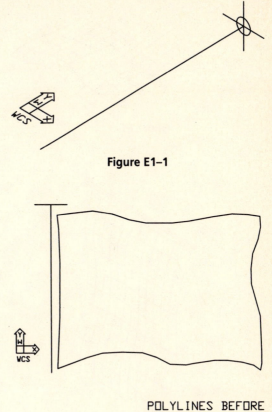

Figure E1–1

POLYLINES BEFORE
ROTATION.

Figure E1–2

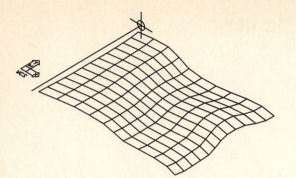

Figure E1–3

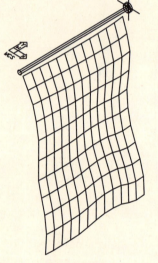

Figure E1–4

4. Create a mesh by Edgsurf. Invoke **Draw> Surfaces> Edge Surface**. Select each of the polylines as edges, then press Enter.

You may adjust *Surftab1* and *Surftab2* by clicking each on at the side menu to set the desired mesh density. This action may be done transparently while you are in the object selection phase of the Edgsurf command.

5. Set UCS to be centered on the circle, with the z-axis set along the straight line. The mesh is 3D rotated about the center of the circle (y-axis rotate) at an angle of 80°.

The original polylines are saved to another layer and turned off.

Using **Draw> Solids> Extrude**, the circle is then extruded (tapered) to form a flag pole.

In Figure E1–4, the circle is offset down and extruded to form a straight pole. The original circle is also extruded slightly to form a base plate for the pole.

Exercise 2. Armchair

Drawing this armchair takes advantage of the ability of AutoCAD R13 to extrude along a curved path.

Set up a new drawing with the following parameters:

Name of drawing: *Armch.dwg*
Drawing units: *Architectural*
Drawing limits: *12′, 10′*
Layers:

Name	Color	Linetype
0	White	Continuous
CHAIR	Cyan	Continuous
CUSHION	Yellow	Continuous
CUSHION2	Green	Continuous
GUIDES	White	Continuous

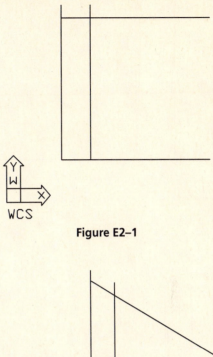

Figure E2–1

1. Begin with drawing some guide lines.
Layer GUIDES is Current.
Layers CHAIR, CUSHION, and CUSHION2 are *Off*.
View is set at plan view, WCS.

With Ortho *On*, click on **Draw> Line**.
Draw 36″ lines at right angles to each other.

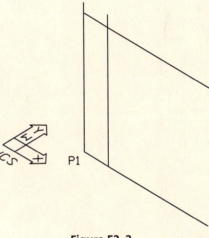

Figure E2–2

Construct> Offset
Distance: *33″*
Pick the horizontal line to offset in the +y direction.

Construct> Offset
Distance: *7*
Pick the vertical line to offset in the +x direction.

Construct> 3D Rotate
Pick all the lines.
Select the x-axis rotate option.
Origin: '*Intersection* at P1
Rotation angle: *90*

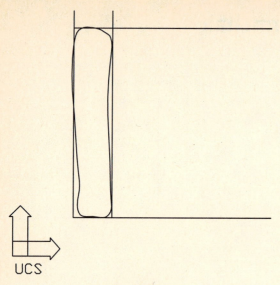

UCS

Figure E2–3

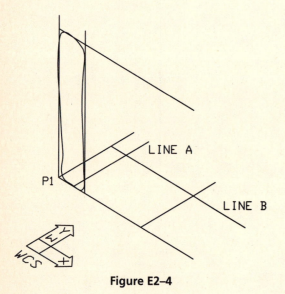

LINE A

P1

LINE B

WCS

Figure E2–4

2. Press **F8** to turn Ortho *Off*.
Select: **View> 3D Vp Presets> SE Isometric**.

Click on **View> Set UCS> X-axis Rotate**.
Rotation angle: *90*

Click **View> Set UCS> Origin**.
Origin: *'Intersection* at P1

Select **View> 3D Vp Presets> Plan View> Current UCS**. The rectangle is now seen in plan view of the UCS, which has been rotated 90° from the WCS.

Set Layer CHAIR *On* and Current.
Draw> Polyline
Draw a closed polyline within the rectangle to resemble the cross-section of an upholstered armchair.

3. Draw an outline of the seat in the x-y plane.
View > 3D Vp Presets> SE Isometric.
Switch to WCS with **View> Set UCS> World**.

Construct> Offset
Distance: *14*
Pick the bottom line, offset in the +y direction (line B).

Draw> Line
From point: *'Intersection* at P1
To point: *@0,20*

Modify> Properties
Change the layer of the line to GUIDES.

Construct> Offset
Distance: *4*
Pick the line you just drew, offset in the +x direction (line A).

Construct> Offset
Distance: *18*
Pick the line you just offset, offset in the +x direction.

4. You now have a rectangular outline of the seat on the x-y plane, but it needs to be further edited.

Modify> Trim

Cutting edge: Pick the line you just offset.

Objects to be trimmed: Pick the protruding end of line B.

Construct> Fillet

Radius: *6*

Press the RMB or click **Construct> Fillet**.

Pick lines A and B near the point where they intersect.

Modify> Edit Polyline

Pick line A; answer *Yes* to turn it into a polyline.

Enter *J* (for Join).

Pick the fillet arc and line B to join together into a single polyline.

This polyline denotes the center line of the chair arm and back in plan view.

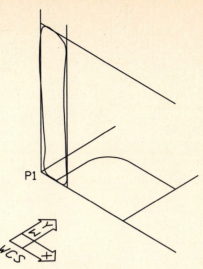

Figure E2–5

5. View> 3D Vp Presets> SE Isometric

Draw> Surfaces> Extruded Surface

Object to extrude: Pick the profile loop.

Enter *Path* and pick the center line drawn in the last step above.

The profile is extruded along the center line to form half of the chair.

Toggle **F8** to turn Ortho *On*.

Construct> Mirror

Pick the extruded object as object to mirror.

First point on mirror line: *'Intersection* at P1

Other point: Pick any point in the +x direction. Do not delete old object.

The chair now has two parts. ACIS solids may not look like they are solids; however, they are and will hide and render as such.

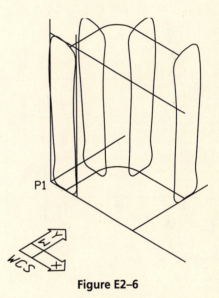

Figure E2–6

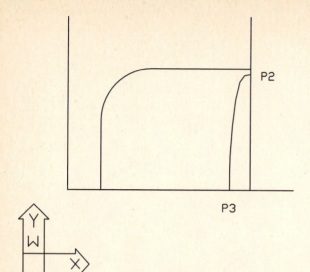

P2

P3

Figure E2–7

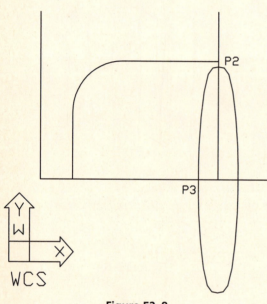

P2

P3

WCS

Figure E2–8

6. You will need a seat for the chair.

Turn layers CHAIR and CUSHION2 *Off*.
Layer GUIDES is still *On*.
Set layer CUSHION *On* and Current.
Set view to plan view, WCS.
Toggle **F8** to turn Ortho *Off*.
Zoom in on the lower guide lines.

Draw> Polyline

Draw a profile of the seat cushion above the guide line from P2 to P3. No point on the polyline should be more than 3″ away from the guide line.

Save a copy of the profile for later use.

Construct> Copy

Pick the polyline just drawn.
Base point: Pick any point.
Displacement: @

Modify> Properties

Pick the copy by entering *L* (for Last).
Change its layer property to CUSHION2, which is turned *Off*.

Return to the original profile line.
Be sure Ortho is still *Off*.

Construct> Mirror

Pick the profile.
First point: Pick P2.
Other point: Pick any point in the -y direction.

Press the RMB to reenter: Mirror
First point: Pick P3.
Other point: Pick any point in the +x direction.

Modify> Edit Polyline

Pick one of the profile lines.
Enter *J* (for Join).
Pick the other four segments of the profile line.

The two halves of the profile have been joined to become a closed loop.

View> 3D Vp Presets> SE Isometric

Construct> 3D Rotate

Pick the profile loop.

Select the y-axis rotate option.

Point on y-axis: Pick P2.

Rotation angle: *90*

Click on **View> Set UCS> Z-axis**.

Point on z-axis: *'Intersection* at P1

Second point: *'Endpoint* at P2

View> Named UCS

In the dialog box, rename the current *No Name* UCS to *U1*.

Draw> Surfaces> Extruded Surface

Pick the rotated profile loop.

Height: *–15* (that is, negative 15″)

The profile has been extruded to form the body of the cushion.

7. Now round off the ends of the cushion.
Turn layer CUSHION *Off*.
Set layer CUSHION2 *On* and Current.
Click **View> Set UCS> World**

The quarter profile line copied in Step 6 is now visible.

Construct> 3D Rotate

Pick the quarter profile.

Enter *Y*, to use the y-axis rotate option.

Point on y-axis: *'Intersection* at P1 (Figure E2–11)

Click on **View> Named UCS**.

Highlight *U1* and click on the Current window.

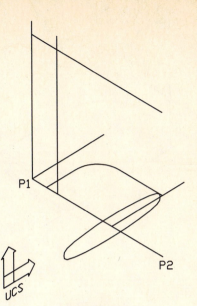

Figure E2–9

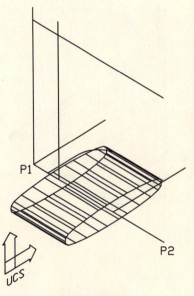

Figure E2–10

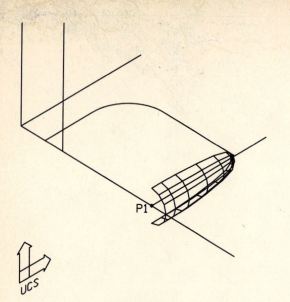

Figure E2–11

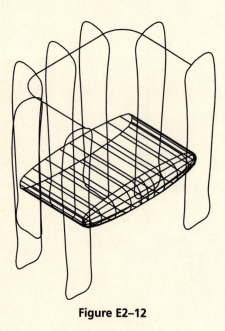

Figure E2–12

Toggle **F8** to turn Ortho *On*.

Draw> Surfaces> Revolved Surface

Object to revolve: Pick the quarter profile. Do not press the RMB.

Axis of revolution: Pick the line parallel to x-axis at a point near P1.

Start angle: *0,* or just press the RMB

Included angle: *180*

Construct> Mirror

Pick the revolved object.

First point: P2

Other point: *@0,4,* or pick any point in the +y direction.

8. Turn layer CUSHION *On*.
Turn layer GUIDES *Off.*
Click on **View> Set UCS> World**.

Modify> Move

Pick all the cushion parts.

Base point: Pick any point.

Displacement: *@0,0,14*

Because you used a 3D Surface command to create a part of the 3D front end (which was then moved), the original quarter profile still exists and is now visible. Change it to layer GUIDES.

9. All parts of the chair have been created.
Turn on layer CHAIR.

You should be able to see the chair in its entirety.

Use **Tools> Hide** to create a hidden-lines removed view of the chair.

Exercise 3. Lamp Sculpture

In drawing this sculpture, it is necessary to maneuver in 3D. Therefore, it is a good exercise for practicing 3D visualizing and modeling functions.

1. Two lines of 4″ are drawn perpendicular to each other at midpoint. A 2″ vertical line is drawn at the intersection of the first two lines. Using **Modify> Point**, change the endpoint of the vertical line to a point @0,0,–2 below the x-y plane. The resultant figure is a 3D cross, with x, y, and z axis lines.

The intersection of these lines will be used as the Origin in further references in this exercise.

A circle is drawn centered on the Origin.

2. In plan view, WCS, objects A and B are drawn using **Draw> Polyline (2D)**.

With **Construct> 3D Rotate>**, object A is rotated at its intersection with the x-axis and –110° about the y-axis.

Object B is similarly rotated two times. The first time, B is 3D rotated –70° about the y-axis, using the point where it intersects the x-axis line as the reference point. The second time, it is rotated –10° on the y-axis and the Origin.

The two polylines, A and B, have been tilted away from the x-y plane on which they were drawn.

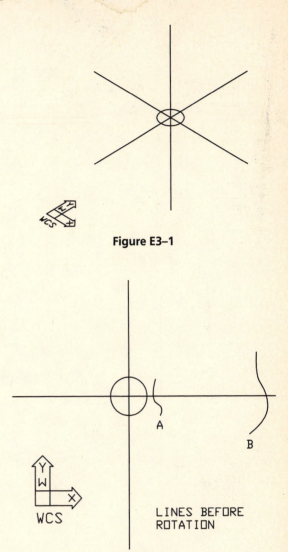

Figure E3–1

LINES BEFORE
ROTATION

Figure E3–2

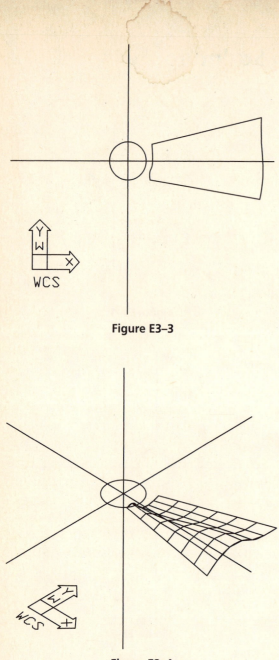

Figure E3–3

Figure E3–4

3. With Ortho *Off*, draw 3D polylines between corresponding endpoints of objects A and B.

Make a 3D mesh with these lines and objects by using **Draw> Surfaces> Edge Surface**.

Set *Surftab1* and *Surftab2* to the desired mesh density.

4. With **Construct> 3D Mirror**, make a copy of the mesh by using the xy option and the Origin as a point on the mirror plane.

Click on **Modify> Move** to raise the upper mesh by a small distance. Use any base point and a displacement of @0,0,.2.

When the upper mesh is moved, the original lines used to define the mesh become visible. Erase them or move them to a turned-off layer.

Shift the lower mesh by using **Construct> Rotate** based on the Origin, z-axis, and an angle of –40°.

5. Make copies of the meshes around the z-axis using the **Construct> Array> Polar** command. In this example, the meshes are rotated a full circle six times.

6. A stand can be made by creating a cylinder out of the circle of Step 1. Use **Draw> Solids> Extrude** to set a height for the circle, making it into a cylinder.

This object may also be used without any other details. Use it as a sculpture as drawn here, or scale it to fit another application. It can be rotated to hang on a wall, to use as a lamp, or to create an ornamental piece.

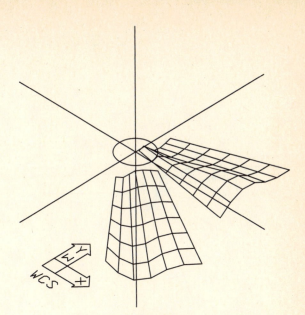

Figure E3–5

Figure E3–6

Exercise 4. Spiral Staircase

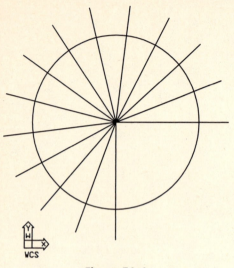

Figure E4–1

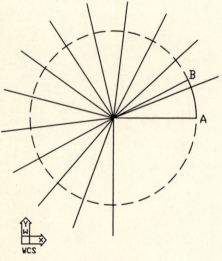

Figure E4–2

Here is one way to draw a spiral staircase without the benefit of an algorithm for drawing spirals. Some parameters:

The staircase is designed to have a radius of 3′0″ and completes a 270° turn. Floor-to-floor height is 9′4″, which divides into 14 risers at 8″ each. The handrail is a spiral tube whose center is 32″ high and 1.5″ in from the edge of a tread. It is held up by rods .75″ in diameter.

1. Use **Draw> Circle>** to create a circle with a 36″ radius.

With Ortho *On,* **Draw> Line** on the x-axis from the center to a point past the circumference of the circle (line A, Figure E4–2).

The line is arrayed 14 times in an arc of 270°, with the **Construct> Array> Polar** command, copying objects as they are arrayed.

2. Dividing 270° by 13 (segments of the 3/4 circle drawn above) yields a result of approximately 21°. This is roughly the angle between two of the arrayed lines. Since stair treads overlap one another, you will make the overlap about 5°, making a tread with a spread of 26°.

A polar array of 2 is made of the first line at 26°, resulting in line marked B in Figure E4–2.

Using the circle as the cutting edge, **Modify> Trim** off the protruding ends of lines A and B.

On a TREAD layer, **Draw> Arc> SCE** between endpoints A and B and centered on the circle. Lines A, B, and the arc form a wedge. Isolate them onto a distinct layer.

3. In **Construct> Offset**, offset the arc segment 1.25″ toward the center. Then polar array line A 10.5°. At the crossing of the new line and arc, draw a circle of 0.75″ diameter. Save the new line and arc on a turned-off layer. They will be used in Step 8.

Draw a 32″ vertical line from the center of the above circle. To specify the length in the z-axis, enter *@0,0,32* from the center of the circle.

The small circle and the line just drawn will be used as references for the handrail and support rod.

4. With **Modify> Edit Polyline> Join**, the lines in the wedge mentioned in Step 2 are made into one polyline.

The polyline is then given a height of –2″ using **Draw> Solids> Extrude**. This object is the prototype of the stair tread. It is extruded downwards so that the top of the step is at the reference for measuring riser height.

5. The tread and the handrail references are arrayed 14 times in 270°.

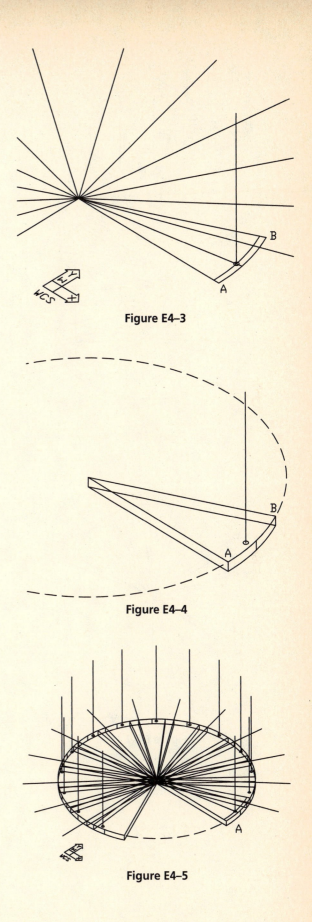

Figure E4–3

Figure E4–4

Figure E4–5

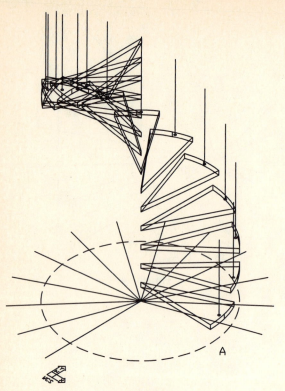

Figure E4–6

6. By using **Modify> Move**, each stair tread and its handrail references are raised 8″ higher than the last.

Zoom in and out and move around the objects to ensure picking the correct set of objects to move. Make a list of multiples of 8 from 8 to 112 (14 times 8), so that you do not make mistakes in adding. Use any point as a base point for moving, and use the relative (@) option to specify, successively, the next higher point.

7. The array done in Step 5 results in an extra step, the last one. Erase that last tread, but leave the small circle and the vertical handrail reference line.

The second to the last tread protrudes past 270°, so the extra portion is taken out by using **Draw> Solids> Slice** to cut the tread with the 270° mark line and a y-z cutting plane. Do this in the plan view of the WCS. Specify the center of the circle as the point on the y-z plane. You will be prompted for the side to save. Pick a point to the left of the 270° line. The **Slice** command will cut the tread and remove the excess part to the right.

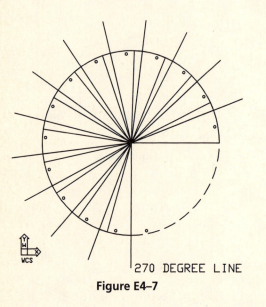

270 DEGREE LINE

Figure E4–7

8. In 3D view, create a spiral with **Draw> 3D Poly-line**, connecting each endpoint of the vertical handrail reference line, beginning from the lowest to the highest. Use *'Endpoint* and a RAIL layer.

Turn on the layer with the guide lines created in Step 3. Click **View> Set UCS> 3Points**.
Origin: *'Endpoint* of Line A at the center of the large circle
+ x point: *'Intersection* of guide line and inner arc
+y point: *@0,0,4*

Draw> Circle> Center, Radius

Center: *'Endpoint* at top of the 32″ vertical line
Radius: *1.25″*

Use **Draw> Solids> Extrude** to create a spiral tube with the above circle and the spline as the extrusion path.

9. Going around the staircase, make each support rod solid. Use its reference circle in the **Extrude** command and the vertical guide line as the extrusion path.

A center post and an ornament on top are added to complete the staircase.

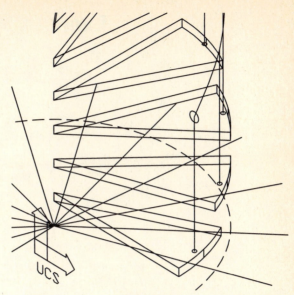

Figure E4–8

Figure E4–9

Exercise 5. Curved Wall

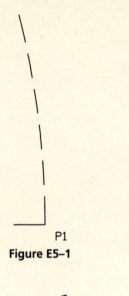

Figure E5–1

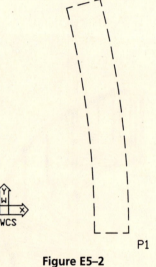

Figure E5–2

To create a curved wall, the basic wall is first created in cross section. Shapers are then created to perforate the wall with window openings. Finally, a column is made to hold up the wall.

Set up a new drawing named: *Curvwal.dwg*
Drawing units: *Architectural*
Drawing limits: *150', 120'*
Create new layers:

Name	Color	Linetype
0	White	Continuous
COLUMN	White	Continuous
GUIDES	White	Dashed 2
SHAPER	Green	Continuous
WALL	Cyan	Continuous

1. Layers: 0 and GUIDES are *On* and GUIDES is Current. Other layers are *Off*.
View is set at plan view, WCS; zoomed: All.

Click on **Draw> line**.
From point: 110',25' (P1)
To point: @–4',0

View> Zoom> Window, zoom in on the line.

Draw> Arc> SCA
Start point: *'Endpoint* of line at right end (P1)
Center: @–100',0
Angle of arc: *15*

Construct> Array> Polar. Pick the line.
Center of array: *'Center* of the arc
Number of items: *2*
Included angle: *15*

Construct> Offset
Distance: *4'*
Pick the arc and offset in the -x direction, toward the center of the arc.

A basic unit of the wall in plan view is done.

2. Construct> Copy

Pick all four objects; enter any point as base point, and then enter @ as displacement.

You have copied the objects in place. To change the copies to another layer, use the cycling method to select objects.

Modify> Properties

Select objects: *L* (for Last). Do not press the RMB. One object is shown in dotted lines.

Hold down Ctrl and pick another object with the LMB. That object is shown in dotted lines.

Hold down Ctrl and pick a third object with the LMB. The third object is shown in dotted lines.

Again, Crtl+LMB, click on the fourth object. Press the RMB.

The **Change Properties** dialog box comes on.

Change the layer property of the objects to that of SHAPER and in Continuous Linetype.

You have made a copy of the arcs and base line, and placed each of them on a turned-off layer to be used later.

3. Returning to the original two arcs and two lines, make another copy and put it on layer WALL.

Then make layer WALL Current, and turn the GUIDES layer *Off*.

Modify> Edit Polyline

Pick one of the lines.

Answer *Yes* to turn the line into a polyline.

Enter *J* (for Join).

Select the other line and the two arcs.

The lines and arcs have been turned into a closed polyline loop.

Draw> Solids> Extrude

Pick the polyline loop.

Height: *22′*

Modify> Move

Pick the extruded object and enter any base point.

Displacement: *@0,0,10′*

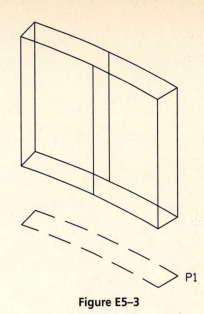

Figure E5–3

P1

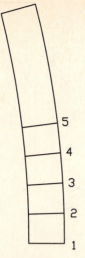

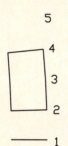

Figure E5–4

5

4

3

2

1

Figure E5–5

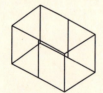

1

Figure E5–6

4. Set layers GUIDES and WALL *Off*.
Make the SHAPER layer Current.

Construct> Array> Polar

Object to array: Pick the base line.

Center of array: *'Center* of arc

Number of items: *5*

Included angle: *7.5*

An array of five lines has been created. Starting from the horizontal baseline, number the lines 1 to 5.

These lines may look like they do not intersect with the arcs. This is due to the regeneration setting of curved objects. Type *Regen* on the Command Prompt Line. The lines and arcs should regenerate in proper resolution.

Modify> Properties

Pick lines 3, 5, and the very top line.

Change the layer property to GUIDES.

Modify> Trim

Cutting edges: Pick lines 2 and 4.

Edges to be trimmed: Pick the ends of the arcs away from one another.

Modify> Edit Polyline

Pick one of the lines.

Answer *Yes* to turn the line into a polyline.

Enter *J* (for Join).

Select the other line and the two arcs.

The lines and arcs have been turned into a closed polyline loop.

Draw> Solids> Extrude

Pick the polyline loop.

Height: *4'*

Modify> Move

Pick the extruded object; enter any base point.

Displacement: *@0,0,13'*

A fan-shaped object has been created to be used as a shaper.

5. Turn layer GUIDES *On*.
Press **F8** to toggle Ortho *Off*.

Construct> Mirror

Select objects: Pick the shaper.

First mirror point: Enter one of the endpoints of line 5 referred to above.

Second mirror point: Pick the other end of line 5.

Delete old object? *No*

Construct> 3D Array> Rectangular

Select objects: Pick the two shapers.

Number of levels: *3*

Distance between tiers: *6'*

You now have an arrangement of six window shapes in two columns on the wall.

Make them openings in the wall.
Set up a 3D view and zoom in so you can see the wall and all the shapers clearly.

Construct> Subtract

Pick the wall as the first object.

Then pick all the shaper objects to subtract from the wall.

6. Make layer COLUMN Current.
Turn layers GUIDES and SHAPER *On*.

Create a column for the wall.

Draw> Solids> Cylinder> Center

Center point: *'Midpoint* of Line 3

Radius: *16"*

Height: *10'*

A 32" diameter column has been created.

Construct> Mirror

Pick the column as object to mirror.

First mirror point: 'Endpoint at inner end of line 5

Other point: 'Endpoint at outer end of line 5

The curved wall segment is done.

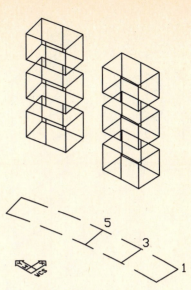

Figure E5–7

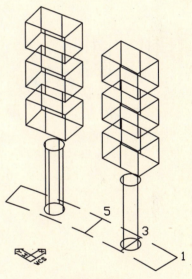

Figure E5–8

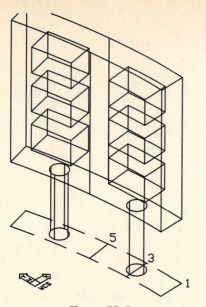

Figure E5–9

7. Leave layer COLUMN current.
Turn layers GUIDES and WALL *On.*

In 3D view, join the wall and column into one object.
Construct> Union
Pick the column and the wall objects.

Now to finish creating the curved wall.
Construct> Array> Polar
Pick the unioned wall object.
Center of array: *'Center* of arc guide
No. of items: *5*
Included angle: *60*

Turn layer GUIDES *Off.*

A curved wall of five segments has been created.

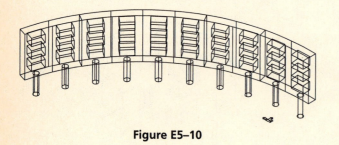

Figure E5–10

Tutorial 1. Customer Waiting Area

ABOUT TUTORIAL 1.   CUSTOMER WAITING AREA

The customer waiting area is located in the lobby next to the window wall outside of the conference room. It is designed to be airy and cheerful, and it takes advantage of the view of the garden outside.

As this is not a high-traffic area, the furnishings are sparse and light with a sophisticated appearance that fits in with the overall design of the bank building.

With AutoCAD, you can begin to get a sense of a space in a building with very few objects. As soon as you put in some parameters, such as horizontal surfaces representing floor or ceiling, and vertical planes, you can see how a space looks by means of one of the 3D viewing commands. Draw as much of the building as necessary to enable you to get some good views of the interior space, which will help you to develop the rest of the building. In this way, you are using the computer to create and not merely as a drafting machine.

T1–1   DRAWING SETUP

Begin drawing the building by setting up some guide lines to mark the exterior corners and internal columns. Then set up a grid to use as a guide for designing the major elements of the building.

When the guide lines and the grid are done, columns and exterior walls will be drawn. After that, the window wall is drawn. The second floor will be sketched in, and then interior walls will be defined. For this tutorial, the building may not be fully detailed. Many of the spaces and areas, particularly the teller counter area, will be drawn and detailed in later tutorials.

T1–1a   Drawing Setup

Set up a new drawing with the following parameters:

Name of Drawing: *T1.dwg*
Data> Units: *Architectural*
Data> Drawing Limits:
Lower left at: 0,0
Upper right at: 160′,130′

Options> Drawing Aids> Grid
Set at x = *40″*, y = *36″* and click the *On* box.

View> Zoom> All

Data> Layer
Set up layers:

Layer Name	Color	Linetype
0	White	Continuous
2NDFLR	Yellow	Continuous
3DFLOOR	Green	Continuous
3DUPPER	White	Continuous
CEILING	Cyan	Continuous
COLGRID	White	Dashed
COLUMNS	White	Continuous
EXTWALL	75	Continuous
GRID	151	Hidden
INTWALL	White	Continuous
ROOF	White	Continuous
WINDWALL	White	Continuous
WINDWALL2	Cyan	Continuous

T1–1b   Draw Guide Lines and Grid Lines

The guide lines mark the exterior outline and interior column centers of the building. After drawing a beginning vertical line and a horizontal line, they will be offset from each other to form a grid of guide lines.

Layer settings:

0	Off
2NDFLR	Off
3DFLOOR	Off
3DUPPER	Off
CEILING	Off
COLGRID	*Current*
COLUMNS	Off
EXTWALL	Off
GRID	*On*
INTWALL	Off
ROOF	Off
WINDWALL	Off
WINDWALL2	Off

16'8,18'

20',15'

Figure T1–1b(1)

1. Be sure to set **View> Zoom> All**.
Press **F8** to toggle Ortho *On*.

2. Begin with **Draw> Line**.
From point: *20',15'* (RMB)
To point: *@0,90'* (RMB)

Again, select **Draw> Line**.
From point: *16'8",18'* (RMB)
To point: *@100',0* (RMB)

Note: From this point on, it is assumed that you know you have to press the RMB or press Enter after you put in requested data or to end a command. You will no longer be reminded to do so with the (RMB) instruction.

Click on **Options> Linetype> Linetype Scale Global**.
Enter: *75*. The lines you have just drawn should appear as broken lines. Enter a larger number if you want the lines to be more open. For tighter dashed lines, enter a smaller number.

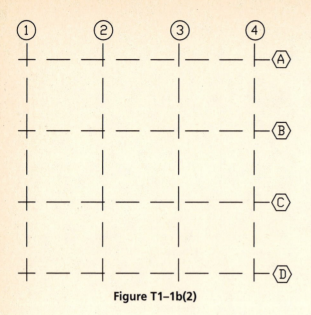

Figure T1–1b(2)

3. Now create the other guide lines by offsetting from the ones already drawn.

Click on **Construct> Offset**.

Distance to offset: *27"*

Pick the horizontal line, successively offsetting it three more times toward the +y direction, for a total of four horizontal lines.

Again, click on **Construct> Offset**.

Distance to offset: *30'*

Pick the vertical line and offset it three times successively toward the +x direction for a total of four vertical lines.

4. Select **Draw> Text> Dynamic Text**.
Pick a point above the leftmost vertical guide line.
For Height of text enter *18"*.
For Text enter *1* (the number one).

Similarly, enter *2*, *3*, and, *4* individually to each of the tops of the other vertical guide lines.

Select **Draw> Text> Dynamic Text** again to enter letters A, B, C, and D successively to each of the right ends of the horizontal grid lines, beginning with the topmost one.

Click on **Draw> Circle> Center**. Draw a 20" radius circle centered on each of the numbers and letters. You can just draw one of the circles, then multiple copy it to the other locations.

Then pick **Draw> Polygon> Polygon> Center**.
Pick the center of one of the circles just drawn.
Number of sides: *6*
Select the option: Circumscribe
Radius: *20"*

A six-sided polygon is drawn around the circle. Move the polygon to around the letter A at the end of the top horizontal guide line. Then multiple copy the polygon around the other letters.

The column guide lines have been drawn. Your drawing should be the same as Figure T1–1b(2).

5. As the basic grid unit measurement for the building is 40″ × 36″, some intermediate grid lines will now be drawn based on that unit measurement. The grid lines will be used later for determining locations of elements in the building.

Set **View> Zoom> All**.

Leave layer COLGRID *On*.

Make current layer GRID.

Set Ortho *On*.

Click on **Construct> Offset**.

Pick vertical column guide line 1.

Distance to offset: *10′*

Offset line *twice* in the +x direction.

Select **Modify> Properties ...** dialog box.

Pick both of the offset objects just created.

In the *Layer* box, scroll to GRID.

Check that the *Linetype* is Hidden.

Click *OK*.

You have changed the offset objects to the GRID layer and made sure that the line type is Hidden. The objects will now be referred to as grid lines.

Under **Construct> Array> Rectangular**.

Array the two vertical grid lines.

Number of columns: *3*

Distance between columns: *30′*

6. Repeat Step 5 with the column guide line D.

Offset guide line D in the +y direction by a distance of 9′, *twice* successively.

Change their layer property to GRID.

Construct> Array the two horizontal grid lines.

Number of rows: *3*

Distance between rows: *27′*

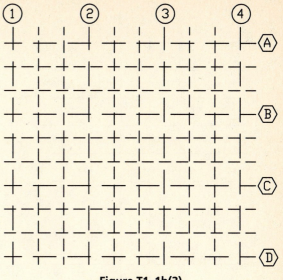

Figure T1–1b(3)

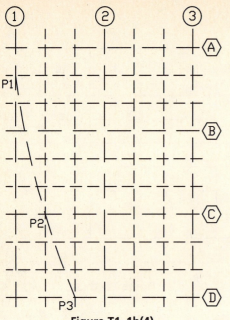

Figure T1–1b(4)

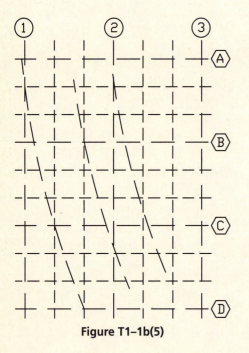

Figure T1–1b(5)

7. Draw guide lines for the window wall, balcony, and teller counter.

Leave layer GRID *On.*

Set layer COLGRID Current.

Set Ortho *Off.*

Click **Options> Running Object Snap**.

Select *Intersection.* (X is in the Intersection box.)

Zoom in on the left side of the drawing.

Click on **Draw> Arc> 3 Points**.

From: P1 to P2 to P3

This is the guide line for the window wall.

8. You will now create a copy of the balcony line to be used as a guide for the teller counter.

Pick **Construct> Offset**.

Pick the curve just created.

Distance: *30′* in the +x direction

Offset the window wall curve again.

Distance: *16′8* in the +x direction

Pick **Modify> Extend**.

Boundary edge: Select guide line A.

Edge to extend: Pick the window wall curve.

All the guide lines and the grid have been drawn.

T1–2   CREATE SOLID HORIZONTAL SURFACES

Surfaces such as a floor slab for the first floor and a ceiling plane covering the second floor will be needed for mapping on materials or textures during rendering. A roof is created for the building, as its shadow may be in view of the lobby area.

T1–2a Create a Solid First Floor

In this section, you will create a solid or 3D floor slab for the lower level by making a 6″ thick block to cover the area of the building. Surface materials and characteristics will be mapped on when you render.

Layer settings:	
0	Off
2NDFLR	Off
3DFLOOR	*Current*
3DUPPER	Off
CEILING	Off
COLGRID	*On*
COLUMNS	Off
EXTWALL	Off
GRID	*On*
INTWALL	Off
ROOF	Off
WINDWALL	Off
WINDWALL2	Off

1. Drawing is set at UCS: World, and View is set at plan view; zoomed: All.

2. Draw> Solids> Box> Corner
First corner: *'From, 'Intersection* at D-1
Offset: *@–3'6",0* (P1)
Other corner: *@93'6",81'*
Height: *6"*

3. Modify> Move
Pick the floor (box just drawn) as object.
Base point: Pick any point.
Displacement: *@0,0,–6.5"*

The floor is moved down slightly from the x-y plane so that it will be separate from the bases of columns and walls, which will rest on the x-y plane. When you render in AutoVision, the lines separating the walls, columns, and floor will be seen distinctly.

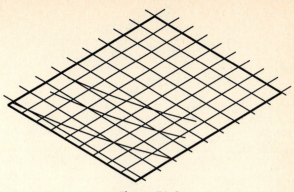

Figure T1–2a

T1–2b   Create a Ceiling Plane

A ceiling plane that covers the entire interior area is positioned at a height of 23′6″ above the lower-level floor. Material characteristics will be attached later in the rendering sessions, so that diffused lights can be seen through the ceiling plane.

Layer settings:	
0	Off
2NDFLR	Off
3DFLOOR	Off
3DUPPER	Off
CEILING	*Current*
COLGRID	*On*
COLUMNS	Off
EXTWALL	Off
GRID	*On*
INTWALL	Off
ROOF	Off
WINDWALL	Off
WINDWALL2	Off

1. Draw> Polyline

First point: *.xy* of P1
Need z: *22'6"*
To point: Enter *A* (for Arc).
Endpoint of arc: Enter *CE* (for Center).
Center point: *'Center*
Center of: Pick a point on the dashed curve line.
End point of arc: Pick P2.
To point: Enter *L* (for Line).
To point: Pick P3.
To point: P4
To point: *C* (for Close)

2. Construct> Region

Pick the polyline loop you just created as object.

The polyline loop has been made into a solid plane, which serves as the ceiling plane above the second floor.

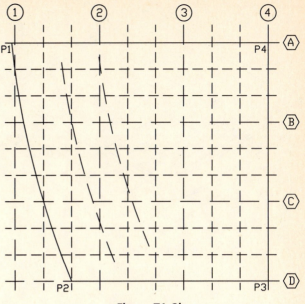

Figure T1–2b

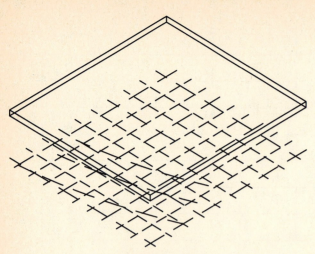

Figure T1–2c

T1–2c   Create a Roof

The roof structure is a space frame 3′ high. The roof is represented here by a simple box for visualization and rendering purposes.

Layer settings:	
0	Off
2NDFLR	Off
3DFLOOR	Off
3DUPPER	Off
CEILING	Off
COLGRID	*On*
COLUMNS	Off
EXTWALL	Off
GRID	*On*
INTWALL	Off
ROOF·	*Current*
WINDWALL	Off
WINDWALL2	Off

1. Draw> Solids> Box
First corner: *'From, 'Intersection* at D-1
Offset: *@–3′4″,–3′,25′*
Other corner: *@96′8″,87'*
Height: *3′*

Notice that you have specified a z coordinate so the box is drawn at the desired height.

T1–3   CREATE EXTERIOR WALLS

In this section, only the walls that are relevant to Tutorial 1 will be drawn, Other perimeter walls will be dealt with in the appropriate tutorials.

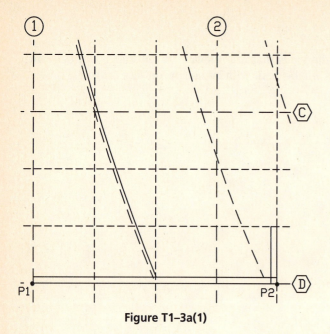

Figure T1–3a(1)

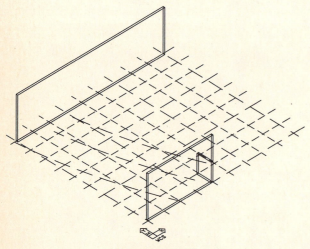

Figure T1–3a(2)

T1–3a Draw Perimeter Walls

Layer settings:

0	Off
2NDFLR	Off
3DFLOOR	Off
3DUPPER	Off
CEILING	Off
COLGRID	*On*
COLUMNS	Off
EXTWALL	*Current*
GRID	*On*
INTWALL	Off
ROOF	Off
WINDWALL	Off
WINDWALL2	Off

1. Zoom in around D-1 and D-2.

Select **Draw> Solids> Box> Corner**.
First corner: Pick '*Intersection* at P1.
Other corner: @*40',1'*
Height: *24'*

Repeat **Draw> Solids> Box> Corner**.
First corner: Pick '*Intersection* at P2.
Other corner: @*–1',9'*
Height: *10'6*

2. Zoom in around columns A-1 and A-4.

Click on **Draw> Solids> Box> Corner**.
First corner: Pick P1 at junction of guide lines A and 1.
Other corner: @*90',–1'*
Height: *24'*

T1–3b   Draw Building Columns

You begin by drawing two of the internal columns. They are copied to put columns on all four internal intersections.

Exterior columns are drawn and arrayed onto their approximate locations. They are then located correctly by using editing commands.

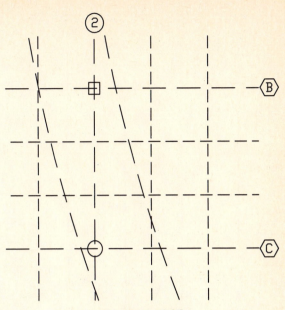

Figure T1–3b(1)

Layer settings:	
0	Off
2NDFLR	Off
3DFLOOR	Off
3DUPPER	Off
CEILING	Off
COLGRID	*On*
COLUMNS	*Current*
EXTWALL	Off
GRID	*On*
INTWALL	Off
ROOF	Off
WINDWALL	Off
WINDWALL2	Off

1. The internal columns are centered on the intersections of the column guide lines.

Use **View> Zoom> Window** to open a window at the intersection of column guide lines at B-2.

Select **Draw> Solids> Box> Corner**.
First corner: *'From*
From point: *'Intersection* at B-2
Offset: *@–12,–12*
Other corner: *@24,24*
Height: *10'6*

Click **Draw> Solids> Cylinder> Center**.
Center: *'Intersection* at C-2
Radius: *16*
Height: *10'6*

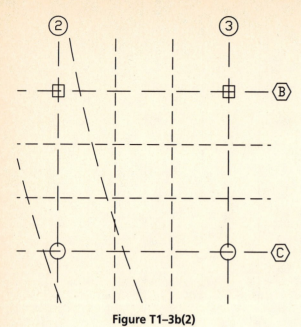

Figure T1–3b(2)

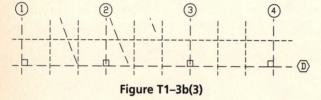

Figure T1–3b(3)

2. You have drawn the columns on one side. Now, copy them to the other side.

Click on **Construct> Copy**.
Select the columns as objects to copy.
Pick any base point.
Displacement: @*30',0*

The internal columns have now been drawn.

3. Create perimeter columns.

Zoom in on intersection at D-1.

Click on **Draw > Solids> Box> Corner**.
First Corner: P1
Other corner: @*2',2'*
Height: *24'*

Click on **Construct> Array> Rectangle**.
Pick the rectangle.
Number of columns: *4*
Distance between columns: *30'*

Set the new columns in their proper positions.

Invoke **Modify> Move**.
Select the columns at D-2 and D-3.
Base point: Select any point.
Displacement: @*–12,0*

Zoom in on intersection D-4.
Invoke **Modify> Move**.
Pick column at D-4 and move it: @*–24,0*

4. Create columns for the opposite wall.

Construct> Array> Rectangular

Pick columns D1, D2, D3, and D4.

Number of rows: *2*

Distance between rows: *79′*

Construct> Array> Rectangle

Pick column D-4 only.

Number of rows: *3*

Distance between rows: *27″*

5. Columns on the back and right side exterior walls have been inserted. Some of them need to be relocated into their proper positions.

Modify> Move column B-4.

Base point: Pick any point.

Displacement: *@0,–12*

Modify> Move column A-1.

Base point: Pick any point.

Displacement: *@–24,12*

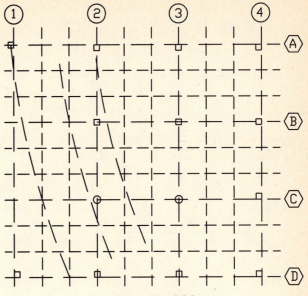

Figure T1–3b(4)

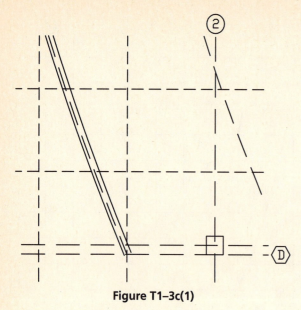

Figure T1–3c(1)

T1–3c Draw Window Wall

The window wall follows the leftmost curved guide line created in Section T1–1b.

After drawing the outline of the window wall, you may calculate the length of the curve of the wall in order to determine the number of mullions needed to create an interesting window design.

Layer settings:	
0	Off
2NDFLR	Off
3DFLOOR	Off
3DUPPER	Off
CEILING	Off
COLGRID	*On*
COLUMNS	Off
EXTWALL	Off
GRID	*On*
INTWALL	Off
ROOF	Off
WINDWALL	*Current*
WINDWALL2	Off

1. Zoom in on the lower part of the left curved guide line.
Click on **Construct> Offset**.
Pick the arc guide.
Offset: *4″* in the -x direction

Construct> Offset again.

Pick the arc guide again.

Offset: *6″* in the +x direction

Click on **Modify>** Properties.

Select the two offset arcs and change their layer to WINDWALL, and make sure Linetype is Continuous.

Again, **Construct> Offset**.

Distance: *12*

Pick guide line D and offset it in the +y direction.

This is a temporary guide line; click **Modify> Properties** to change its layer to Layer 0.

Click on **Draw> Line**.

From point: '*Intersection* at P1 [Figure T1–3c(2)]

To point: '*Center*

Center of: Pick the left arc. Press the RMB.

A line is drawn from P1 to the center of the left arc.

Modify> Extend

Boundary edge: Pick the left arc.

Edge to extend: Pick the line just drawn.

Modify> Properties

Pick the line just drawn and change its layer property to Layer 0.

2. Draw> Solids> Box> Corner

First corner: Pick P1 [Figure T1–3c(3)]

Second corner: @*10,6*

Height: *21′*

Toggle **F8** to turn Ortho *On*.

Select **Modify> Align**.

Pick the box as object or enter *L* (for Last).

First source point: Pick P1.

First destination point: @

Second source point: Pick any point in the +x direction.

Second destination point: '*Center*

Center of: Pick the left arc.

Third source point: Press the RMB.

Third destination point: Press the RMB.

The bottom of the box is aligned with the center of the arc.

Toggle **F8** to turn Ortho *Off*.

Click **Modify> Trim**.

Cutting edge: Pick the line to the center of the arc.

Edges to trim: Pick the lower protruding ends of all three arcs.

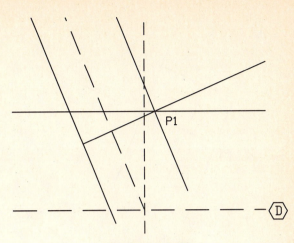

Figure T1–3c(2)

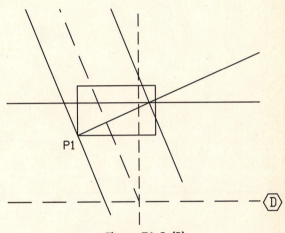

Figure T1–3c(3)

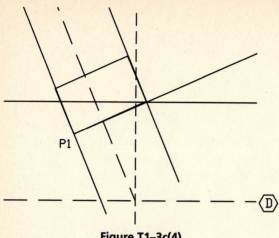

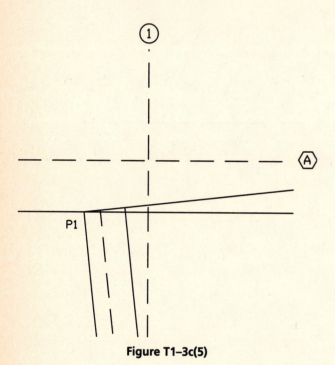

3. Zoom in on column A1.
Draw> Line
From: *'Intersection* at P1 [Figure T1–3c(4)]
To point: *'Center* of left arc

Use this line to trim off the upper parts of all three curved lines.

Click on **Construct> Offset**.

Distance: 12

Pick guide line A.

Offset line A 12″ in the -y direction [Figure T1–3c(5)]

In **Modify> Properties**.

Change the layer property of the line just offset to Layer 0.

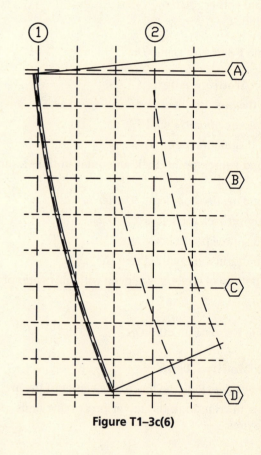

Figure T1–3c(4)

Figure T1–3c(5)

Figure T1–3c(6)

4. Calculating the length of an arc.

You do not have to do this step of the tutorial. You can just take the result from calculating the length of the arc and use it subsequently in Step 5. However, if you are curious about how to use the geometry calculator of R13, here is an opportunity to go through the motions of doing some basic mathematical functions.

It is known that the length of an arc can be determined by the formula:

$$\text{length} = \frac{\pi\, r\, \theta}{180}$$

where r = radius and θ = included angle of the arc.

You have drawn the arc, and you have drawn lines from each end to the center of that arc. R13 will give you the distance and angular direction of each one of the lines. The difference between the angular measurements of the two lines will give you the included angle, θ.

Here is how to find the distance and the angle.

a. Make layer 0 Current.
Turn all other layers *Off*.

b. Click on **Assist> Inquiry> Distance**.
First point: Pick *'Intersection* at P1.
Second point: *'Endpoint* at P2
AutoCAD returns a distance of 275'10″ and angle of 186°.

c. Switch to the lower line.
Repeat the above step to determine the distance between P1 and P3.
AutoCAD returns a distance of 275'10″ and an angle of 203°.

d. The difference between the two angles is
203° − 183° = 17°.
The radius is 275'10″, which is also expressed as:
(275*12+10) inches.

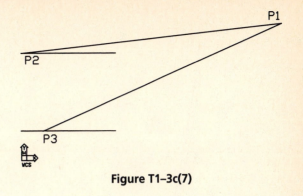

Figure T1–3c(7)

Figure T1–3c(8)

e. Click on **Tools> Calculator**.
Expression: Enter: *pi*(275*12+10)*17/180*

AutoCAD returns 82′ as the length of the arc. The figures are rounded out here.

5. Dividing the window wall with mullions.

Given that the arc is about 82′ in length, you can say that a division of roughly 9′ fits well into our unit measurement of 40″ × 36″, since 3′ is a division of 9′ and 9 × 9′ equals 81′.

Turn layers COLGRID and WINDWALL *On*.
Make layer WINDWALL Current
Turn layer 0 *Off*.

Zoom in on the lower end of the arcs.
Click on **Construct> Array**.
Pick the rectangle at the lower end of the arc.
Select Polar array.
Center of array: '*Center* of left arc
Number of items: *9*
Angle included: *–17*
Rotate objects? *Yes*

An array of nine mullions has been arranged along the arc across the window wall.

Note: In plan view, the mullions may not look like they are aligned with the arcs. This is due to the display resolution of arcs and has nothing to do with whether or not the shapes are correctly aligned.

6. Now to create the horizontal members of the window wall.

Set view to plan view, WCS.
In **Data> Layer**, set layer WINDWALL2 Current.
Make sure layers 0 and COLGRID are *On*.

Zoom in on the lower end of the window wall on the left side of the drawing.

Pick the two arcs on either side of the dashed guide curve.
In **Modify> Properties**, change their layer to WINDWALL2.

Click on **View> Set UCS> 3 Points**.
Origin: P1
+x axis point: P2
+y axis point: *@4<90*

Click on **View> Set UCS> Named UCS**.
Save the UCS as *U1*.

Draw> Polygon> Rectangle
First corner: P1
Other corner: *@10,6*

Construct> 3D Rotate
For object to rotate, enter *L* (for Last, the rectangle you just drew).
Enter *X* to use the x-axis option.
Point on x-axis: Pick *'Endpoint* at P1.
Rotation: *90*

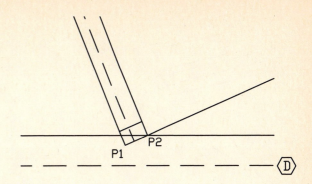

Figure T1–3c(9)

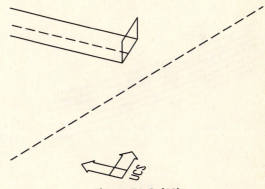

Figure T1–3c(10)

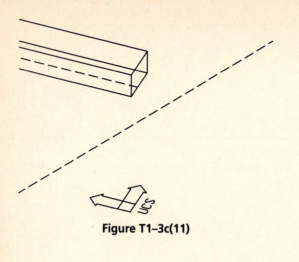

Figure T1–3c(11)

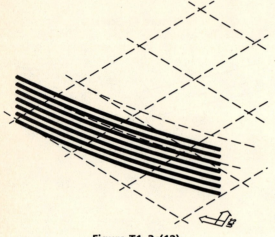

Figure T1–3c(12)

7. Turn layer 0 *Off*.
Set **View> 3D Viewpoint Presets> SW Isometric**.
View> Zoom in on the lower end of the window wall until you can clearly pick out the rotated rectangle created above.

Draw> Solids> Extrude

Pick the rotated rectangle of Step 5 above.

Enter *P* (for Path).

Select the dashed curve line as Path.

The rectangle is extruded along the path to become the window sill plate. It is copied upwards to form horizontal crossing mullions.

Construct> 3D Array> Rectangular

Pick the sill plate.

Number of rows: *1*

Number of columns: *1*

Number of levels: *7*

Distance between levels: *3'*

8. Drawing the lintel beam.

Toggle **F8** to turn Ortho *Off*.
Set view to plan view, WCS.
Check that UCS is still set at *U1*.
Current layer is WINDWALL2.

Draw> Polygon> Rectangle
First point: *.xy* of *'Endpoint* at P1
Need z: Enter: *0*
Other corner: *@10,36*

Construct> 3D Rotate
Pick the rectangle just drawn as the object to rotate.
Enter *X* to use the x-axis option.
Point on x-axis: Pick P1.
Rotation: *90*

Set View to SW Isometric and zoom in tightly on the rectangle.

Draw> Solids> Extrude
Pick the rotated rectangle, or enter *L*.
Path: Pick the dashed curve guide line.

A 3′ tall curved beam has been created; now move it up to the proper height.

Modify> Move
Select the beam.
Base point: Pick any point.
Displacement: *@0,0,21′*

9. Make layer WINDWALL Current.

Construct> Union
Pick all vertical and horizontal window members as well as the lintel beam. They are unioned into one object.

Check to see that the unioned wall is on the current layer. Then delete layer WINDWALL2 with the **Data> Purge** command.

Zoom all and erase the guide lines on Layer 0 that are drawn to the center of the arcs.

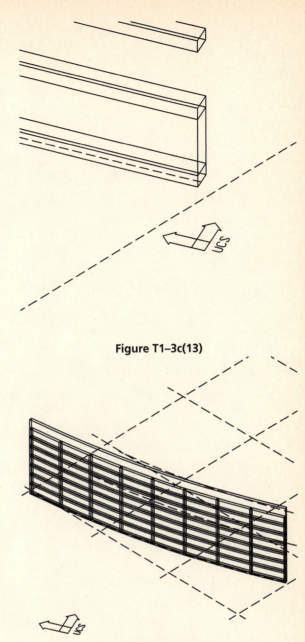

Figure T1–3c(13)

Figure T1–3c(14)

T1–3d Draw Conference Room Walls

On the first floor, you will draw walls around the conference room, the interior of which is dealt with in Tutorial 2.

Layer settings:	
0	*On*
2NDFLR	Off
3DFLOOR	Off
3DUPPER	Off
CEILING	Off
COLGRID	*On*
COLUMNS	*On*
EXTWALL	Off
GRID	*On*
INTWALL	*Current*
ROOF	Off
WINDWALL	*On*

1. First, draw the walls around the conference room. Toggle **F8** to turn Ortho *On*.

View is set at plan view, WCS.

Zoom in on the upper left hand area at the intersection of the second grid line and the temporary guide line offset from A.

Draw> Line

From point: *'From, 'Intersection* at P1

Offset distance: *@3,0*

To point: *@0,–25'*

Construct> Offset the line *6"* in the -x direction.

Draw> Line

Draw a 6" horizontal line joining the upper ends of the two lines you have just drawn.

2. Zoom in on the third mullion from the top.

Draw> Line

From point: *.xy* of *'Endpoint* of the lower right corner of the third mullion (P2).

Need z: Enter: *0*.

To point: *@25',0*

Construct> Offset the line *6"* in the +y direction.

You are still zoomed in around P2.

Click **Draw> Line**.

Draw a 6" vertical line to join the ends of the horizontal lines you have just drawn.

3. Change the view to the area where the 25' lines meet. Clean up the corners with **Modify> Trim**. The conference room has been outlined.

Click **Modify> Edit Polyline**.

Pick one of the wall lines of the conference room; answer *Yes* to change the line into a polyline, then enter *J* (for Join).

Pick the other lines defining the conference room, including the 6" lines at both ends. This is now a polyline loop.

Draw> Solids> Extrude

Pick the polyline loop and extrude it to a height of 10'6.

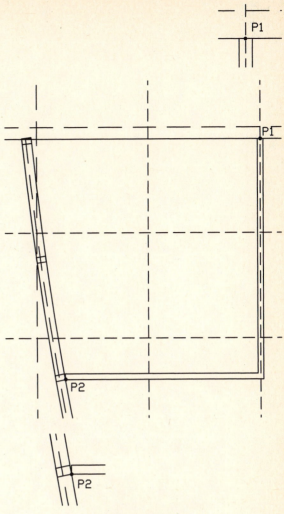

Figure T1–3d

T1–3e Save Drawing for Tutorial 2

When you have finished Section T1–3, make a copy of the current drawing to be used for Tutorial 2.

1. The current drawing is *T1.dwg*. Save it and exit AutoCAD.

2. Make two copies of *T1.dwg*. Save one copy as a backup of T1 to date. Rename the other *T2.dwg*.

3. If you are doing Tutorial 2 as an independent project, skip the rest of this tutorial. Go to Tutorial 2 and use *T2.dwg* as the opening drawing.

4. To do Tutorials 1 and 3, reload AutoCAD, open *T1.dwg*, and continue with the next section.

T1–4   CREATE A PARTIAL SECOND FLOOR

Most of the second floor cannot be seen from the first floor; therefore, only parts of the upper story will be drawn.

The underside of the second floor serves as the ceiling over the open office and teller areas. First, draw a polyline loop that outlines the second floor. The loop is extruded to become a solid object, which is then moved into position.

Layer settings:	
0	Off
2NDFLR	*Current*
3DFLOOR	Off
3DUPPER	Off
CEILING	Off
COLGRID	*On*
COLUMNS	Off
EXTWALL	Off
GRID	*On*
INTWALL	Off
ROOF	Off
WINDWALL	*On*

1. With Ortho *On*, click **Draw> Line**.

From point: *.xy* of *'Endpoint* at P2. (This is the lower right corner of the fourth mullion just below guide line B.)

To point: *'Perpendicular* to guide line 2

Check to be sure both ends of this line are on the x-y plane.

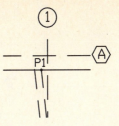

Modify> Trim

Cutting edge: Pick the line just drawn.

Object to trim: Pick the upper part of the middle dashed arc.

2. Zoom out to see the entire plan.
Switch views and zoom in as necessary.
Set Running Object Snap to Intersection.

Draw> Polyline

From point: Pick P1. [See inset, Figure T1–4a(1)]

Enter: *A*, to change to drawing arcs.

Endpoint of arc: Enter: *CE* (for Center).

Center of: *'Center* of the arc between P1 and P2.

Endpoint of arc: Pick P2.

Enter *L*, to change to drawing lines.

Endpoint of line: Pick P3.

At P3, enter *A*, to change to drawing arcs.

Endpoint of arc: Enter *CE* (for Center).

Center of: *'Center* of the dashed arc between P3 and P4.

Endpoint of arc: Pick P4.

At P4, enter *L*, to change to drawing lines.

Endpoint of line: Pick P5.

Endpoint of line: Pick P6.

At P6, enter *C*, to close the polyline from P6 back to P1.

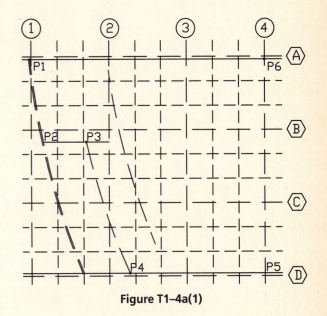

Figure T1–4a(1)

2. Draw> Solids> Extrude

Pick the polyline as object.

Height: *18*

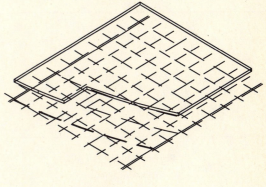

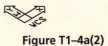

Figure T1–4a(2)

Modify> Move

Pick the extruded polyline, which is now a solid.

Base point: Pick any point.

Displacement: *@0,0,10'6*

You have created a solid second floor slab and moved it so that the top of the floor is at 12' elevation.

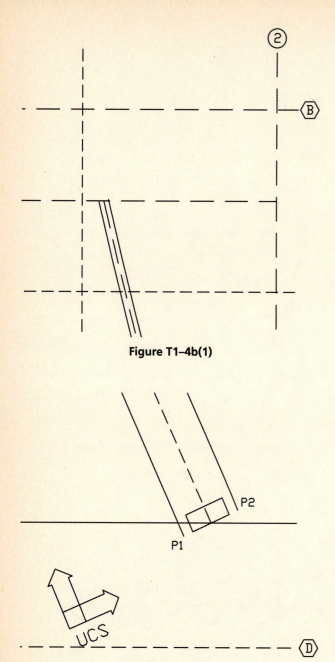

Figure T1–4b(1)

Figure T1–4b(2)

T1–4b   Create a Balcony Bulkhead and Railing

In this section, a partial upper-level floor plan and the balcony details will be drawn.

Layer settings:

0	*On*
2NDFLR	Off
3DFLOOR	Off
3DUPPER	*Current*
CEILING	Off
COLGRID	*On*
COLUMNS	Off
EXTWALL	Off
GRID	*On*
INTWALL	Off
ROOF	Off
WINDWALL	Off

1. In plan view, WCS, zoom in around guide lines B and 2.
Click **Construct> Offset**.
Pick the middle curved guideline.
Offset it *3″* to *each* side.

2. Draw the uprights or stanchions of the railing.

Zoom in on the other (lower) end of the arcs.
Click on **View> Set UCS> 3 Points**.
Origin: '*Endpoint* at P1
+x point: '*Endpoint* at P2
+y point: *@4<90*

Click **View> Named UCS**.
In the dialog box, name the current UCS to *U2*.

Draw> Solids> Box> Corner
First corner: *1,0*
Other corner: *@4″,1.75″*
Height: *36*

Construct> Array> Polar

Pick the box just drawn.

Center of polar array: *'Center*

Center of: Pick the middle dashed guide arc.

Number of items: *12*

Angle: *–11.3*

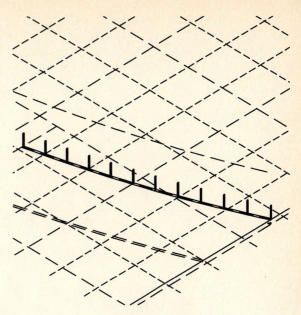

The stanchions are arrayed along the railing.

Since 3D objects can vastly increase the size of a drawing file, the railing will not be elaborately detailed. It will have a simple baffle drawn between the stanchions.

3. Make sure the current UCS is still set at *U2*. Set view at plan view of current UCS and zoom in on the lower end of the railing.

Figure T1–4b(3)

Make layer 0 Current.

Turn layer 3DUPPER *Off*.

Draw> Polygon> Rectangle

First corner: *2.5,3*

Other corner: *@1,30*

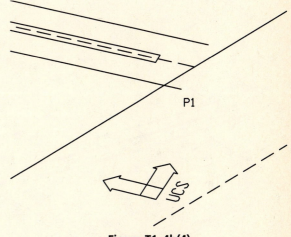

Construct> 3D Rotate

Pick the object just drawn.

Enter *X* to select the x-axis option.

Point on x-axis: Enter: *0,0* or pick P1.

Angle: *90*

View> Set UCS> World

Set view to SW Isometric and zoom in.

Figure T1–4b(4)

Draw> Solids> Extrude

Pick the rectangle just drawn.

Enter *P* (for Path).

Pick the middle dashed guide arc as path.

Make layer 3DUPPER Current.

In **Modify> Properties**, change the layer property of the extruded baffle just drawn to 3DUPPER.

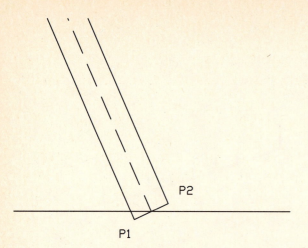

P2

P1

Figure T1–4b(5)

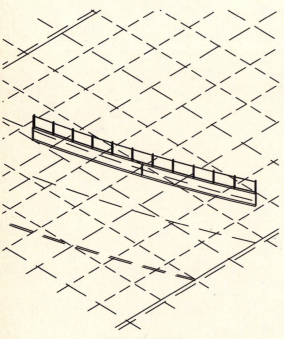

Figure T1–4b(6)

4. Do not union the baffle and stanchions. You may assign different materials to them at rendering time.

Click on **Modify> Move.**

Pick the baffle and all the stanchions.

Pick any base point.

Displacement: *@0,0,12'*

The railing has been moved to the upper floor. Now create a header beam under the railing.

5. Make layer 0 Current.

Turn layer 3DUPPER *Off.*

Set view at SW Isometric and window around the curved railing guidelines on the ground floor (x-y plane.)

Draw> Line from P1 to P2.

Again, **Draw> Line** to close the other ends of the curves.

Click on **Modify> Properties.**

One at a time, pick the two lines just drawn and the offset lines on each side of the dashed guide line. Change the layer and linetype to 3DUPPER and Continuous.

Make layer 3DUPPER Current.

Modify> Edit Polyline

Select the line from P1 to P2.

You will be asked if you want to turn this line into a polyline. Enter *Y* (for Yes).

Then enter *J* (for Join).

Object to join: Pick the two curved lines marking the railing and the line drawn from P3 to P4.

The curves and end lines are joined into a polyline loop.

Draw> Solids> Extrude

Pick the polyline loop.

Height: *3'*

Modify> Move the extrusion. Use any base point.

Enter: *@0,0,9'* to put the bottom of the beam at 9' high.

The header beam and railing are complete.

T1–5 CREATE SOME INTERIOR DETAILS

In this section, you will draw walls in the vault and block out the teller counter, as they are partially visible from the customer waiting area. However, details for the teller counter will be developed in Tutorial 4.

T1–5a Draw the Vault and Teller Counter

Layer settings:

0	*On*
2NDFLR	Off
3DFLOOR	Off
3DUPPER	Off
CEILING	Off
COLGRID	*On*
COLUMNS	Off
EXTWALL	Off
GRID	*On*
INTWALL	*Current*
ROOF	Off
WINDWALL	*On*

1. Drawing is set at plan view, WCS.
Change view to around guide lines B and 2.

Draw> Solids> Box> Corner

First corner: *'Intersection* at B-2

Other corner: *@12',6*

Height: *10'6*

Again, click **Draw> Solids> Box> Corner**.

First corner: *'Intersection* at B-2

Other corner: *@6",–26'*

Height: *10'6*

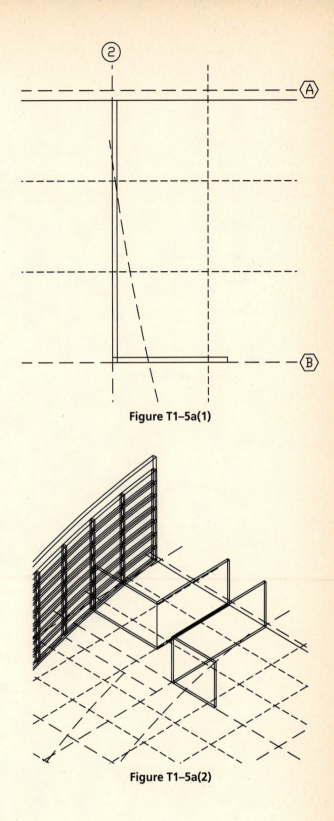

Figure T1–5a(1)

Figure T1–5a(2)

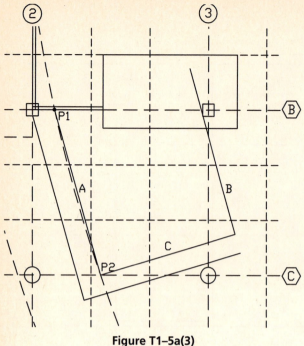

Figure T1–5a(3)

2. Drawing the vault.

Zoom in on column B-3.

Draw> Solids> Box> Corner
First corner: *'From, 'Intersection* at guide lines B-3
Offset: *@5',–3'*
Other corner: *@–23',12'*
Height: *10'6*

3. Drawing the teller counter.
Zoom out to see all four interior columns.
Make layer 0 Current.

Draw> Line from P1 to P2. Use *'Intersection.*
This is line A.

Construct> Offset
Offset Distance: *24'*
Object to offset: Pick the line and a point in the +x direction. This is line B.

Click on **Draw > Line**.
From point: Pick *P2.*
To point: *'Endpoint* of lower end of line B
This is line C.

4. Zoom in on the upper end of line A.

Construct> Copy
Pick line A.
Base point: *'Endpoint* of line A
Displacement: *'Intersection* at center of column B-2

Construct> Offset
Offset line C at a distance of 3'2" in the -y direction.

Modify> Extend
Pick both copied line A and offset line C.

As they do not actually cross each other, use the Project/View and Extend options to make the lines meet.

5. Make layer INTWALL Current.

Refer to Figure T1–5a(4) for the following P points.

Draw> Polyline

Draw from P1 successively through P4.
At P4, enter *C* to close back to P1.
You have created a polyline loop.

Draw> Solids> Extrude

For object, enter *L*, or pick the last polyline loop.
Height: *3'5"*

6. Again, click **Draw> Polyline**.
From point: P5 (Intersection at B-2)
To point: P6, successively through P7
At P7, enter: *'Perpendicular* to guide line B at P8
At P8, enter C to close back to P5.
You have created another polyline loop.

Draw> Solids> Extrude

For object, enter *L*, or pick the last polyline loop.
Height: *18"*

Modify> Move

Pick the last polyline loop and any base point.
Displacement: *@0,0,9'*

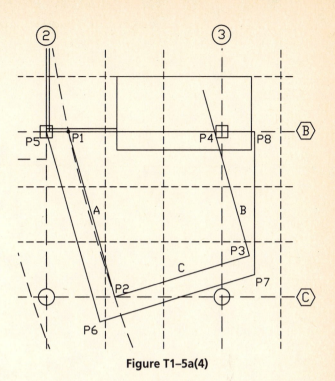

Figure T1–5a(4)

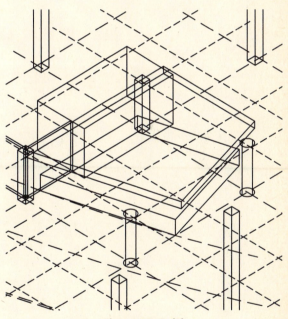

Figure T1–5a(5)

T1–5b   Save Drawing for Tutorial 3

At this stage, you should save the current *T1.dwg* drawing so that you can continue on to Tutorials 3, or complete the rest of Tutorial 1.

1. At the end of Section T1–5, you are still working in drawing *T1.dwg*. Save current drawing and exit AutoCAD.

2. Make two copies of *T1.dwg*. Save one copy as a backup. Rename another copy as *T3.dwg*.

3. To do Tutorial 3, follow the instructions in Tutorial 3 and use drawing *T3.dwg*.

4. To complete Tutorial 1, reload AutoCAD and *T1.dwg*. Continue to the next section: T1–6.

About the only thing left to do around the customer waiting area is the wall at the end of the balcony railing on the second floor. This wall is quite a prominent feature of the design. If you are viewing from the lobby toward the customer waiting area, this wall can be seen. Therefore, it needs to be included in Tutorial 1.

T1–6a   Draw a 3D Wall for the Second-Floor End Room

The wall consists of a tier of horizontal members. The bottom one is a support beam, while the ones above are perforated with windows.

Create the following new layer:

Name	Color	Linetype
WPANE	Green	Continuous

Layer settings:

0	*On*
2NDFLR	Off
3DFLOOR	Off
3DUPPER	*Current*
CEILING	Off
COLGRID	*On*
COLUMNS	*On*
EXTWALL	Off
GRID	*On*
INTWALL	*On*
ROOF	Off
WINDWALL	Off
WPANE	Off

1. Toggle **F8** to turn Ortho *Off*.

Set View to plan view, WCS.

Zoom in on the end of the balcony.

You should be able to see the horizontal line drawn in step 1 of T1–4a and the line from step 4, T1–5a.

Modify> Extend

Pick line from T1-5a as boundary edge.

Pick the horizontal line drawn in T1–4a as object to extend.

Click File> Inquiry> Distance.

Measure the length of the line just extended by using its endpoints.

AutoCAD reports a distance of 26'10" (approximate).

Click Draw> Solids> Box> Corner.

First corner: *.xy* of *'Endpoint* at P1

Need Z: Enter: *9'*

Other corner: *@26'10",6"*

Height: *3'*

You have drawn the beam at the base of the wall. Now make a copy of it to be used as the first tier of the windows.

2. Construct> Copy

Pick the box just drawn and any base point.

Displacement: *@0,0,3'*

View is still set at plan view, WCS.

Change view to around the middle of the beam.

Make layer 0 Current.

Turn layer 3DUPPER *Off*.

Click Draw> Solids> Box> Corner.

First corner: *'Intersection* at P1

Other corner: *@–18,12*

Height: *18*

Modify> Move

Pick the box just drawn.

Displacement: *@–9,–3,12'9"*

Make layer 3DUPPER Current.

Modify> Properties

Change the layer property of the box just drawn to layer 3DUPPER.

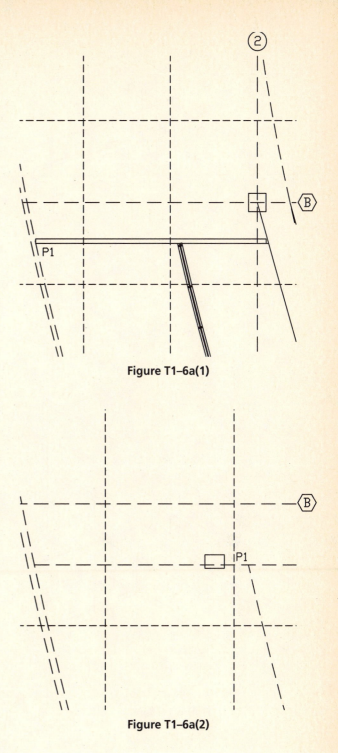

Figure T1–6a(1)

Figure T1–6a(2)

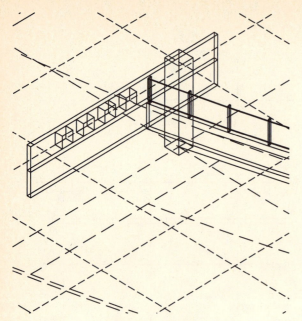

Figure T1–6a(3)

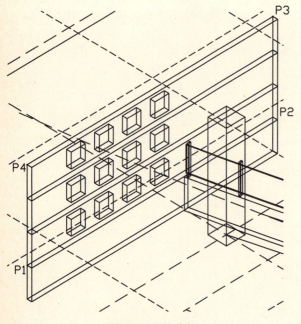

Figure T1–6a(4)

3. The small box you have been working with is the prototype of one of the windows. It will now be copied laterally to put window shapes on the rest of the beam.

Click **Construct> Array> Rectangular**.

Number of columns: *4*

Distance between columns: *–3′*

Switch to a SW Isometric view and zoom in on the beam.

Construct> Subtract

Pick the beam with the windows.

Then pick all four of the window shapes to subtract.

4. The beam now has window holes in it. It is then arrayed upwards to fill the rest of the wall.

Construct> 3D Array> Rectangular

Number of levels: *3*

Distance between levels: *3′*

5. Draw a 3D Face behind the windows so that you can assign a material to the window holes during rendering.

Still in SW Isometric, zoom in on the end of the lowest window beam.

Draw> Surfaces> 3D Face

First point: *'Endpoint* at P1

For second, third, and fourth points, be sure to pick the endpoints at the other end of the same side of the window beam. Cycle around that side of the beam and the fourth point will be directly above P1. After picking the fourth point, you will be prompted for another "third Point." Just press the RMB to exit the 3D Face command.

A 3D Face is drawn on the inside of the wall. You can assign a material and adjust the degree of transparency later during rendering.

T1–6b   Save Work for Tutorial 1

As far as visibility and relevance to the customer waiting area is concerned, all the building elements have been drawn. Save your drawing at this point. As the rest of the elements for Tutorial 1 are individual furniture pieces, do them on separate files.

1. The current drawing is *T1.dwg.* Save it and exit AutoCAD.

2. Make a copy of *T1.dwg* and save it as a backup.

3. Continue on Tutorial 1 with sections T1–7, 8, and 9.

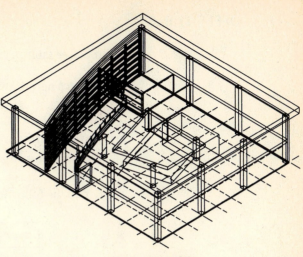

Figure T1–6a(5)

A coffee table is created for the customer waiting area.

Set up a new drawing with the following parameters:

Name of Drawing: *Coffee.dwg*
Data> Units: *Architectural*
Data> Drawing Limits: Lower Left at *0,0*; Upper Right at *20′,16′*

Set up the following layers through **Data> Layer:**

Layer Name	Color	Linetype
0	White	Continuous
BASE	Green	Continuous
GUIDES	White	Continuous
TOP	Cyan	Continuous

T1–7a Draw Guide Lines

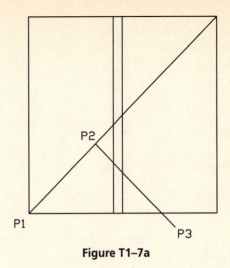

Figure T1–7a

View is zoomed: All, at plan view, WCS.

1. Draw> Polygon> Rectangle
First corner: _6',6'_ (P1)
Other corner: _@40,40_

Draw> Line
From point: '_Midpoint_ of bottom edge
To point: '_Midpoint_ of top edge

Construct> Offset
Pick the line and offset it 2″ in the -x direction.

Draw> Line
From the lower left corner to the upper right corner.

2. Draw> Line
From point: 'From, '_Intersection_ at P1
Offset: _@20<45_ (P2)
To point: _@24<-45_ (P3)

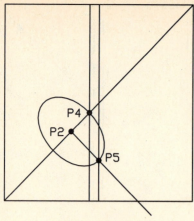

Figure T1–7b

T1–7b   Draw the Base

Layer settings:	
0	Off
BASE	*Current*
GUIDES	*On*
TOP	Off

1. Options> Running Snap> Intersection

Draw> Solids> Cylinder> Elliptical

Enter *C* (for Center).

Center: *'Intersection* at P2

Axis endpoint: *'Intersection* at P4

Other axis endpoint: *'Intersection* at P5

Height: *18*

The elliptical base is drawn.

T1–7c   Draw the Top

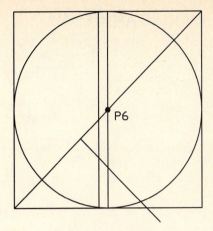

Figure T1–7c(1)

Layer settings:	
0	Off
BASE	Off
GUIDES	*On*
TOP	*Current*

1. Draw> Solids> Cylinder> Center

Center: *'Intersection* at P6

Radius: *20*

Height: *0.75"*

Modify> Move

Pick the cylinder.

Base point: Pick any point.

Displacement: *@0,0,18*

All the parts for the coffee table have been drawn.

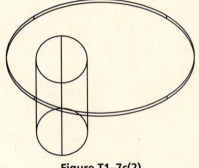

Figure T1–7c(2)

2. Turn *Off* the Layer GUIDES and turn *On* layers: BASE and TOP.

Set **View> 3D Viewpoint Presets> SE Isometric** to see the table in 3D.

Save your drawing.

Invoke **File> Export> Block**.

Name of drawing: *T1-tab.dwg*

Block name: Press the RMB

Insertion point: *0,0*

Objects: Select the base and the top only.

Save and exit AutoCAD. Make a copy each of the *coffee.dwg* and *T1-tab.dwg* files. Use the copy of *T1-tab.dwg* for insertion into the perspective drawings when you get to Chapter 5.

The chair consists of a molded frame, a seat cushion, and a matching cushion for the back.

A frontal profile of the frame is first created by editing lines and arcs. The profile is then extruded horizontally to the depth of the chair.

The cushions are created separately by using a similar sequence of steps.

Set up a new drawing with the following parameters:

Name of Drawing: *Wchair.dwg*
Data> Units: *Architectural*
Data> Drawing Limits: Lower Left at *0,0*;
Upper Right at: *20',16'*

Set up the following layers through **Data> Layer:**

Layer Name	Color	Linetype
0	White	Continuous
BACK	Green	Continuous
FRAME	White	Continuous
GUIDES	White	Continuous
SEAT	White	Continuous

T1–8a Guide Lines for the Frame

To begin the frame, you need to draw some guide lines.

Layer settings:

0	Off
BACK	Off
FRAME	Off
GUIDES	*Current*
SEAT	Off

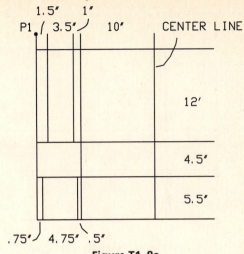

Figure T1–8a

1. Draw a series of guide lines according to Figure T1–8a.

Set **View> 3D Vp Presets> Plan View> World**.
Set Ortho *On*.
Click on **Draw> Line**.
From point: *5',8'* (P1) (arbitrary location)
To point: *@0,–24*
To point: *@24,0*

Use **Construct> Offset** to create the other vertical guide lines. Be sure to set the correct offset distance. The inner line (the one on the right) is the center line of the frontal profile of the chair.

Draw the four horizontal guide lines. Use **Modify> Trim** to cut off excess ends of the lines.

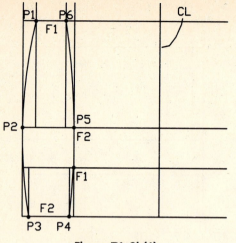

Figure T1–8b(1)

T1–8b   Draw the Frame

Layer settings:	
0	Off
BACK	Off
FRAME	*Current*
GUIDES	*On*
SEAT	Off

1. Set **Options> Running Object Snap** to **Intersection**.

Use **Draw> Arc> 3 Points** to draw an arc from P1 to P2 to P3.

Draw another arc from P4 to P5 to P6.

Modify> Trim

Trimming edges: Pick the two middle horizontal guide lines.

Objects to trim: Pick the part of the inner arc between the cutting edges [between P5 and F1, Figure T1–8b(1)].

The inner arc has been broken into two separate segments.

2. **Construct> Fillet**

Enter *R* to set radius.

Enter *0.5* (for the radius of the first fillet).

Pick the adjoining lines at a point marked F1.

The corner between the two lines is filleted at a radius of *0.5″*.

Fillet the other intersections marked F1 (there are three in all). When you repeat the **Fillet** command, the radius is set to the previously defined radius value. You do not have to reset the radius every time unless you want to change the fillet radius, as you are going to do in the following step.

3. Construct> Fillet

Enter *R* to set radius.

Enter *0.3*

Pick the adjoining lines at a point marked F2.

The corner between the two lines is filleted at a new radius of *0.3″*. There are three intersections marked F2.

Click on **Modify> Trim**.

For the cutting edge, pick the center line.

For edges to trim, pick the two protruding ends of the horizontal lines.

4. Consolidate lines for the frontal profile.

Click on **Modify> Properties**.

Use a crossing window to select all objects on the screen. Do NOT press Enter or the RMB.

Instead, enter *R* (for Remove).

Objects to remove: Pick the remaining segments of vertical guide lines. (They should be the only objects remaining on the screen that are not a part of the frontal profile.) Now press the RMB to return to the **Change Properties** dialog box.

Change the layer property of the remaining objects to layer FRAME.

Turn layer GUIDES *Off*. Your drawing should look like Figure T1–8b(3).

5. Modify> Edit Polyline

Pick any line on the screen except the CL.

Answer *Yes* to change the object into a polyline.

Then, enter *J* (for Join).

Select objects: Pick all the lines except the CL.

Exit the **Edit Polyline** command. If you click the LMB on any part of the line on the screen, you should be able to see that all the line segments have been linked into one polyline.

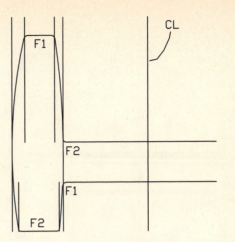

Figure T1–8b(2)

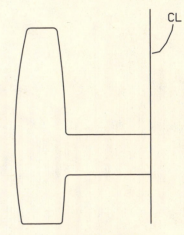

Figure T1–8b(3)

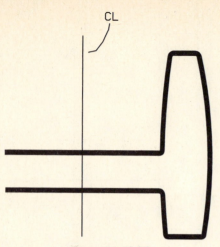

Figure T1–8b(4)

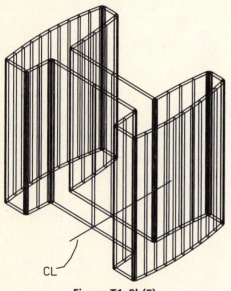

Figure T1–8b(5)

6. With Ortho *On*, click on **Construct> Mirror**.
Pick the polyline.
First point on mirror line: *'Endpoint* at P1
Second point: Pick any point above or below P1.
Delete old objects? *No*

The polyline has been mirrored to the other side.

Modify> Edit Polyline
Pick the polyline on one side of the center line.
Enter *J* (for Join).
Pick the polyline on the other side of the center line.
Enter *W* (for Weight).
Enter: *0.6″*

The two halves have been joined into one 0.6″ wide polyline.

7. Modify> Properties
Pick the polyline loop.
The **Modify Polyline** dialog box comes on.
In the Thickness window, enter *28*.

The polyline loop has been "extruded" to 28″ high to be a 3D object.

Set view to SE Isometric.

Rotate it so that the object lies flat on the x-y plane.
Construct> 3D Rotate
Pick the 3D polyline.
Select the x-axis rotate option.
Point on x-axis: Pick the left (front) end of the center line.
Rotation angle: *90*

The base frame of the chair has been created and placed in the correct orientation.

T1–8c   Create the Seat Cushion

Layer settings:

0	Off
BACK	Off
FRAME	Off
GUIDES	*Current*
SEAT	*On*

1. Set **View> 3D Viewpoint Presets** to plan view, WCS.

With the above layer settings, the only object visible should be the center guide line.

Draw > Polygon> Rectangle

First corner: Pick a point next to the center guide line.

Other corner: @ *2'3", 7*

Use **Draw> Circle> Center, Radius** to position 3″ and 4″ radii circles within the rectangle roughly as shown in Figure T1–8c(1). You do not have to be very precise in placing the circles, but do put smaller circles at the ends.

2. Change layer SEAT to Current.
Check to be sure Ortho is *Off.*

Draw> Polyline

Draw a curved line with the circles as guides. For the last endpoint, use the Close option to make the polyline a loop.

Modify> Edit Polyline

Pick the polyline loop and enter F (for Fit).

The polyline should smooth out. Do not use Spline, as that would greatly increase the size of the drawing file. Press the RMB to exit command.

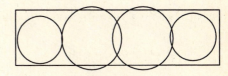

Figure T1–8c(1)

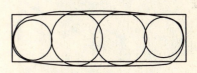

GUIDELINE

Figure T1–8c(2)

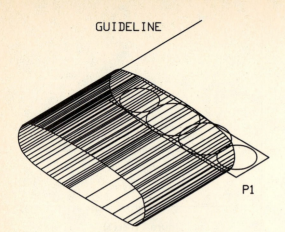

GUIDELINE

Figure T1–8c(3)

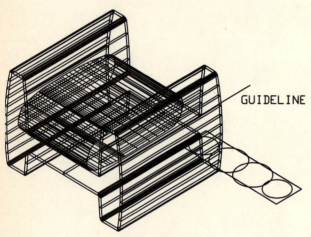

P1

GUIDELINE

Figure T1–8c(4)

3. Set **View> 3D Viewpoint Presets> SE Isometric**.

Draw> Solids> Extrude

Pick the polyline loop.

Height: *19*

Construct> 3D Rotate

Pick the extruded object.

Use x-axis Rotate and P1 as the point on x-axis.

Rotation angle: *90*

4. Set **View> 3D Viewpoint Presets** to plan view, WCS.

Click **Modify> Rotate**.

Pick a point near the center of the seat as the base point; rotate the seat 90°.

The seat has been drawn and rotated into the proper orientation.

5. Turn layer FRAME *On*.

Modify> Move

Pick the seat and move it over the seat frame with about 3″ protruding at the front.

Set **View> 3D Viewpoint Presets** to **Front**.

Again, click on **Modify> Move**.

Pick the block and move it to sit on the seat frame.

Switch to a 3D view to check on your drawing.

T1–8d   Create the Cushion for the Back

Layer settings:

0	Off
BACK	*On*
FRAME	Off
GUIDES	*Current*
SEAT	Off

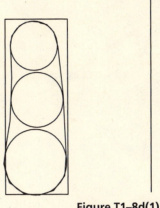

GUIDELINE

Figure T1–8d(1)

Follow the same procedure as in Section T1–8c to create the cushion for the back.

1. First, change the layer property of the existing rectangle to layer 0.

Draw> Polygon> Rectangle

Pick a point to the left of the center guide line.

Other corner: *6,16*

Use **Draw> Circle> Center, Radius** to position circles with radii at 2.25″, 2.5″ and 3″, starting from the top as in Figure T1–8d(1). Slant the circles slightly to the left. The bottom of the figure will become the front face of the back when the figure is rotated into its proper position.

2. Change layer BACK to Current.

Draw> Polyline

Draw from tangent to tangent and around the end circles. Be sure you end the polyline with the Close option. If your loop is not smooth, try Fit Curve to make it smoother. See Step 2, T1–8c.

Draw> Solids> Extrude

Pick the polyline loop.

Height: *17*

Construct> 3D Rotate

Pick the extruded object.

Enter Y to use the y-axis option.

Point on y-axis: Pick the lower right corner of the rectangle.

Rotation angle: *–90* (that is *negative* 90°)

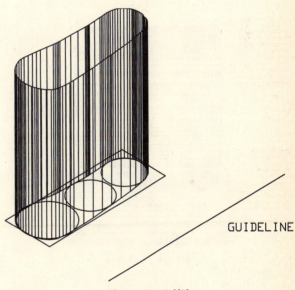

GUIDELINE

Figure T1–8d(2)

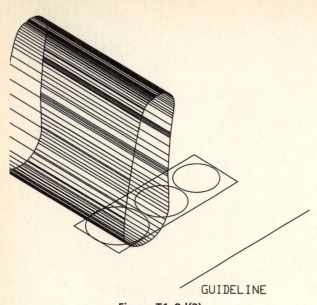

GUIDELINE

Figure T1–8d(3)

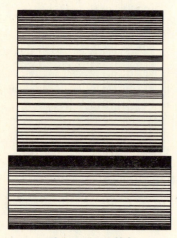

Figure T1–8d(4)

3. Set **View> 3D Viewpoint Presets** to plan view, WCS.

Construct> 3D Rotate

Pick the extruded object.

Select the x-axis rotate option.

Point on x-axis: Pick the lower end point of the guide line.

Rotation angle: *83*

The back cushion has been rotated twice into its correct orientation.

4. Turn layer SEAT *On*.
Turn layer GUIDES *Off*.
Layer BACK is Current.
View is set at plan view, WCS.

Modify> Move

Pick the block and move it over the seat frame to about where the back should be.

Set **View> 3D Viewpoint Presets** to **Left**.

Again, click on **Modify> Move**.
Pick the block and move it to sit on the seat cushion.

Check the position of the back by **View> 3D Viewpoint Presets** to **Front**. If necessary, move it again until it is seated properly.

The waiting room chair has been created.

5. Make sure layer GUIDES is *Off* and that layers FRAME and SEAT are *On*.

Set **View> 3D Viewpoint Presets> SE Isometric** to see the chair in 3D.

Save your drawing.

Invoke **File> Export> Block**.

Name of drawing: *T1-chr.dwg*

Block name: Press the RMB

Insertion point: *0,0*

Objects: Select the frame and cushions

Exit AutoCAD and make a copy each of the *Wchair.dwg* and *T1-chr.dwg* files. Use the copy of *T1-chr.dwg* for insertion into the perspective drawings when you get to Chapter 5.

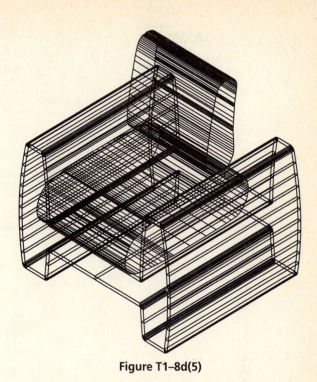

Figure T1–8d(5)

A sideboard is created for the customer waiting area.

Set up a new drawing with the following parameters:

Name of Drawing: *Side.dwg*
Data> Units: *Architectural*
Data> Drawing Limits: Lower Left at *0,0*;
Upper Right at *20',16'*

Set up the following layers through **Data> Layer:**

Layer Name	Color	Linetype
0		
BODY	White	Continuous
GUIDES	Cyan	Continuous
LEGS	White	Continuous
SB	White	Continuous
TOP	Green	Continuous

T1–9a Create Guide Lines for the Sideboard

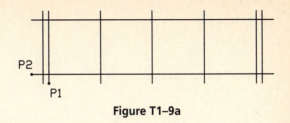

Figure T1–9a

Layer settings:

0	Off
BODY	Off
GUIDES	*Current*
LEGS	Off
SB	Off
TOP	Off

View is set to zoom: All, at plan view, WCS.

1. To begin the sideboard, you need to draw some guide lines.
Click on **Draw> Line**.
From point: Enter *7″,7″* (P1)
To point: *@0,24*
Construct> Array> Rectangular
Pick the line as subject.
Number of columns: *5*
Distance between columns: *18*

Construct> Offset

Distance to offset: *2*

Select one of the end lines.

Side to offset: Pick a point away from the center.

Repeat **Offset** with the other end line.

2. Draw> Line
From point: *6′6,7′3.*(P2)
To point: *@7″,0*

Construct> Offset

Distance: *18*

Offset the line in the +y direction.

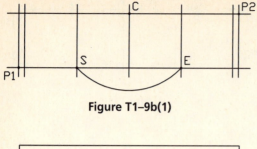

Figure T1–9b(1)

Figure T1–9b(2)

Layer settings:	
0	Off
BODY	Off
GUIDES	*On*
LEGS	Off
SB	Off
TOP	*Current*

1. Draw> Polygon> Rectangle

First corner at P1.
Other corner at P2.

Draw> Arc> S,C,E

Start point: Pick point S.

Center: Pick point C.

End point: Pick point E.

Modify> Trim

Cutting edge: Pick the lines on each side of the center line.

Objects to trim: Pick the lower edge of the rectangle between the cutting edges.

The segment of the rectangle between the arc has been trimmed.

2. Turn layer GUIDES *Off*.

Modify> Edit Polylines

Select the arc and enter *Yes* to change the arc into a polyline.

Enter *J* (for Join).

Select all the remaining segments of the rectangle.

The arc and modified rectangle are now joined to become one closed polyline loop.

3. Construct> Offset

Offset the loop *1"* in toward the center.

Modify> Change Properties

Select the inner polyline loop.

Change its layer property to BODY.

You have created the outline of the body of the sideboard with a modified copy of the top.

4. Draw> Solids> Extrude

Pick the polyline loop. (It should be the only visible thing, as the copy has been relocated to the BODY layer, which is turned *Off* and is not currently visible.)
Height: *1"*

Modify> Move

Pick the polyline loop.

Base point: Pick any point.

Displacement: *@0,0,30*

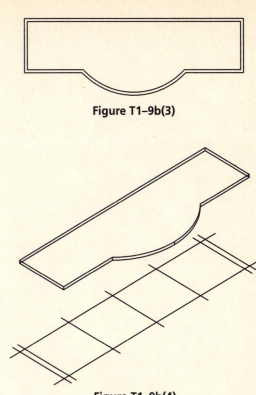

Figure T1–9b(3)

Figure T1–9b(4)

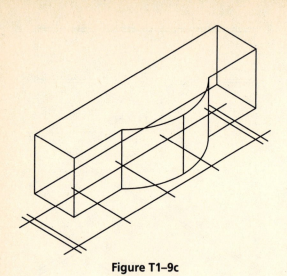

Figure T1–9c

Layer settings:

0	Off
BODY	*Current*
GUIDES	*On*
LEGS	Off
SB	Off
TOP	Off

The polyline loop modified in Section T1–9b, Step 3, should be the only object on this layer.

1. Draw> Solids> Extrude
Pick the polyline loop.
Height: *20*

The 2D polyline loop has been made into a solid 3D object.

Modify> Move

Pick the solid.

Base point: Pick any point.

Displacement: *@0,0,9.5″*

There is a ½″ gap or reveal between the top and body of the sideboard.

T1–9d   Create the Legs

Layer settings:	
0	Off
BODY	Off
GUIDES	*On*
LEGS	*Current*
SB	Off
TOP	Off

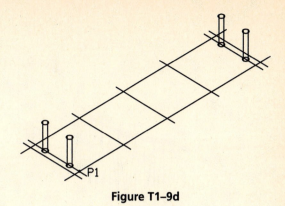

Figure T1–9d

1. You will draw some cylinder to represent legs for the sideboard.

Draw> Solids> Cylinder> Center
Center: *'From, 'Intersection* at P1
Offset: *@0,4*
Radius: *1"*
Height: *9.5"*

Construct> Array> Rectangular

Pick the cylinder.

Number of rows: *2*

Number of columns: *2*

Distance between rows: *10"*

Distance between columns: *6'* (that is, 6 feet).

The legs for the sideboard are complete.

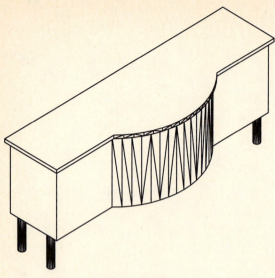

Figure T1–9e

T1–9e   Finish Up

Now that you have created the legs, you have made all the parts for the sideboard.

Turn layer GUIDES *Off*; turn layers BODY, TOP, and SB *On*.

Switch to a SE Isometric view to see the sideboard in 3D.

Save your drawing.

To limit the proliferation of layers when you insert this drawing into a perspective view, organize the parts of the sideboard into a single layer: SB.

Click on **Modify> Change Properties**.

Pick the legs, body, and top of the sideboard.

Change their layer properties to SB.

Turn all layers *Off* except SB.

Invoke **File> Export> Block**.

Name of drawing: *T1-cab.dwg*

Block name: Press the RMB

Insertion point: *0,0*

Select all the parts on layer SB. Exit AutoCAD and make a copy each of the *Side.dwg* and *T1-cab.dwg* files. Use the copy of *T1-cab.dwg* for insertion into the perspective drawings when you get to Chapter 5.

Tutorial 2. Conference Room

ABOUT TUTORIAL 2.   CONFERENCE ROOM

The conference room is located at one corner of the bank building next to the customer waiting area. The room is quite small, with a one-story height, and is a part of the building at the curved window wall.

In this tutorial, you have occasion to draw some close-up details in such items as cabinets, tables and chairs, and the entry doors to the conference room. Because some of the elements are quite simple, you will build many of the models directly in 3D.

You can do this tutorial as an independent project. Begin by following Tutorial 1 from Section T1–1 through T1–3. At the end of Section T1–3, save the drawing and rename a copy of it as *T2.dwg*. Use the copy to continue in this tutorial beginning at Section T2–3.

If you are doing this tutorial after having completed Tutorial 1, open a copy of the drawing saved at the end of Section T1–6. In this section, the building has already been drawn. Rename the copy of the drawing as *T2.dwg*, then go to Section T2–3 to begin this tutorial.

T2–1   DOING TUTORIAL 2 AS AN INDEPENDENT PROJECT

As the tutorials emphasize different areas of the bank building, you can do this tutorial as a project independent of the other tutorials.

1. Still, you need to begin by following Tutorial 1 from Section T1–1 until you have finished Section T1–3.

2. At the end of Section T1–3, save the drawing as *T2.dwg*. Exit AutoCAD.

3. Make a copy of *T2.dwg*. Save it as a backup.

4. Reload AutoCAD.
Click on **File> Open**.
Name of file: *T2.dwg*

5. Go to Section T2–3 in this tutorial to continue.

T2–2   DOING TUTORIAL AFTER HAVING COMPLETED TUTORIAL 1

1. Ready a copy of the drawing you saved at the end of Section T1–6. This is the section where you completed the building, but not the furnishings.

2. Make a copy of the drawing and rename it as *T2.dwg*.

3. Reload AutoCAD.
Click on **File> Open**.
Name of file: *T2.dwg*

4. Go to Section T2–3 in this tutorial to continue.

T2–3   CREATING NEW 3D ELEMENTS FOR THE CONFERENCE ROOM

Having completed a part of the bank building, you can now turn your attention to creating some solid elements particular to the interior of the conference room.

T2–3a   Create New Layers

Click on **Data> Layers**.
Create the following new layers:

Layer name	Color	Linetype
CONCLG	Magenta	Continuous
CONDOR	53	Continuous
T2LTG	Cyan	Continuous
DPANE	White	Continuous

T2–3b Draw Ceiling Panels

The multilevel ceiling of the conference room steps
down from the entry toward the window wall. The
ceiling is drawn as three panels suspended at different
heights. There can be vertical soffits in between the
ceiling panels, but you can leave them out at this time.
There will be fill lights coming through the gaps between the panels. If there seems to be too much of
void showing during rendering, you may create some
soffits.

Layer settings:

0	*On*
2NDFLR	Off
3DFLOOR	Off
CEILING	Off
COLGRID	*Current*
COLUMNS	Off
CONCLG	Off
CONDOR	Off
DPANE	Off
EXTWALL	Off
GRID	*On*
INTWALL	Off
ROOF	Off
T2LTG	*On*
TEMP	*On*
WINDWALL	Off

---

1. View is set at plan view, WCS. Zoom in tightly around the column at the upper left-hand corner.

The window wall center guide line and its offset to the right, representing the inner edge of the window wall, should be visible.

The inner arc will be referred to as arc A.

Construct> Offset

Distance: *6'8*

Pick arc A and offset it in the +x direction. This is arc 2.

Construct> Offset

Distance: *16'8*

Pick arc A again and offset it in the +x direction. This is arc 3.

2. Check to see that the temporary line offset 12″ down from *guide line A* is visible.

Construct> Copy

Pick the temporary offset line.

Base point: *'Endpoint* at P1

Displacement: *'Endpoint* at P2

Draw> Line

From point: P1

To point: P2

Modify> Properties

For objects, enter *L* (for Last).

In the dialog box, change the layer of the line to CONCLG.

Turn layer INTWALL *Off.*

Modify> Trim

Use the just-copied guide line to trim off the excess ends of arc A, arc 2, and arc 3. Also trim off any excess at the upper ends of the arcs.

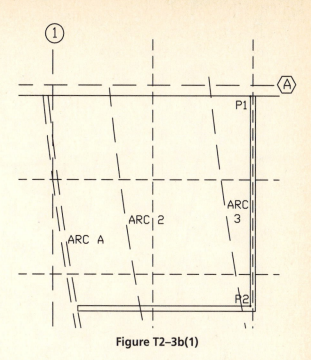

Figure T2–3b(1)

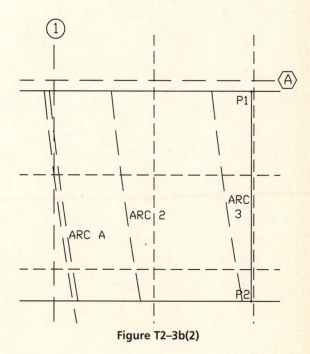

Figure T2–3b(2)

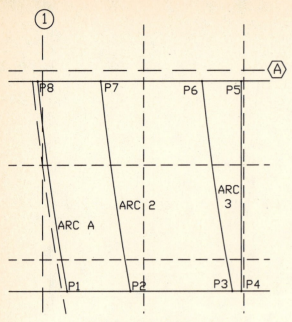

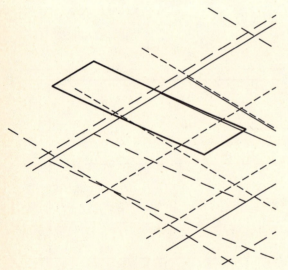

Figure T2–3b(3)

Figure T2–3b(4)

3. Click on **Construct> Copy**.
Pick arc 2 and arc 3.
Base point: Pick any point.
Displacement: @

Modify> Properties

For object, enter *L* (for Last). DO NOT press the RMB.
(Arc 3, the last object referenced, is shown dotted.)
Place the cursor on arc 2, hold down the Ctrl key, and
click the LMB.

AutoCAD cycles the selection set to pick arc 2 and displays it in dotted line.

Now click the RMB twice.

The **Modify Properties** dialog box appears. In the
Layer window, scroll to and click on Layer CONCLG.

You have just made a copy of the two arcs by using the
Selection Cycling method.

4. To create the ceiling panels, begin with the left one.

Make layer TEMP Current.

Modify> Properties

Change the property of arc A to TEMP and Continuous
linetype.

Draw> Line. Use *'Endpoint.*
From P1 to P2.

Draw> Line again.
From P7 to P8.

Turn layer COLGRID *Off.*
Turn layer CONCLG *On.*

Modify> Edit Polyline

Pick arc A. Enter *Yes* to turn it into a polyline.
Enter *J* (for Join).
Pick arc 2 and the two lines just drawn.

The two arcs and end lines have been joined into a closed loop.

Draw> Solids> Extrude

For object, enter *L* (for Last).

Height: *1″*

Modify> Move

For object, enter *L.*

Base point: Pick any point.

Displacement: *@0,0,9′*

The ceiling panel on the left has been created and moved into position.

Make layer CONCLG Current and turn layer TEMP *Off.*

The panel is put on a turned-off layer temporarily so that it will not interfere with the next step.

5. Now create the middle ceiling panel following a similar method.

Turn layer COLGRID *On.*

Change the layer of arc 2 to CONCLG and Continuous linetype.

Turn layer COLGRID *Off.*

Draw> Line. Use P numbers in Figure T2–3b(3).

From P2 to P3. Use *'Endpoint.*

Draw> Line

From P6 to P7.

Modify> Edit Polyline

Pick arc 2.

Enter *J* (for Join).

Pick arc 3 and the end lines just drawn.

The two arcs and end lines have been joined into a closed loop.

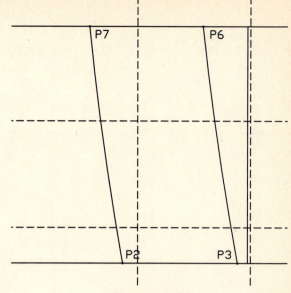

Figure T2–3b(5)

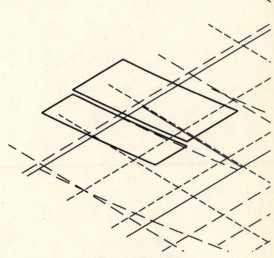

Figure T2–3b(6)

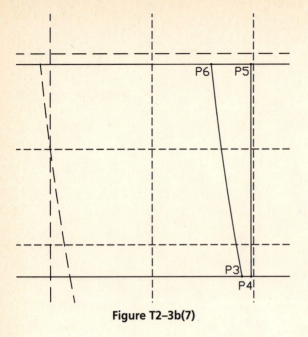

Figure T2–3b(7)

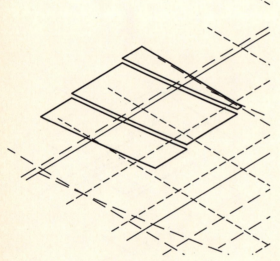

Figure T2–3b(8)

Draw> Solids> Extrude
For object, enter *L* (for Last).
Height: *1"*

Modify> Move
For object, enter *L* (for Last).
Base point: Pick any point.
Displacement: *@0,0,9'9"*

Modify> Properties
For object: Pick the panel.
Change its layer to TEMP.

The panel is also put on a turned-off layer temporarily so that it will not interfere with the next step.

6. Create the last panel.

Layer CONCLG is Current.
Turn layer COLGRID.
Change arc 3 to layer CONCLG.

Draw> Line. Use P numbers in Figure T2–3b(3).
From P3 to P4. Use *'Endpoint*.

Again, **Draw> Line**.
From P5 to P6.

Modify> Edit Polyline
Pick arc 3 and enter *Yes* to turn it into a polyline.
Enter *J* (for Join).

Draw> Solids> Extrude
For object, enter *L* (for Last).
Height: *1"*

Modify> Move
For object, enter *L* (for Last).
Base point: Pick any point.
Displacement: *@0,0,10'6*

The ceiling panel on the right has been created and moved into position.

7. View> 3D Vp Presets> SW Isometric
Turn layer TEMP *On*.

Modify> Properties
Pick the two panels that were stored on this layer.
Change their layer property to CONCLG.

Turn layer TEMP 0 *Off*.

All the ceiling panels are now done. There are gaps between the panels that may have to be filled. For now, leave them alone until you have assigned lighting and tried some rendered views.

T2–3c Draw Lighting Fixtures

Much of the lighting will be from above the suspended ceiling panels and/or diffused through the panels. The degree of opacity of the panels as well as the effects of lights in the ceiling will be created through adjusting the lights to be specified before you render the scene.

The only visible light fixtures will be some wall washers at both ends of the room. These will be drawn as holes in the ceiling panels, created by subtracting solid cylinders from the panels.

Layer settings:

0	*On*
2NDFLR	Off
3DFLOOR	Off
CEILING	Off
COLGRID	*On*
COLUMNS	Off
CONCLG	*On*
CONDOR	Off
DPANE	Off
EXTWALL	Off
GRID	*On*
INTWALL	Off
ROOF	Off
T2LTG	*Current*
TEMP	*On*
WINDWALL	Off

1. Create a prototype cylinder to be subtracted from the ceiling panels to form circular holes for the lights to shine through. As the panels are only 1″ thick, the cylinder to be subtracted from the panels does not need to be deep.

The light fixtures are numbered from 1 to 11 in Figure T2–3c(1).

View is set at plan view, WCS.

Draw fixture L3 first by centering it at *30′,81′*.

Draw> Solids> Cylinder> Center

Center point: *30′,81′*

Radius: *3″*

Height: *6*

2. Use **Construct> Copy** and the Multiple option to space the center point of each symbol 36″ apart. Do fixtures 3, 4, and 5 first; copy 3 and 4 to the left to become fixtures 1 and 2. Then copy the whole line up 14′ and adjust the fixtures laterally.

When you have finished inserting the cylinders, use **Modify> Move** to raise each one according to the following specifications:

Fixture symbol #:

1, 2, 6, and 7	Move to 9′ high
3, 4, 5, 8, 9, and 10	Move to 9′9″ high
11	Move to 10′6″ high

3. Set a 3D view and zoom in on the ceiling.

Construct> Subtract

First pick all three ceiling panels. Press the RMB.

Then pick all 11 of the cylinders.

Subtracting the cylinders from the panels leaves holes in the panels for light to shine through.

Lighting for the conference room is done.

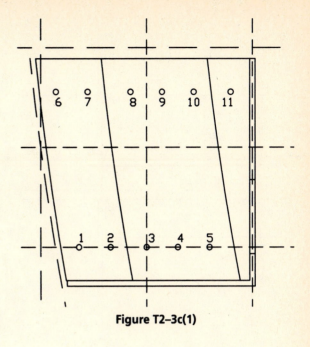

Figure T2–3c(1)

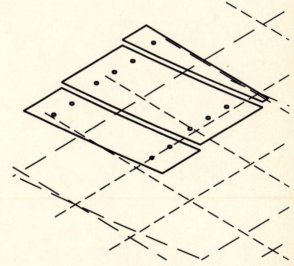

Figure T2–3c(2)

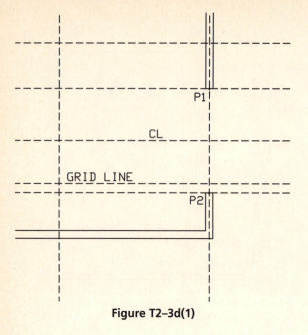

Figure T2–3d(1)

P1
CL
GRID_LINE
P2

T2–3d   Draw Entry Doors

To accommodate the entry doors into the conference room, you need to make an opening in the wall. The opening is made just a little larger than the doors so that the doors will appear to be distinct entities when you render the scene.

Layer settings:	
0	*On*
2NDFLR	Off
3DFLOOR	Off
CEILING	Off
COLGRID	*On*
COLUMNS	Off
CONCLG	Off
CONDOR	Off
DPANE	Off
EXTWALL	Off
GRID	*On*
INTWALL	*Current*
ROOF	Off
T2LTG	Off
TEMP	Off
WINDWALL	Off

1. View is set at plan view, WCS.
Zoom in around the conference room.

Construct> Offset

Distance: *2′9″*

Pick the grid line between the corridor and offset it in the +y direction. This is the center line: CL.

Construct> Offset

Distance: *40″* (that is, *3′4″*)

Object to offset: Pick line CL.

Side to offset? Pick a point on *each side* in the +y and -y directions.

Draw> Solids> Slice

Pick an edge of the conference room wall.

Select the ZX option.

Point on the x-axis: *'Intersection* at P1

Elect to retain both sides.

Select **Draw> Solids> Slice** again.

Specify the ZX option and *'Intersection* at P2.

Retain the bottom side to create the door opening.

Create a lintel with **Draw> Solids> Box> Corner**.

First corner: P2

Other corner: *@6,80*

Height: *18*

Modify> Move

Pick the lintel and any base point.

Displacement: *@0,0,9'*

2. Create the outer door frame.
Make layer CONDOR Current.
Turn layer INTWALL *Off*.

Draw> Solids> Box> Corner

Corner of box: Pick P

Other corner: *@2,40*

Height: *9'*

Make an opening for the frame.

Draw> Solids> Box> Corner

Corner of box: Pick P2

Other corner: *@4,34*

Height: *100*

Modify> Move

Object to move: Enter *L* (for Last).

Base point: Pick any point.

Displacement: *@-1",3.5",4"*

Construct> Subtract

First object: Pick the outer frame.

Object to subtract: Enter *L* (the second, smaller box).

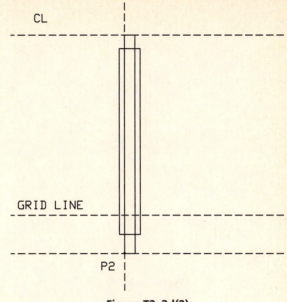

Figure T2–3d(2)

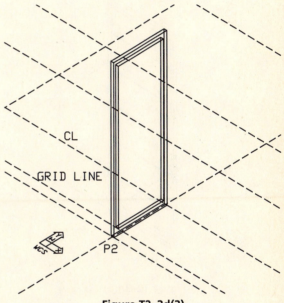

Figure T2–3d(3)

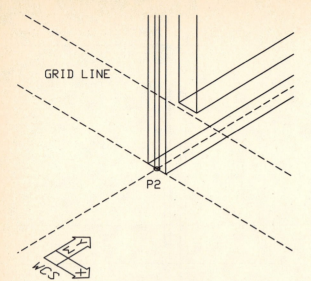

GRID LINE

P2

WCS

Figure T2–3d(4)

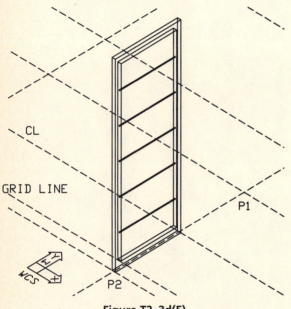

CL

GRID LINE

P1

P2

WCS

Figure T2–3d(5)

Now move the frame laterally to center on the door opening.

Modify> Move

Object to move: Pick the outer frame.

Base point: Pick any point.

Displacement: @–1″,0

3. Create some cross muntins for the opening in the door.

Set **View> 3D Vp Presets> SE Isometric**.

View> Zoom> Window, zoom in on the door.

Draw> Solids> Cylinder> Center

Center: Pick 'Intersection at P2.

Radius: 0.25

Height: 39

Construct: 3D Rotate

For object to rotate, enter L.

Select x-axis rotate.

Point on x-axis: P2.

Rotation angle: –90

Modify> Move

Object to move: L

Base point: Pick any point.

Displacement: @0″,0.5″,18″

Construct> 3D Array> Rectangular

For object to array, enter L, or pick the muntin.

Select: 1 row, 1 column, 5 levels

Distance between levels: 18

Construct> Union

Pick the outer frame and all muntins.

The frame and muntins have been combined into a single object.

4. Create a pane for the door so that you can experiment with assigning materials later, when you render the scene.

Set layer DPANE Current.

Turn layer 3DINTWALL *Off*.

View is set at SE Isometric.

Zoom in on lower left corner of opening in door frame.

Draw> Surfaces> 3Dface

From *'Midpoint* to *'Midpoint* of the inside of opening, beginning at point MP [Figure T2–3d(6)], and continuing counterclockwise around the opening. After picking the fourth point (at the upper-left corner), press the RMB to exit the command.

When you are done, you have drawn a pane that bisects the muntins in the opening. You can later specify materials, including different degrees of transparency, when you render the conference room.

5. For door pulls, first create a pull on one side, then copy it to the other side.

Make layer CONDOR Current.

Turn layer DPANE *Off*.

View is set at SE Isometric.

Zoom in on the area around the middle left-hand side of the door frame.

View> Set UCS> 3 point

Origin: *'Midpoint,* outer edge of door frame on the right (the edge closest to you, the viewer).

Point on +x axis: *@0,4*

Point on +y axis: *@0,0,4*

View> Named UCS

In the dialog box, rename Current UCS to *U2.*

(*U1* was named in Tutorial 1.)

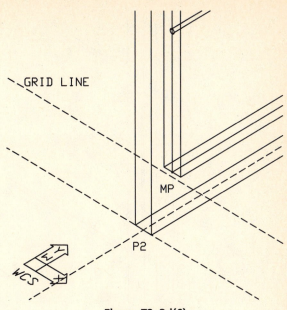

Figure T2–3d(6)

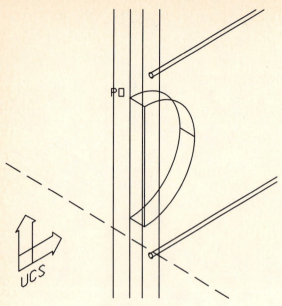

Figure T2–3d(7)

Draw> Polyline

From point: *0,0.* (PO)

To point: *@0,–12*

To point: Enter *A* (for Arc).

Options list: Enter *A* (for Angle).

Included angle: *180*

End of arc: *0,0.* Press the RMB.

Draw> Solids> Extrude

Pick the polyline just drawn.

Height: *1.75″*

Construct> Copy

For object, pick the extruded object.

From point: Pick any point.

Displacement: *@1.25″,0″,–0.75″*

Construct> Subtract

For object to subtract from: Pick the original extruded object.

For object to be subtracted: Pick the object just copied.

Modify> Move

Pick the modified object or enter *L* (for Last).

Base point: Pick any point.

Displacement: *@0,–12*

Examine the drawing from different angles to be sure that the pull is aligned correctly. Try **View> 3D Vp Presets> Right** and **Top**.

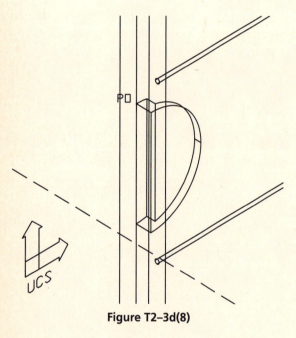

Figure T2–3d(8)

6. View> Set UCS> World

UCS is set to WCS.

View> 3D Vp Presets> Plan View> World

Zoom in tight on the door pull.

Toggle **F8** to turn Ortho *On*.

Construct> Mirror

Pick the door pull.

First mirror point: *'Intersection* at P1

Second mirror point: Pick any point above or below P1.

Choose not to delete old object.

The door pull is mirrored to the other side of the door frame. One of the double doors is now complete, except that it is drawn as a right-hand door, but placed at the left-hand side.

Click on **Modify> Move**, and any base point, with a displacement of *@0,40*. Now the door is in its correct position.

7. Turn layer DPANE *On*.
Be sure Ortho is *On*.
View is at plan view, WCS.

Construct> Mirror

Pick the door and pulls with a right-opening crossing window.

First mirror point: *'Intersection* at P1

Second mirror point: Pick any point left or right of P1.

Choose not to delete old object.

The double doors and architectural elements of the conference room are done.

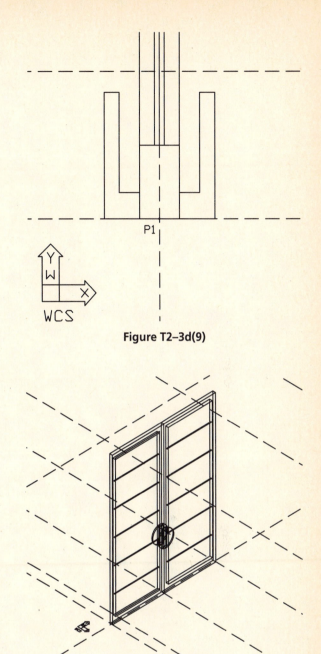

Figure T2–3d(9)

Figure T2–3d(10)

T2–3e   Save Work for Tutorial 2

Save this drawing, which is still named *T2.dwg*, and exit AutoCAD. Save the original as a backup, and use a copy for insertion in Chapter 5.

The interior walls, doors, and ceiling panels are the only new elements created in this tutorial. You can incorporate them into Tutorial 1 by substituting the interior walls with a Wblock file containing the new architectural elements. However, keep in mind that the drawing file will increase in size, perhaps in excess of the capacity of a high-density diskette.

Continue with the following sections to draw furnishings for the conference room. They are drawn as separate files so that they do not affect the size of the conference room drawing.

T2–4   BUILT-IN CABINETRY

Some modular cabinets are built in for the conference room. The units of the modules are based on the basic design grid units (40″ × 36″) of the building.

Begin a new drawing named: *Cabinet.dwg*
Drawing Units: *Architectural*
Drawing Limits: *30′,26′*

Create new layers:

Layer name	Color	Linetype
0	White	Continuous
BASE	Yellow	Continuous
GUIDES	White	Continuous
UNIT_A	White	Continuous
UNIT_B	Cyan	Continuous

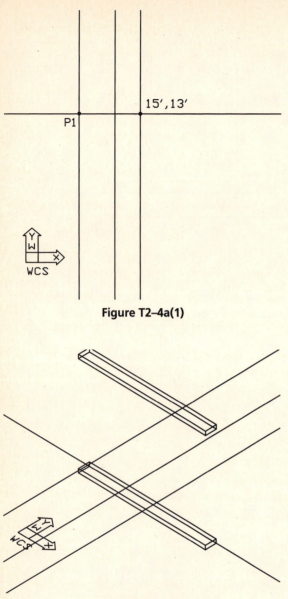

Figure T2–4a(1)

Figure T2–4a(2)

Layer settings:

0	Off
BASE	Off
GUIDES	*Current*
UNIT A	Off
UNIT B	Off

1. View is set at plan view, WCS; zoomed: All. Press **F8** to turn Ortho *On*.

Draw> Construction Line

From point: '*15',13'*

To point: Pick any point in the +x direction.

To point: Pick any point in the +y direction.

To point: Press the RMB.

Construct> Offset

Distance: *30*

Pick the vertical construction line, offset it in the -x direction.

Click on **Construct> Offset**.

Distance: *72*

Pick the vertical construction line again and offset it in the -x direction.

2. Make layer BASE Current.

Draw> Solids> Box> Corner

First corner: '*From,* '*Intersection at P1*

Offset: *@2,0*

Other corner: *@140,–12*

Height: *4*

Construct> Copy

Pick the box just drawn.

From point: Pick any point.

Displacement: *@0,0,104*

T2–4b   Create Unit A Cabinets

Layer settings:

0	Off
BASE	Off
GUIDES	*On*
UNIT A	*Current*
UNIT B	Off

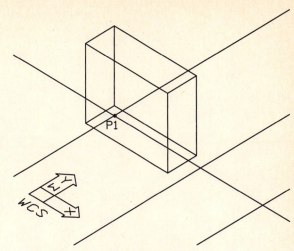

Figure T2–4b(1)

1. Draw> Solids> Box> Corner

First corner: *'Intersection* at P1
Other corner: *@40,–14*
Height: *32*

Modify> Move

For object, enter *L* (for Last).
Base point: Pick any point.
Displacement: *@0,0,4*

Construct> 3D Array> Rectangular

For object, enter *L*.
Array with the following settings:

  1 row

  2 columns, distance: *104"*

  3 levels, distance: *34"*

The sides of the cabinet consisting of tiers of Unit A
modules have been created.

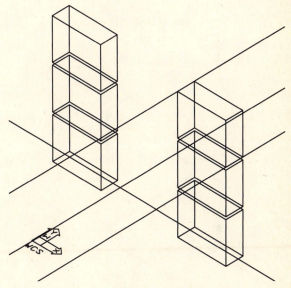

Figure T2–4b(2)

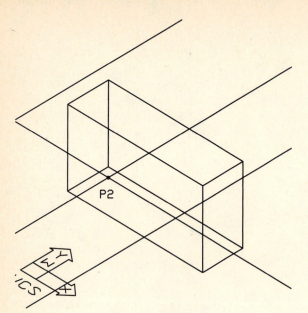

Figure T2–4c(1)

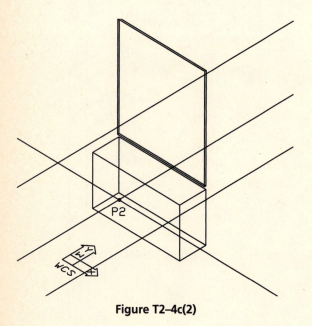

Figure T2–4c(2)

T2–4c Create Unit B Cabinet

Layer settings:

0	Off
BASE	Off
GUIDES	*On*
UNIT A	Off
UNIT B	*Current*

1. Draw> Solids> Box> Corner

First corner: '*Intersection* at P2
Other corner: *@60,–18*
Height: *32*

Modify> Move

For object, enter *L* (for Last).
Base point: Pick any point.
Displacement: *@0,0,4*

2. Create a marker board above Unit B.

Draw> Solids> Box> Corner

First corner: '*From,* '*Intersection* at P2
Offset: *@0,0,38*
Other corner: *@60,–1"*
Height: *66*

T2–4d   Finish Up Built-In Cabinets

All components of the built-in cabinets have been created. Block the components into a single block to be
inserted into the conference room.

Layer settings:

0	On
BASE	*On*
GUIDES	Off Freeze
UNIT A	*On*
UNIT B	*Current*

1. View is set at plan view, WCS; zoomed: *All*.
File> Export> Block
Name: *T2-cab.dwg*
Name of block: Press the RMB.
Insertion point: *0,0*
Select objects: Use a crossing window to select all
objects in the current view.

Enter *Oops* to redisplay objects.

All visible objects are blocked into a separate drawing
called *T2-cab.dwg*.

2. Use *T2-cab.dwg* for insertion into the drawing
when you get to Chapter 5 for perspective views and
Chapter 6 for rendering.

The cabinets are inserted into the conference room
drawing. Move and rotate them into the proper position in the conference room by using the **Modify>
Move** and **Modify> Rotate** commands.

3. Save the drawing and exit AutoCAD, or go on to the
next section.

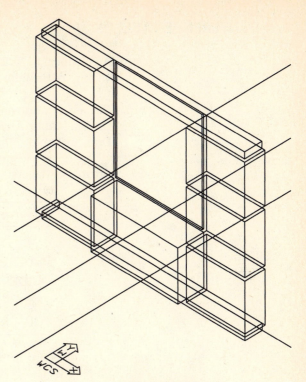

Figure T2–4d

An elliptical table is created for the conference room. The drawing takes advantage of the improved capability in AutoCAD R13 to draw true ellipses.

Begin a new drawing named: *Conftab.dwg*
Drawing Units: *Architectural*
Drawing Limits: *30',26'*

Create new layers:

Layer name	Color	Linetype
0	White	Continuous
PEDEST	Yellow	Continuous
GUIDES	White	Continuous
TEMP	Green	Continuous
TOP	Cyan	Continuous

T2–5a Draw Guide Lines

Layer settings:

0	Off
PEDEST	Off
GUIDES	*Current*
TEMP	Off
TOP	Off

1. View is set at plan view, WCS.
Toggle **F8** to turn Ortho *On*.

Draw> Construction Line

From point: *10',10'*

To point: Pick a point in the +x direction.

To point: Pick a point in the +y direction.

The intersection of these two lines at 10',10' is marked as P1.

2. Construct> Offset

Distance: *20*

Pick the vertical line and offset it 20″ to each side.

Construct> Offset

Distance: *18*

Pick the horizontal line and offset it to each side

3. Click on **Options> Running Object Snap> Intersection**

Draw> Line

From point: P1

To point: P3 [Figure T2–5a(3)]

A diagonal line is drawn.

P1

Figure T2–5a(1)

P1

Figure T2–5a(2)

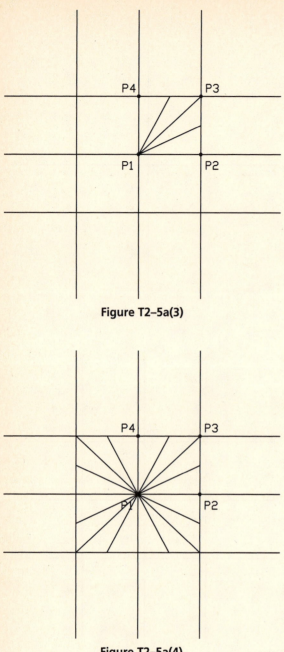

Figure T2–5a(3)

Figure T2–5a(4)

4. Modify> Trim
Cutting edge: Pick P1-4 and P2-3 vertical lines.
Edge to trim: Pick the line segment between P3 and P4.

Draw> Line

From: P3 to P4

Click on **Draw> Line** again.

From: P1 to '*Midpoint* of line between P3 and P4.

5. Repeat Step 3 with the horizontal guide lines.

Modify> Trim

Cutting edge: Pick P1-2 and P4-3 horizontal lines.

Edge to trim: Pick the line segment between P2 and P3.

Draw> Line

From: P2 to P3

Click on **Draw> Line** again.

From: P1 to '*Midpoint* of line between P2 and P3.

6. With Ortho *On*, click on **Construct> Mirror**.
Pick the three slanted lines drawn in Steps 3, 4, and 5.
First point of mirror line: P1
Second point: P4

Construct> Mirror

Pick all six slanted lines.

First mirror point: Pick P1

Other mirror point: Pick P2

Do not delete old objects.

T2–5b Create the Pedestal

Layer settings:

0	Off
PEDEST	*Current*
GUIDES	*On*
TEMP	Off
TOP	Off

1. Set **Options> Running Object Snap> Inter-section**.
Toggle **F8** to turn Ortho *Off*.

Draw> Ellipse> Center

Center: P1

Axis end: P2

Other axis end point: P4

Construct> Copy

Object: *L* (for Last).

Base point: Pick any point.

Displacement: @

Modify> Properties

Object: *L*

Change the layer of the copied ellipse to TEMP.

2. Draw> Solids> Cylinder> Center
Center: P2
Radius: *1.75*
Height: *24*

Modify> Copy

Pick the cylinder, enter *M* (for Multiple).

Base point: P2

Displacement: Successively pick the intersections of guide lines and ellipse.

A total of 16 cylinders are copied around the ellipse.

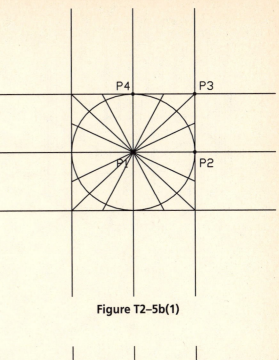

Figure T2–5b(1)

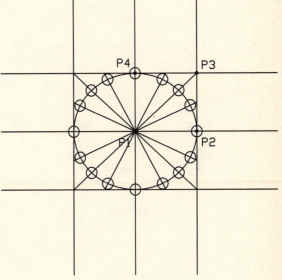

Figure T2–5b(2)

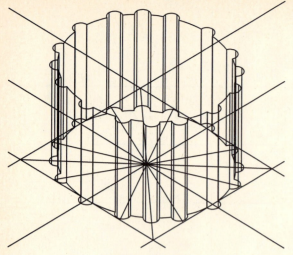

Figure T2–5b(3)

Figure T2–5b(4)

3. Set **View> 3D Vp Presets> SE Isometric**

Draw> Solids> Extrude

Pick the ellipse drawn in Step 1.

Height: *24*

The ellipse has been turned into a solid column.

Construct> Union

Select the column and all the cylinders.

Modify> Move

Pick the unioned column.

Base point: Pick any point.

Displacement: *@0,0,3*

The column and cylinders are combined into one object and moved into place.

4. Turn Ortho and Running Osnap *Off.*
Make layer TEMP Current.
Turn layer PEDEST *Off.*
View is set at SE Isometric.

The ellipse copied in Step 1 above is visible.
Zoom in on the ellipse.

Construct> Offset

Distance: *1.5″*

Pick the ellipse as object and offset it toward the center.

Draw> Solids> Extrude

Pick the inner ellipse as object.

Height: *2*

Modify> Move

Pick the elliptical disk just extruded.

Base point: Pick any point.

Displacement: *@0,0,1*

This disk represents the core of the reveal feature of the pedestal.

There is a similar reveal at the top of the pedestal column, so a copy of the bottom disk will be placed above the column.

Construct> Copy

Pick the elliptical disk.

From point: Pick any point.

Displacement: *@0,0,26*

5. Return to viewing the bottom of the pedestal. The ellipse copied in Step 1 should be visible.

Draw> Solids> Extrude

Pick the ellipse as object.

Height: *1″*

Construct> Copy

Pick the extruded elliptical disk.

From point: Pick any point.

Displacement: *@0,0,29*

6. Modify> Properties

Pick the two reveal disks and the two disks just created.

Change the layer to PEDEST.

Make layer PEDEST Current.

Construct> Union

Pick all the pedestal parts: column, reveals, top, and bottom disks.

Turn layer TEMP *Off*.

The pedestal base is complete.

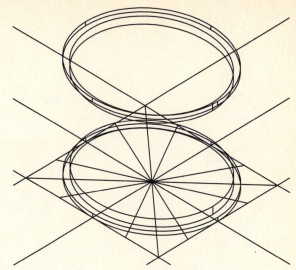

Figure T2–5b(5)

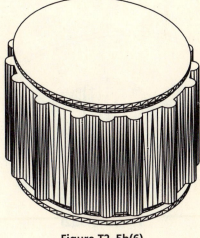

Figure T2–5b(6)

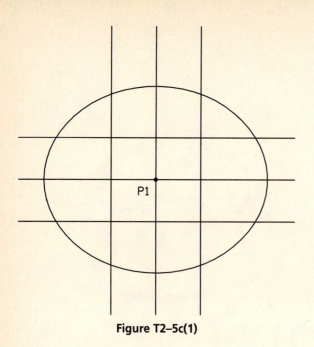

Figure T2–5c(1)

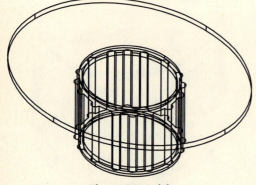

Figure T2–5c(2)

T2–5c Create the Top

Layer settings:	
0	Off
PEDEST	Off
GUIDES	*On*
TEMP	Off
TOP	*Current*

1. View is set at plan view, WCS.
Toggle **F8** to turn Ortho *Off*.
Zoom in to see the lines drawn at the start of Step 1, clearly.

Draw> Solids> Cylinder> Elliptical
Center: '*From*, '*Intersection* at P1
Offset: *@50,0*
Axis endpoint 2: *@–100,0*
Other axis endpoint: *@0,40*
Height: *2*

2. Modify> Move
Pick the solid ellipse.
Base point: Pick any point.
Displacement: *@0,0,30*

3. The top and all the parts of the conference table are now complete.

Turn layers GUIDES and TEMP *Off* and freeze them.

Turn layer 0 *On* and make it Current.

Under **File> Export> Block**, write-block just the top and pedestal as objects to a file, named: *T2-tab.dwg*. Use it in Chapter 5 for perspective viewing and in Chapter 6 for rendering.

T2–6 CONFERENCE CHAIR

A number of solid elements are created in 3D to construct the conference chair.

Begin a new drawing named: *Confch.dwg*
Drawing Units: *Architectural*
Drawing Limits: *12',10'*

Create new layers:

Layer name	Color	Linetype
0	White	Continuous
GUIDES	White	Continuous
BASE	Yellow	Continuous
BODY	Cyan	Continuous
SEAT	Green	Continuous

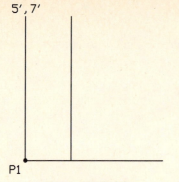

5′, 7′

P1

Figure T2–6a(1)

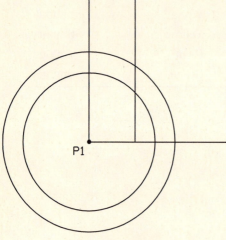

P1

Figure T2–6a(2)

T2–6a   Create the Chair Body

Layer settings:	
0	Off
GUIDES	*Current*
BASE	Off
BODY	*On*
SEAT	Off

1. Set **View> 3D Vp Preset> Plan view> WCS**.
Click on **View> Zoom> All**.
Options> Drawing Aides. Set Grid at 6″ × 6″ and
turn it on.

Draw> Line
From point: *5′,7′*
To point: *@0,–2′*
To point: *@2′,0*

This puts the intersection of the lines at 5′,5′ (P1).

Construct> Offset
Distance: *8*
Offset the vertical line in the +x direction.

2. Make layer BODY Current.

Draw> Solids> Cylinder> Center
Center: *'Intersection* at P1
Radius: *15*
Height: *23*

Draw> Solids> Cylinder> Center
Center: *'Intersection* at P1
Radius: *11.5*
Height: *36*

Modify> Move

For object, enter *L* (for Last).

Base point: Pick any point.

Displacement: *@3,0,2*

Set **View> 3D Vp Presets> SE Isometric**.

Construct> 3D Rotate

Enter *L*, or pick the smaller cylinder.

Enter *Y* to select the y-axis option.

Point on y-axis: *'Center*

Center of: Pick the base of the smaller cylinder.

Rotation angle: *–2* (that is, negative 2°)

The smaller cylinder has been shifted along the x-axis, moved up, and tilted.

3. Now, the large cylinder will be sliced.

View is reset to plan view, WCS.

Press **F8** to toggle Ortho *On*.

Draw> Solids> Slice

Object to slice: Pick the large cylinder.

For slicing plane, enter *YZ*.

Point on plane: *'Intersection* at P1

Point normal to plane: Pick a point above P1.

Desired side of object: Pick a point to the left of P1.

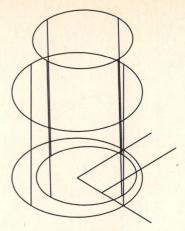

Figure T2–6a(3)

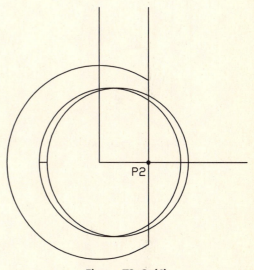

Figure T2–6a(4)

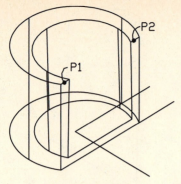

Figure T2–6a(5)

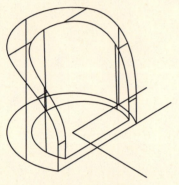

Figure T2–6a(6)

4. Return to SE Isometric view.

Construct> Subtract

Pick the large cylinder and press the RMB.

Then pick the small cylinder.

The inside of the large cylinder has been carved out by the volume of the smaller cylinder.

Construct> Fillet

Enter *R* to set the radius.

Radius: *16*. Press the RMB.

Press the RMB again, to reissue the Fillet command.

For objects to fillet, pick edges at P1 and P2.

The arms of the cylinder are rounded.

T2–6b Draw a Seat Cushion

Layer settings:

0	Off
GUIDES	*Current*
BASE	Off
BODY	Off
SEAT	*On*

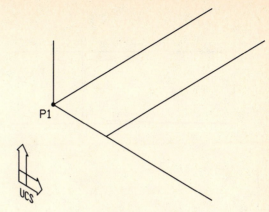

Figure T2–6b(1)

1. View> 3D Vp Presets> Plan view> SE Iso-metric.

Draw> Line
From point: *'Intersection* at P1
To point: *@0,0,8*

View> Set UCS> 3 point
Origin: *'Intersection* at P1
Point in +x direction: *@4,0*
Point in +y direction: *@0,0,4*

View> Named UCS
Rename the *No Name* current UCS to *U1*.

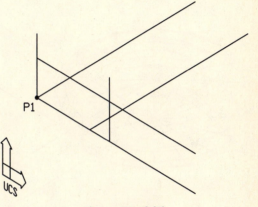

Figure T2–6b(2)

2. Construct> Offset
Distance: *5*
Offset the horizontal line in the +y direction.

Click **Construct> Offset** again.
Distance: *11*
Offset the vertical line in the +x direction.

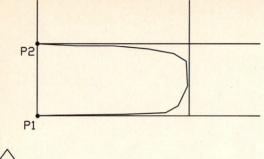

UCS

Figure T2–6b(3)

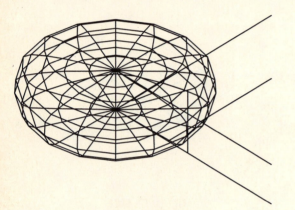

Figure T2–6b(4)

3. View> 3D Vp Presets> Plan view> Current UCS

Make layer SEAT Current.

Draw> Polyline

From Point: '*Intersection* at P1

Draw a profile of the seat cushion generally within the confines of the rectangle formed by the offset lines. Be sure to end the polyline at the intersection at P2.

Modify> Move

For object, pick the polyline or enter *L*.

Base point: Pick any point.

Displacement: @*0,2*

Reset **View> 3D Vp Presets> SE Isometric**.

View> Set UCS> World

On the side menu, click on **DRAW2: SURFACES: Surftab1** and enter *16* on the keyboard.

Click on **DRAW2: SURFACES: Surftab2** and enter *12* on the keyboard.

Draw> Surfaces> Revolved Surface

For path curve, pick the polyline profile. Do not press the RMB.

Pick the P1–P2 vertical line as axis of rotation.

Rotate 360°.

Construct> 3D Rotate

For object, enter *L*.

Enter *Y* to choose the y-axis option.

Point on axis: Pick '*Intersection* at P1

Angle: *–2*

4. Make sure view is set to SE Isometric and the co-ordinate system is set at WCS.

Turn layer BODY *On*.

Set view at plan view, WCS.

Toggle **F8** to turn Ortho *On*.

With **Modify> Move**, shift the seat cushion to the left so that it is in the cavity of the chair body.

Return to SE Isometric.

Click on **Construct> 3D Rotate**.

Pick both seat and body.

Select the y-axis rotate option.

Point on y-axis: *5′,5′* (the original P1 point)

Rotation angle: *–4*

Modify> Move

Pick the seat cushion and any base point.

Displacement: *@0,0,3*

Click on **Modify> Move** again.

Pick the seat and body.

Base point: Pick any point.

Displacement: *@0,0,12*

The chair body and seat cushion are complete and placed in the correct position.

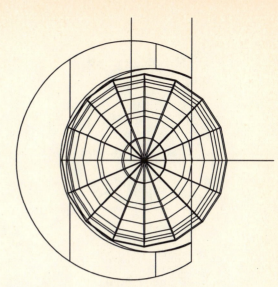

Figure T2–6b(5)

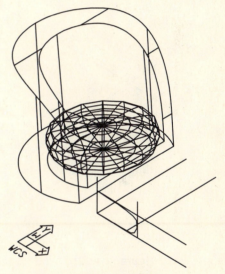

Figure T2–6b(6)

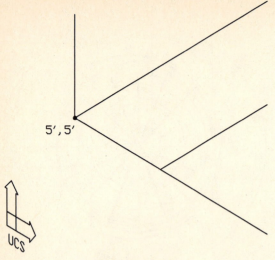

5', 5'

UCS

Figure T2–6c(1)

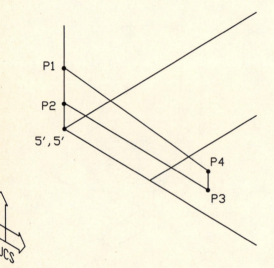

P1

P2

5', 5'

P4

P3

UCS

Figure T2–6c(2)

T2–6c Draw the Base

Layer settings:

0	Off
GUIDES	*On*
BASE	*Current*
BODY	Off
SEAT	Off

1. View> Named UCS> U1

Use **Modify> Erase** to delete both vertical lines that were offset in Step 2, Section T2–6b.

Your drawing should look like Figure T2–6c(1).

2. Draw a leg for the base.

Draw> Polyline
From point: *0,4.75* (P1)
To point: *@0,–2.75* (P2)
To point: *@13.5",0* (P3)
To point: *@0,1.5"* (P4)
To point: *C* (back to P1)

Draw> Solids> Extrude
Pick the polyline.
Height: *2*

Modify> Move
Pick the extruded polyline, or enter *L*.
Base point: Pick any point.
Displacement: *@0,0,–1*

As the polyline was extruded 2″ out from the current x-y plane, the extruded object had to be moved back 1″ so that it is centered on the x-y plane.

3. Zoom in on the small end of the leg.
View> Set UCS> World.

Construct> Fillet

Enter *R* (for Radius).

Radius: *0.25″*

Press the RMB to reissue the Fillet command.

For objects to fillet, pick the three front edges of the leg.

You may fillet the other edges of the leg to make it more refined and softer in outline, if you wish. Remember that the more facets there are in a drawing, the longer it will take to render.

4. Draw the casters.
Make sure UCS is set at *U1*.
View is set at SE Isometric.

Draw> Solids> Cylinder> Center

Center: *13″,0.875″,–1.125″*

Radius: *0.875″*

Height: *2.25″*

Set **View> Set UCS> World**.

Modify> Rotate

Pick the cylinder just drawn.

Base point: *'Midpoint* at P1

Angle: *15*

The cylinder is now configured as the caster.

5. Click **Modify> Rotate** again.
Pick the leg and the caster.
Base point: *'Intersection* at P2
Rotation: *20*

Construct> Array> Polar

Pick the leg and caster.

Number of items: *5*

Array 360° and copy during array.

Center: P1

Second point of array: *@0,0,4*

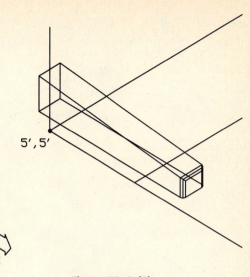

Figure T2–6c(3)

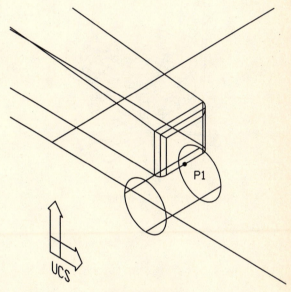

Figure T2–6c(4)

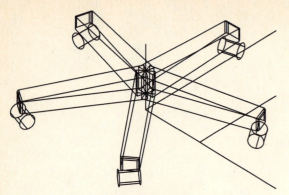

Figure T2–6c(5)

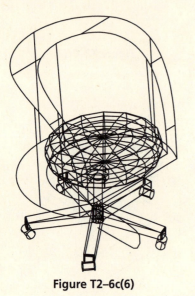

Figure T2–6c(6)

6. Draw an upright support.

Draw> Solids> Cylinder
Center: '*From*, '*Intersection* at P1
Offset: *@0,0,1.75″*
Radius: *1.125″*
Height: *9.25″*

Draw a connecting plate.
Draw> Solids> Cylinder
Center: '*From*, '*Intersection* at P1
Offset: *@0,0,11″*
Radius: *2*
Height: *1*

Construct> Union
Pick the plate, support, and the five legs.

The base is done.

7. Turn layers BODY and SEAT *On*.
Make sure layer GUIDES is *Off*.
View is set at SE Isometric.

File> Export> Block
Name: *T2-chr.dwg*
Name of Block: Press the RMB.
Insertion point: 0,0
Objects: Use crossing window to pick all visible objects: the body, seat cushion, base, and casters.

Enter *Oops* to redisplay the objects.

Use *T2-chr.dwg* for insertion into the conference room drawing in Chapters 5 and 6.

Tutorial 3. Open Offices and Teller Section

ABOUT TUTORIAL 3.   OPEN OFFICES AND TELLER SECTION

The area in front of the teller counter is the open office space for bank officials. The offices are "open" in the sense that there are no walls between the spaces. The offices are furnished by component furniture pieces that make up work stations for the bank officers.

To do this tutorial as an independent project, follow Tutorial 1 through Section T1–5. Save the drawing. Make a copy renamed as *T3.dwg*, then continue with Section T3–3 of this tutorial.

If you have completed Tutorial 1, use a copy of that drawing and continue with Tutorial 3 beginning at Section T3–3.

Either way, you will have drawn much of the bank building by following Tutorial 1. You only need to detail some minor parts of the interior in the area of the open offices, which begins on Section T3–3.

T3–1   DOING TUTORIAL 3 AS AN INDEPENDENT PROJECT

1. To do Tutorial 3 as an independent project, follow Tutorial 1 from Section T1–1 through T1–5. At the end of T1–5, save the drawing. Exit AutoCAD. Make two copies of the drawing.

2. Rename one copy as *T3.dwg*.

3. Reload AutoCAD.
Under **File> Open**, open *T3.dwg*.

4. Go on to Section T3–3 in this tutorial.

T3–2   DOING TUTORIAL 3 AFTER HAVING COMPLETED TUTORIAL 1

Having completed Tutorial 1, you can continue with the same drawing file to work on the open office area in front of the teller counter. For protection of the drawing file, you should use a copy of it to continue to Tutorial 3.

1. Complete Tutorial 1 through Section T1–6. Save the drawing and exit Auto-CAD. Make two copies of the drawing.

2. Rename one copy as *T3.dwg*.

3. Reload AutoCAD.
Click on **File> Open**.
Name of file: *T3.dwg*

4. Go on to Section T3–3 in this tutorial.

T3–3   DETAIL THE OPEN OFFICE AREA

By the time you reach this stage, much of the bank building has been completed. There are only a few details that need to be drawn.

Create the following new layers.

Name	Color	Linetype
T3LTG	Yellow	Continuous
TELLER	Cyan	Continuous

T3–3a   Draw Some Additional Interior Elements

Layer settings:

0	Off
2NDFLR	Off
3DFLOOR	Off
3DUPPER	Off
CEILING	Off
COLGRID	*On*
COLUMNS	*On*
EXTWALL	*Current*
GRID	*On*
INTWALL	*On*
ROOF	Off
T3LTG	Off
TELLER	Off
WINDWALL	Off

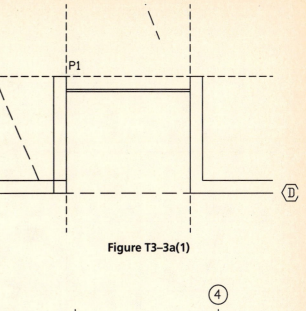

Figure T3–3a(1)

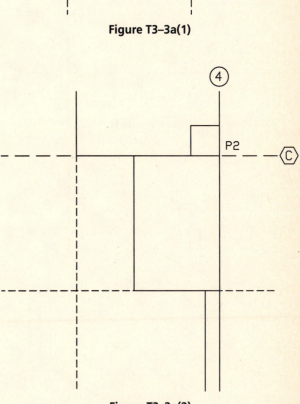

Figure T3–3a(2)

1. Some "doors" need to be drawn at the entrances.

View is set at plan view, WCS.

Zoom in on the area between columns D-2 and D-3.

Draw> Solids> Box> Corner
First corner: *'From 'Intersection* at P1
Offset: *@0,–12*
Other corner: *@10',–2*
Height: *10'6*

Zoom in on the entrance below column C-4.

Draw> Solids> Box> Corner
First corner: *'Intersection* at P2
Other corner: *@–6',–9'*
Height: *10'6*

The last two objects represent entry doors. They provide solid surfaces upon which you can map textures or other features when you render the scene.

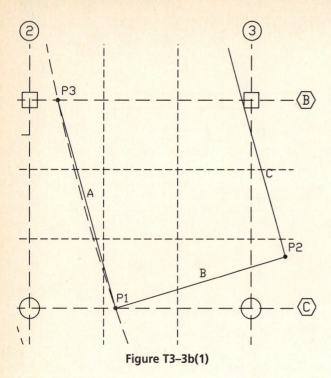

Figure T3–3b(1)

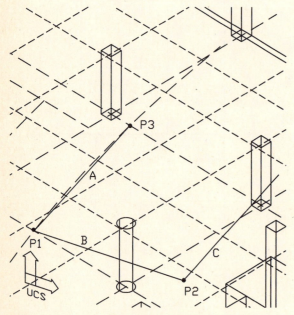

Figure T3–3b(2)

T3–3b   Create Teller Counter

Layer settings:

0	*On*
2NDFLR	Off
3DFLOOR	Off
3DUPPER	Off
CEILING	Off
COLGRID	*On*
COLUMNS	*On*
EXTWALL	Off
GRID	*On*
INTWALL	*Current*
ROOF	Off
T3LTG	Off
TELLER	*On*
WINDWALL	Off

1. First, create some walls behind the teller counter.

Recall that some guide lines were drawn and stored on Layer 0, which is now *On*, and the guide lines are visible. These lines are marked as A, B, and C.

UCS is set at WCS.
Current view is at plan view, WCS.
Zoom in on the counter guide lines.

View> Set UCS> 3 points

Origin: '*Intersection* at P1

+x point: '*Intersection* at P2

+y point: '*Intersection* at P3

View> Named UCS

Rename current UCS to *U1*

2. View> 3D Vp Presets> SE Isometric

Zoom in tightly on the intersection at P1.

View> Set UCS> 3 points

Origin: '*Intersection* at P1

+x point: *@4,0*

+y point: *@0,0,4*

View> Named UCS

Rename current UCS to *U2*

3. Use guide lines A, B, and C to create the walls behind the teller counter.

View> Named UCS

Make *U1* the current UCS.

Turn layer COLUMNS *Off*.

Construct> Offset

Offset Line A *9′* in the +x direction.

Again, offset Line A *10′6″* in the +y direction.

Construct> Offset

Offset Line C *6″* in the +x direction (that's 6″).

Click **Construct> Offset**

Offset Line B *6′6″* in the +y direction.

Again, offset Line B *10′6″* in the +y direction.

4. Make sure that layer INTWALL is Current.

Draw> Polyline. Use *'Intersection*.

Draw from P1 successively to P8.

At P8, enter *C* to close the line back to P1.

Draw> Solids> Extrude

Pick the loop just drawn.

Height: *9′*

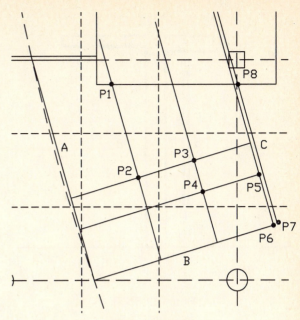

Figure T3–3b(3)

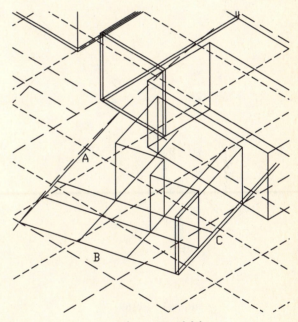

Figure T3–3b(4)

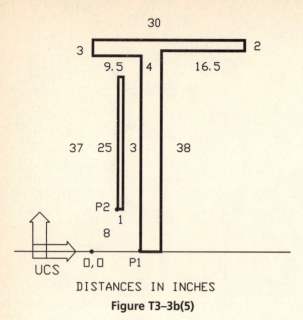

DISTANCES IN INCHES

Figure T3–3b(5)

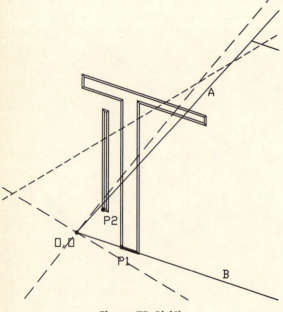

Figure T3–3b(6)

5. Now to create the teller counter.

Set View> Named UCS.
Make *U2* the current UCS.

Make layer TELLER Current.

Draw the profile of the counter and light panel in front as shown in Figure T3–3b(5).

Use **Draw> Polyline**; begin at P1 for the counter. Begin at P2 for the light panel.

Use relative distances from point to point, and close the loop at the last point back to the first point.

When you are done, invoke **Construct> Block**.
Name of block: *Profile*
Insertion point: *0,0*
Select both polyline loops as objects to block.

The objects disappear from the screen.
Enter *Oops* to redisplay counter profile objects.

The Profile block has been made; the objects redisplayed are the original objects before they were blocked so you can work with them as separate polyline loops.

6. Now, leave this part of the counter to first create the lowered counter for the handicapped-accessible section.

View is still at SE Isometric. Zoom in on P1.

Construct> Copy
Objects: Pick both profile loops.
Base point: Pick any point.
Displacement: *@0,0,–20′6″* (negative number)!

Zoom in on the copied objects.

Draw> Solids> Extrude
Pick both copied profile loops.
Height: *–9′6″* (note negative number)

7. Turn layer COLUMNS *Off*.
Set UCS to WCS.
View is still set at SE Isometric.
Zoom in on the counter where it meets the wall.

Draw> Solids> Slice

Pick both extruded counter objects.

Enter *ZX* to use the z-x plane for slicing.

Point on axis: '*Intersection* at P1 (at column B-2)

Side to retain? Pick a point *below* P1 to remove the portion of the counter above guide line B.

Draw> Circle> Center, Radius

Center: '*From,* '*Intersection* at P1

Offset: @0,0,8

Radius: 4

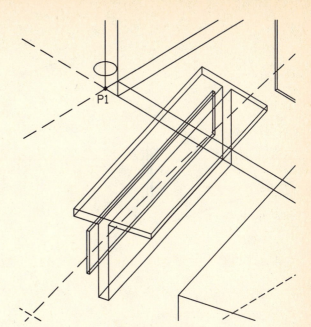

Figure T3–3b(7)

Draw> Solids> Slice

Pick the counter, then the Object option.

Side to retain? Pick a point *above* P1.

Modify> Move the counter and front panel at a displacement of *@0,0,–8*. Then remove the bottom 8″ of the *front panel* only by slicing with the circle.

8. Return to the first corner of the teller counter.
View Named UCS
Make *U2* the current UCS.

View is still set at SE Isometric.
Zoom out to see the profiles created in Step 5.

Draw> Solids> Extrude

Pick both copied profile loops.

Height: *–20′6″*

This side of the counter top is done. Draw some work bins. As they will not be seen from the back side, simply use solid boxes to simulate the bins.

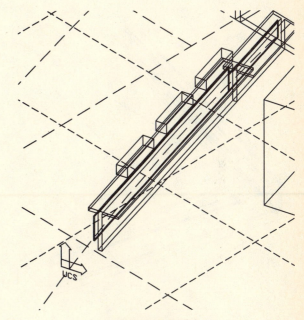

Figure T3–3b(8)

Draw> Solids> Box> Corner

First corner: *0,40,–54*

Other corner: *@11,10*

Height: *–48*

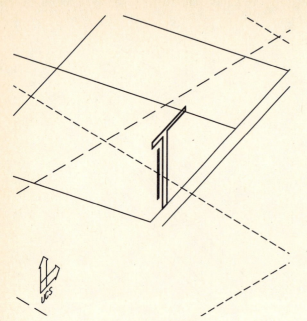

Figure T3–3b(9)

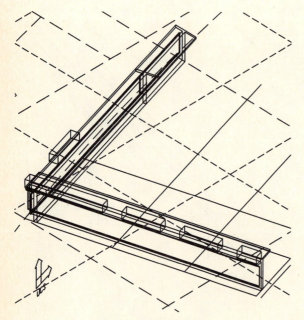

Figure T3–3b(10)

Construct> Copy

Pick the box, use *M*ultiple, and any base point.

Displacement: *@0,0,–72*

Displacement: *@0,0,–144* (that's negative 12′)

Draw> Solids> Box> Corner

First corner: *0,40*

Other corner: *@11,10*

Height: *–30*

9. Now create the other arm of the teller counter.

Set UCS to *U1*.

Set view to SE Isometric.

Turn layers COLUMNS and INTWALL *Off*.

Zoom in on the right side of the teller area.

View> Set UCS> 3 points

Origin: '*Intersection* at P1

+x point: *@0,4*

+y point: *@0,0,4*

View> Named UCS

Rename the current *No Name* to *U3*.

Draw> Insert

Name of Block: *Profile*

Insertion point: *0,0*

Modify> Explode

Pick the block.

Now you can work with the individual profile loops.

Draw> Solids> Extrude

Pick both profile loops.

Height: *–24′*

10. You can create some work bins with a similar process used in Step 8.

Draw> Solids> Box> Corner

First corner: *0,40,–16′* (that is, negative 16 feet)

Other corner: *@11,10*

Height: *–8′*

Draw> Solids> Box> Corner

First corner: *0,40,–48*

Other corner: *@11,10*

Height: *–48*

Construct> Copy

Pick the box just created.

Base point: Pick any point.

Displacement: *@0,0,–72*

Draw> Solids> Box> Corner

First corner: *0,40*

Other corner: *@11,10*

Height: *–24*

11. Zoom in tightly on the corner where the two counters meet to the left of the screen.

Click on **Construct> Union**.
Pick the two boxes at the ends of the counters. They are unioned into a single object.

Then invoke **Construct> Union** again and pick the counters to be unioned. Repeat the command to union the two front panels. Notice that the panels form a cross at the intersection after they are unioned.

12. The teller counter is complete. A dropped ceiling over the area was created in Tutorial 1 so all you have to do here is to turn the CEILING layer *On* to see it.

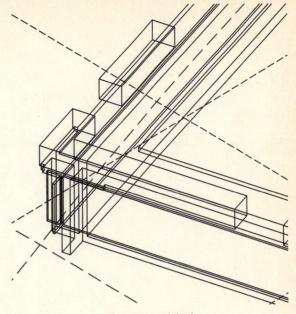

Figure T3–3b(11)

T3-3c   Lighting for the Open Office Area

Layer settings:	
0	Off
2NDFLR	*On*
3DFLOOR	Off
3DUPPER	Off
CEILING	Off
COLGRID	*On*
COLUMNS	*On*
EXTWALL	Off
GRID	*On*
INTWALL	Off
ROOF	Off
T3LTG	*Current*
TELLER	Off
WINDWALL	Off

1. Lighting for the open offices area.

Built-in lighting for this area consists of "can" lights or recessed downlights built into the ceiling. To simulate this type of lighting in the computer model, locate solid cylinders in the appropriate places, then subtract them from the ceiling solid to create holes in which to locate lights later in the rendering tutorials.

There are size C and size D lights. C lights are 8″ × 12″ cylinders, while D lights are 10″ × 12″ cylinders.

2. Create and locate D lights.
Set view to plan view, World.
UCS is set at WCS.

Draw> Solids> Cylinder> Center

Center: *65′,31′,10′6″*

Radius: *5*

Height: *2*. This is fixture D1.

Construct> Array> Rectangular

Pick the cylinder as object to array.

Number of rows: *2*

Number of columns: *2*

Distance between rows: *9′*

Distance between columns: *10′*

There are eight D-size lights.

3. Switch to 3D views to check that all the lights are located at the proper height.

Construct> Subtract

Pick the ceiling solid; press the RMB.
Then pick all the D lights to be subtracted.

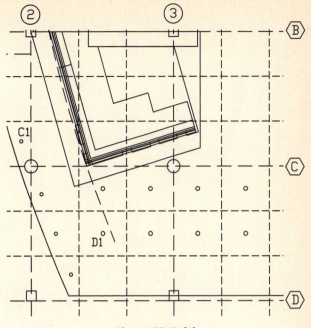

Figure T3–3c(1)

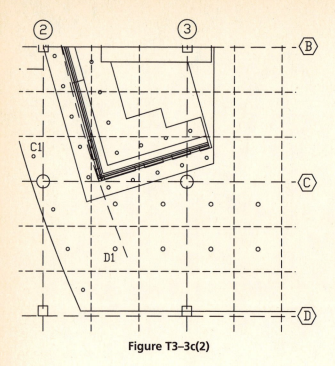

Figure T3–3c(2)

4. To draw size C lights, zoom in on the area above column C-2 in plan view, WCS.

Draw> Solids> Cylinder> Center

Center: *48′,50′,10′6*

Radius: *4*

Height: *10*

Construct> Copy

Pick the cylinder.

Enter *M* (for Multiple).

Base point: Pick any point.

Displacement: Pick a point about 48″ on the other side of column C-2 and about the same distance away from the balcony line. Continue to insert cylinders visually down the balcony line until you have inserted four lights.

When you are done subtract them from the ceiling solid, which is the floor object on layer 2NDFLR.

5. Lighting for the teller section.

There are C-size lights behind the teller counter.

Draw> Solids> Cylinder> Center

Center: *60′,69′,9′*

Radius: *4*

Height: *10*

With **Construct>Array> Rectangular**, pick the cylinder and array it *4* rows at distance *–6′4″*. Then pick the last, or lowest, light and array it *4* columns at distance *5′4″*. Subtract these lights from the ceiling solid.

6. There are also some small spotlights over the teller counters. These are size A lights. Draw a 4″ × 8″ cylinder and copy it to 9′ high at the positions shown in Figure T3–3c(2). Subtract them from the dropped ceiling.

T3–3d Finish Up

1. All the architectural and interior elements for Tutorial 3 have been done.

Save the current *T3.dwg* drawing and exit AutoCAD.

Make a copy of *T3.dwg* and use it for making perspective views in Chapter 5.

2. Go on to the following sections to create some furniture.

In this section, you will create the furniture components that make up a typical work station for the bank officials. The components consist of a work surface and a return, joined by a corner unit, where there is an adjustable keyboard tray and a computer display terminal.

The components can be blocked separately into individual AutoCAD drawings, which you can insert into the bank building according to a custom configuration. To maintain simplicity, the components created in this tutorial are blocked together as a suite, so that you can furnish the open office area with standard setup. After insertion, you can, of course, use the **Explode** command to break down a blocked drawing to work with its individual parts.

Start a new drawing with the following parameters:

Name of drawing: *Wkstn.dwg*
Drawing Units: *Architectural*
Drawing Limits: *20′ × 16′*
Grid is set at 9″ × 9″

Create the layer:

Layer name	Color	Linetype
0	White	Continuous
BASE	Green	Continuous
CORNER	Yellow	Continuous
GUIDES	White	Continuous
LATERAL	White	Continuous
TEMP	Green	Continuous
WKSURF	Cyan	Continuous

T3–4a   Create a Work Surface

Layer settings:

0	*Off*
BASE	*On*
CORNER	*Off*
GUIDES	*Current*
LATERAL	*Off*
TEMP	*Off*
WKSURF	*On*

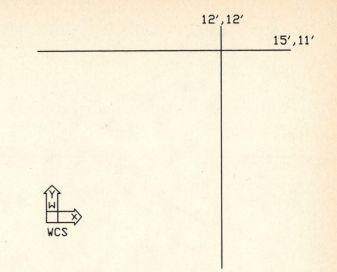

Figure T3–4a(1)

1. First, draw some guide lines.

View is set at zoom, *All*; plan view, WCS.

Click on **Draw> Line**.
From point: *12′,12′*
To point: *@0,–12′*

Select **Draw> Line** again.
From point: *15′,11′*
To point: *@–12′,0*

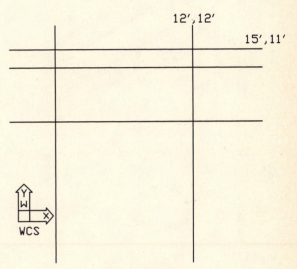

Figure T3–4a(2)

Two guide lines are drawn, crossing approximately at the center of the drawing field.

Offset the horizontal line 9″ and 36″ in the -y direction, using **Construct> Offset**.

Be sure to pick the original horizontal line each time and then reset the distance.

Similarly, offset the vertical line in the -x direction at distances of 72″.

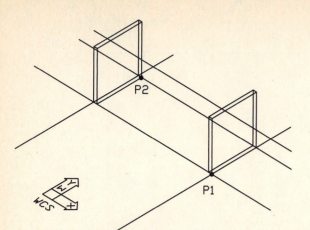

Figure T3–4a(3)

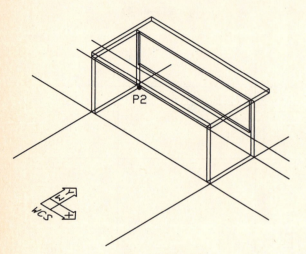

Figure T3–4a(4)

2. Make layer BASE Current.
First create legs for the work surface.

Click on **Draw> Solids> Box> Corner**.

First corner: '*Intersection* at P1

Other corner: @–2,27

Height: *28*

Construct> Copy

Objects: Pick the box, or enter *L*.

Base point: Pick any point.

Displacement: @–70,0

3. Now make a cross brace or privacy panel.
View> 3D Viewpoint Presets> SE Isometric.
Zoom in on P2.

Draw> Solids> Box> Corner

First corner: '*Endpoint* at P2

Other corner: @–68,–1

Height: *16*

Modify> Move

Objects: Pick the box, or enter *L*.

Base point: Pick any point.

Displacement: @0,0,12

4. Draw a top for the work surface.
Make layer WKSURF Current.

Draw> Solids> Box> Corner

First corner: '*Intersection* at P1

Other corner: @–72,36

Height: *2*

Modify> Move

Pick the box, or enter *L*.

Pick any base point.

Displacement: @0,0,28

The work surface is done.

T3–4b   Create a Return

A return, or side work surface, has similar end panels and cross brace as the main work surface.

Layer settings:

0	Off
BASE	*Current*
CORNER	Off
GUIDES	*On*
LATERAL	Off
TEMP	Off
WKSURF	Off

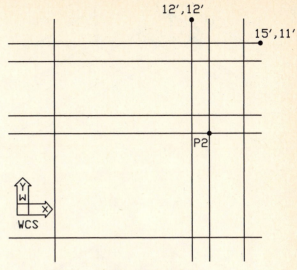

Figure T3–4b(1)

1. Set **View> 3D Vp Presets> SW Isometric**.

Using **Construct> Offset**, offset the vertical guide line on the right to distances of 9″ and 27″ in the +x direction.

Repeat **Construct> Offset**, and offset the bottom horizontal guide line 9″ and 61″ in the -y direction.

Make sure you are using the original guide lines for offsetting each time.

2. Make layer BASE Current.

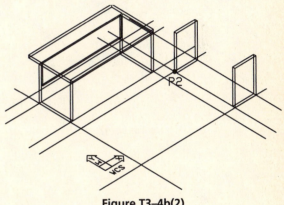

Figure T3–4b(2)

Draw> Solids> Box> Corner
First corner: 'Intersection at P2
Other corner: @18,–2
Height: 28

Construct> Copy
Objects: Pick the box.
Base point: Pick any point.
Displacement: @0,–50

The end legs are complete.

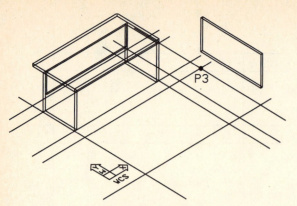

Figure T3–4b(3)

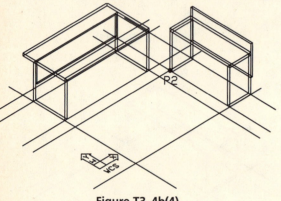

Figure T3–4b(4)

3. Now create a cross brace, which also acts as a back panel for the return.

Zoom in around the intersection at P3.

Draw> Solids> Box> Corner
First corner: *.xy* of *'Intersection* at P3
Need Z: 12
Other corner: @*1.5″,–52″*
Height: *24*

Modify> Move
Pick the box, or enter *L.*
Pick any base point.
Displacement: @*0,0,12*

The legs for the return are complete.

4. Draw a top for the return.
Make layer WKSURF Current.

Draw> Solids> Box> Corner
First corner: *.xy* of *'Intersection* at P2
Need Z: *28*
Other corner: @*18,–52*
Height: *2*

The return is complete.

T3–4c Create a Corner Unit

The corner unit joins the work surface and return.

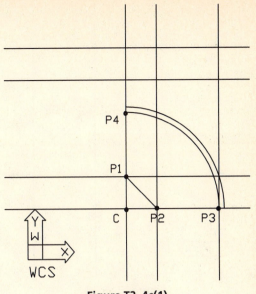

Figure T3–4c(1)

Layer settings:

0	Off
BASE	Off
CORNER	*On*
GUIDES	*Current*
LATERAL	Off
TEMP	Off
WKSURF	Off

1. View is set at plan view, WCS.
Zoom in on the area of the corner unit.

Draw> Arc> S,C,A
Start point: *'Intersection* at P3
Center: *'Intersection* at C
Angle: *90*

Construct> Offset
Distance: *1.5"*
Pick the arc.
Side to offset: Pick a point in the +x direction.

2. Set layer CORNER Current.

Draw> Polyline
From point: *'Intersection* at P1
To point: *'Intersection* at P2
To point: *'Intersection* at P3
At P3, enter *A* (for Arc).
End point of Arc: Enter *CE* (for Center).
Center: *'Intersection* at C
End point of arc: *'Intersection* at P4
At P4, enter *L* (for Line).
To point: *C*, to close line back to P1.

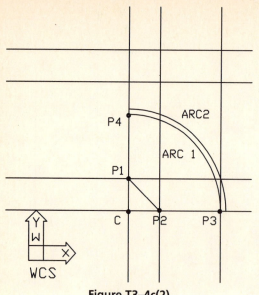

Figure T3–4c(2)

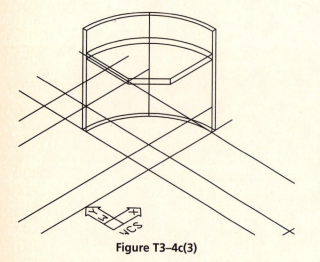

Figure T3–4c(3)

Draw> Solids> Extrude

For objects, pick the polyline loop just drawn.

Height: *2*

Modify> Move

Pick the extruded polyline and any base point.

Displacement: *@0,0,26*

3. In **Data> Layer**, make layer TEMP Current.

Turn layer CORNER *Off*.

The two arcs drawn in Step 1 are visible.

Set view to SW Isometric and zoom in.

Using **Draw> Line**, draw a line connecting the end points at each end of the two arcs; a horizontal line from P3, and a vertical line from P4.

Click on **Modify> Edit Polyline**.

Pick one of the arcs; answer *Yes* to turn it into a polyline. Do not press the RMB.

Enter *J*(for Join).

Then pick the other arc and the end lines.

The arcs and end lines are joined to become a closed polyline loop.

Draw> Solids> Extrude

Pick the polyline loop.

Height: *36*

Modify> Properties

Pick the extrusion and change its layer to CORNER.

Data> Layer

Turn layer CORNER *On* and make it Current.

Turn layer GUIDES *Off*.

The corner unit is done.

4. Draw a computer keyboard tray.

View is set at SW Isometric, zoomed in around P1.

Make layer TEMP Current.

Turn layer CORNER *Off*; make sure layer GUIDES is *On*.

Draw> Solids> Box> Corner

First corner: '*Intersection* at P1

Other corner: *@20,7*

Height: *1.5"*

Draw> Circle> Center, Radius

Center: '*Endpoint* at P2, top corner of box

Radius: *4*

Construct> 3D Rotate

Pick the circle.

Enter *X* to use the x-axis rotate option.

Point on x-axis: '*Center* of the circle

Rotation angle: *4*

Draw> Solids> Slice

Pick the box.

Enter *O* to use the slice by Object option.

Pick the circle as object.

Enter *B* to retain both sides.

The box has been sliced into two parts. Use **Modify> Erase** to remove the top part, leaving a box with a sloped top. In a 3D view, it is sometimes not clear as to which is the desired side of the slicing plane. It is less confusing to retain both parts of a sliced object and then simply erase the undesirable part or parts. Erase the circle as well.

Modify> Rotate

Pick the box and P1 as base point.

Rotate it –45° along the z-axis.

Use **Modify> Move**, 2 times.

Pick the box and any base point.

First time: Displacement at *@10<135*

Second time: Displacement at *@0,0,25*

Change the layer of the box to CORNER.

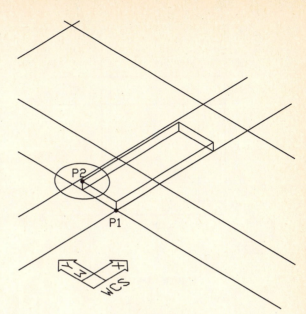

Figure T3–4c(4)

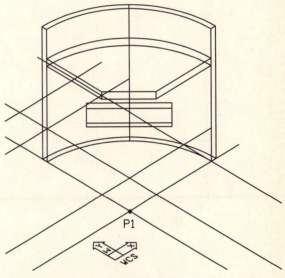

Figure T3–4c(5)

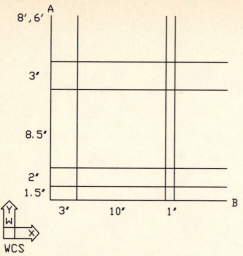

Figure T3–4c(6)

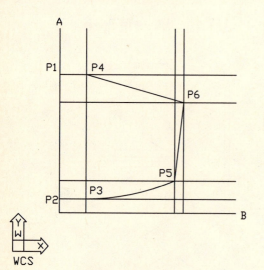

Figure T3–4c(7)

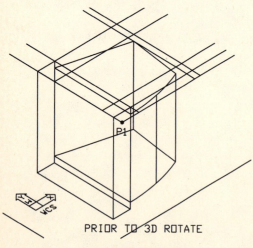

PRIOR TO 3D ROTATE

Figure T3–4c(8)

5. Create a display monitor.

View> 3D Vp Presets> Plan view> World.
Data> Layer
Set layer GUIDES Current.
Turn layer CORNER *Off.*
Turn layer TEMP *On.*

Draw> Line
From point: *8´,6´* (Absolute coordinates. This point is at an empty space within the grid of guide lines for the work station.)
To point: *@0,–20* (line A)
To point: *@20,0* (line B)

Click on Construct> Offset
Set distances as noted in Figure T3–4c(6) and offset lines A and B accordingly.

6. Make layer TEMP Current.

Draw> Polyline
From P1 successively to P4. Use '*Intersection.*
At P4, enter *C* (for Close), back to P1.

Draw> Solids> Extrude
Pick the polyline loop just drawn.
Height: *–15*

Draw> Polyline
From point: P3
End point of line: *A* (for Arc)
End point of arc: P5
End point of arc: *L* (for Line)
End point of line: P6
End point of line: P4
At P4, enter *C* (for Close), back to P3.

Modify> Move
Pick the last loop and any base point.
Displacement: *@0,0,–1*

Draw> Solids> Extrude
Pick the polyline loop.
Height: *–13*

7. View> 3D Vp Presets> SW Isometric

Construct> 3D Rotate

Pick both parts of the monitor.

Enter *X* for x-axis rotate.

Point on x-axis: *'Intersection* at P1

Angle: *90*

Click on **Construct> 3D Rotate** again.

Pick both parts of the monitor.

Enter *Y* for y-axis rotate.

Point on y-axis: *'Intersection* at P1

Angle: *5*

Construct> Union

Pick the front and back objects of the monitor.

The front and back are made into a single solid.

8. Still in SW Isometric view, draw a base.
Make layer 0 Current.
Turn layer TEMP *Off*.

Draw> Solids> Cylinder> Center

Center: *'Intersection* at P1

Radius: *3*

Height: *0.5"*

Draw> Solids> Cylinder> Center

Center: *'Intersection* at P1

Radius: *1.75"*

Height: *1.5"*

Construct> Union

Pick the two cylinders. They are made into one object.

Modify> Move

Pick the unioned object and any base point.

Displacement: *@8",7.5"*

The base moved to be under the display monitor.

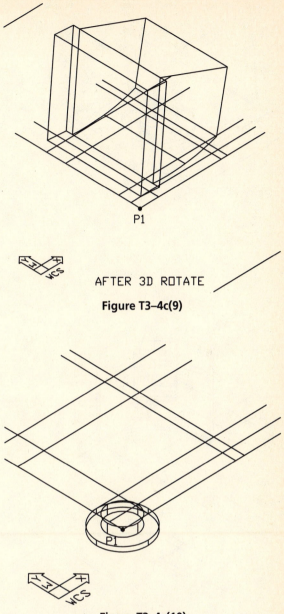

AFTER 3D ROTATE

Figure T3–4c(9)

Figure T3–4c(10)

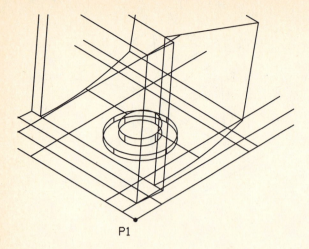

P1

Figure T3–4c(11)

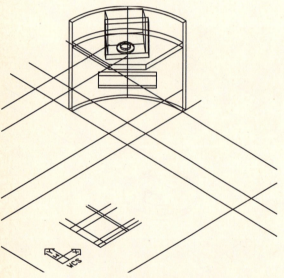

Figure T3–4c(12)

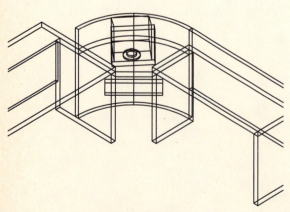

Figure T3–4c(13)

9. Modify> Properties
Pick the base.
In the dialog box, change its layer to CORNER.

Turn layers TEMP and CORNER *On*.
Modify> Properties
Pick the monitor.
In the dialog box, change its layer to CORNER.

Construct> Union
Pick the monitor and its base.

The units are made into one object. If you want to adjust the tilt of the monitor, do not union the units. If you have already, you can click **Assist> Undo** to go back to the previous state.

10. Now you need to move the monitor onto the top of the corner unit.

Set view to plan view, WCS.
Zoom in on the monitor.

Modify> Rotate
Pick the monitor unit.
Base point: Pick a point in the center of the unit.
Angle: *50*

Modify> Move
Pick all of the monitor unit.
Base point: Pick any point.
Visually move the monitor to the center of the corner unit.

Click on **Modify> Move** again.
Pick the monitor unit and any base point.
Displacement: *@0,0,28*

The monitor has been turned to face the person at the work surface and moved onto the top of the corner unit.

T3–4d Create a Lateral File

The lateral file is a simple box. Its distinctive feature lies in the drawer pulls.

Layer settings:

0	Off
BASE	Off
CORNER	Off
GUIDES	Off
LATERAL	*Current*
TEMP	Off
WKSURF	Off

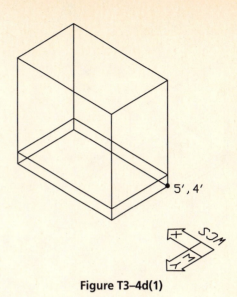

Figure T3–4d(1)

1. View> 3D Viewpoints Presets> NW Isometric

First, draw a base.

Draw>Solids> Box> Corner

First corner: *5'4'* (absolute coordinates of an arbitrarily selected point)

Other corner: *@30,18*

Height: *3*

Now draw the file cabinet.

Click on **Draw>Solids> Box** again.

First corner: *60,48,3*

Other corner: *@30,18*

Height: *25*

The base and body of the file cabinet are complete.

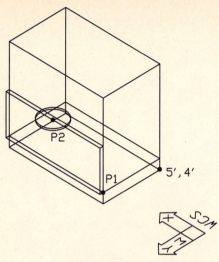

P2

P1

5′, 4′

WCS

Figure T3–4d(2)

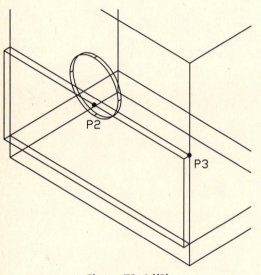

P2

P3

Figure T3–4d(3)

2. Now to create drawer fronts.

Draw>Solids> Box> Corner
First corner: *'Endpoint* at P1
Other corner: *@30,1*
Height: *12.25″*

Draw> Solids> Cylinder> Center
Center: *'Midpoint* at P2
Radius: *4*
Height: *0.5″*

Construct> 3D Rotate
Pick the cylinder.
Use the X-axis rotate option.
Point on x-axis: *'Midpoint* at P2
Angle: *90*

Modify> Move
Pick the cylinder.
Base point: Pick any point.
Displacement: *@0,0,2.5*

Construct> Subtract
Pick the box.
Pick the cylinder.

Construct> 3D Mirror
Pick the drawer front box.
Pick the XY plane option.
Point on x-axis: *'Endpoint* at P3
Do not delete old object.

Modify> Move
Pick the upper box.
Base point: Pick any point.
Displacement: *@0,0,0.5″*

The file drawer fronts are drawn, and the lateral file cabinet is complete.

3. View> Set UCS> World
View> 3D Vp Presets> Plan view> World

File> Export> Block

Name of drawing: *T3-cab.dwg*

Name of block: Press the RMB

Insertion point: Pick the lower left corner of the lateral file.

For objects, use a crossing window to pick all the objects.

The objects disappear from the screen.

Enter *Oops* to bring the objects back.

The file is blocked as *T3-cab.dwg*. Use it to insert into the bank building before setting up perspective views in Chapter 5.

4. Make layer 0 Current.
Turn layers BASE, CORNER and WKSURF *On*.

Turn layers GUIDES, LATERAL and TEMP *Off* and freeze.

File> Export> Block

Name of drawing: *T3-wkn.dwg*

Name of block: Press the RMB

Insertion point: 0,0

For objects, use a crossing window to pick all the objects of the work station.

The objects disappear from the screen.

Enter *Oops* to bring the objects back.

To insert the work station into a perspective view in Chapter 5, use the drawing *T3-wkn.dwg*.

5. Save the current drawing *Compon.dwg*.
Make a copy and save the original as a backup.

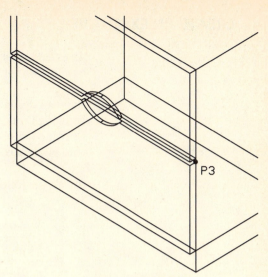

Figure T3–4d(4)

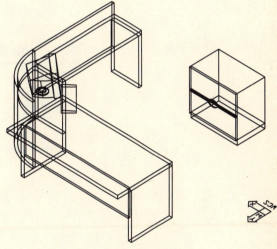

Figure T3–4d(5)

An executive-style swivel chair is created for the work station. You can use the base drawn for the conference room chair, if you completed Tutorial 2.

Name of drawing: *Swchair.dwg*
Drawing Units: *Architectural*
Drawing Limits: *10',12'*
Grid is set at 6" × 6"

Create the following layers:

Layer name	Color	Linetype
0	White	Continuous
BASE	White	Continuous
CHAIR	White	Continuous
GUIDES	Cyan	Continuous
GUIDES2	Green	Continuous
SEAT	Red	Continuous
SEAT2	Yellow	Continuous

T3–5a   Create the Seat and Back

Layer settings:

0 (Default layer)	Off
BASE	Off
CHAIR	Off
GUIDES	_Current_
GUIDES2	Off
SEAT	Off
SEAT2	Off

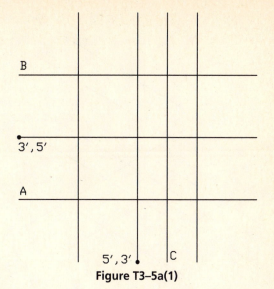

Figure T3–5a(1)

1. You need some basic guide lines for the chair. View is set at plan view, WCS.

Draw> Line
From point: _3',5'_
To point: _@4',0_

Click on **Draw> Line** again.
From point: _5',3'_
To point: _@0,4'_

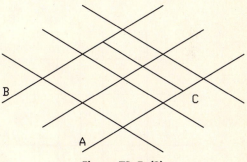

Figure T3–5a(2)

The intersection of these two lines is at 5', 5', absolute coordinates.

Construct> Offset

Offset the horizontal line 12″ in the -y direction (this is line A).

Again, offset it 12″ in the +y direction (line B).

Click on **Construct> Offset** again
Pick the vertical line.
Offset it 12″ in the -x direction.
Then offset it 12″ in the +x direction.

Click **Construct> Offset**, reset distance to _6″_.
And offset the original vertical line 6″ in the +x direction (line C).

View> 3D Viewpoint Preset> SW Isometric

Modify> Trim
Cutting edges: Pick lines A and B.
Objects to trim: Pick the ends of line C.

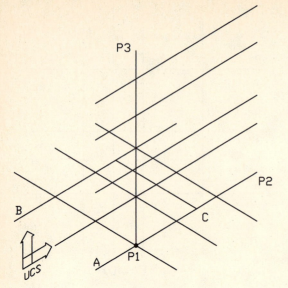

P3

P2

B

C

A   P1

UCS

Figure T3–5a(3)

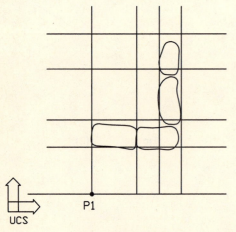

P1

UCS

Figure T3–5a(4)

2. Make layer GUIDES2 Current.

Construct> Copy
Pick line A.
Enter *M* (for Multiple).
Base point: Pick any point.
Displacement: *@0,0,12*
Displacement: *@0,0,19*
Displacement: *@0,0,32*
Displacement: *@0,0,41*

Modify> Properties
Change the layer property of the four lines just offset to that of layer GUIDES2.

Draw> Line
From point: *'Intersection* at P1
To point: *@0,0,48*

View> Set UCS> 3 Point
Origin: *'Intersection* at P1
+x-axis point: *'Endpoint* at P2
+y point: *'Endpoint* at P3

View> Named UCS
Rename the current UCS to *U1*.

3. Set **View> 3D Vp Presets> Plan view> UCS**.
Make layer SEAT Current.

Construct> Offset
Offset the vertical line successively at 12″, 6″, and 6″ again.

Click on **Draw> Polyline**.
Draw closed polyline loops roughly within the guide lines as shown in Figure T3–5a(4).

View> Set 3D Vp> SW Isometric
View> Set UCS> World

Draw> Solids> Extrude
Pick all four of the polyline loops just completed.
Enter *P* (for Path).
Pick the trimmed off line C as path.

4. Turn layers GUIDES2 and SEAT *Off*.
Make layer SEAT2 Current.

Set **View> Set UCS> World**.
Set **View> 3D Vp Presets> Plan view> World**.

Click on **Draw> Polyline**.
Draw closed polyline loops roughly within the guide lines for the back (loop A).

Modify> Move
Pick the loop just drawn.
Base point: Pick any point.
Displacement: *@0,0,19*

Draw> Polyline
Draw another closed polyline loop within the guide lines for the chair seat (loop B). This loop covers the entire 24″ × 24″ seat outline.

Modify> Move
Pick the last object, Loop B, and any base point.
Displacement: *@0,0,12*

5. Set view to SW Isometric.

Draw> Solids> Extrude
Pick loop A.
Extrusion height: *29″*

Click on **Draw> Solids> Extrude** again.
Pick loop B.
Extrusion height: *6″*. See Figure T3–5a(7).

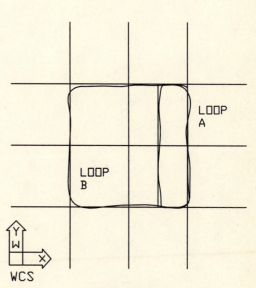

Figure T3–5a(5)

Figure T3–5a(6)

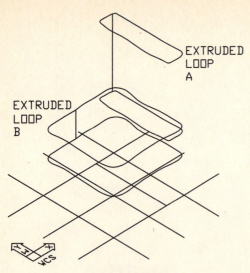

EXTRUDED
LOOP
A

EXTRUDED
LOOP
B

Figure T3–5a(7)

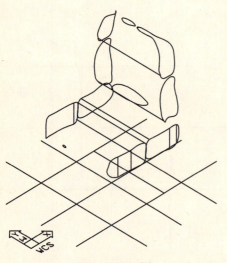

Figure T3–5a(8)

6. Leave layer SEAT2 Current.
Turn layer GUIDES *Off*.
Turn layer SEAT *On*.

Draw> Solids> Interference

Pick the extruded solids of the chair *back*.

Answer *Yes* to create an interference object.

Modify> Properties

Enter L (for Last), or pick the interference object just created. (Use this option, because it is difficult to pick out the interference object among the extrusion lines.)

Change the layer property to CHAIR.

Repeat **Draw> Solids> Interference**.

Pick the solids representing the seat.

Again, click on **Modify> Properties**.

For object, enter L (for Last).

Change the layer to CHAIR.

7. Make layer CHAIR Current.
Turn layers SEAT and SEAT2 *Off*.

The seat and back of the swivel chair are done.

T3–5b Create the Swivel Base

A. If you have completed Tutorial 2, you can use the base created for the conference room chair for the executive chair here.

1. Save and exit the current drawing *Swchair.dwg*.

2. Load the *Confchr.dwg* file and isolate the base for the chair. Use **File> Export> Block** to Write-block the base to a separate drawing, named *Base.dwg*, with insertion point set at *5',5'*.

3. Reload drawing *Swchair.dwg*.
Click on **Draw> Insert> Block> File**.
Insert the base at *5',5'*.

4. The chair is done. Go on to Section T3–5c.

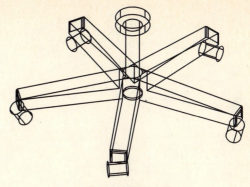

Figure T3–5b(1)

Figure T3–5b(2)

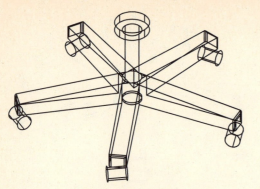

Figure T3–5b(3)

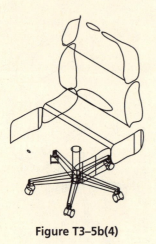

Figure T3–5b(4)

B. Do the following steps only if you have to create a swivel base for the executive chair.

If you did not do Tutorial 2, create a base using the steps detailed in Section T2–6c of Tutorial 2.

1. The layer setup, coordinates, and drawing limits used are the same as the ones set up for this drawing. So you can begin the base by drawing a line at coordinates 5′,5′, as instructed in Step 1 of Section T2–6a.

2. When you have finished the base, the chair is done.

Go to Section T3–5c.

Layer settings:

0	*On*
BASE	*On*
CHAIR	*Current*
GUIDES	*Off Freeze*
GUIDES2	*Off Freeze*
SEAT	*Off Freeze*
SEAT2	*Off Freeze*

A. If you have imported the base from Tutorial 2, it would have been placed on the BASE layer and is now visible on the screen, along with the chair seat and back.

B. If you just created the base in the previous section, it also should be visible, along with the seat and the back of the chair.

Click on **File> Export> Block**.

Name of drawing: *T3-xchr.dwg*

Block name: Press the RMB

Insertion point: Pick a point at the center of the seat.

Objects to block: Pick all seat, back, and base objects with a crossing window.

Enter *Oops* to redisplay the block objects.

Save the current drawing: *Swchair.dwg*.

Make a copy of it for use as a backup.

Use the exported drawing *T3-xchr.dwg* for insertion into the bank building when you set up perspective views in Chapter 5.

A chair is created for use by clients in the open offices area. The legs and arms on each side of the chair form a continuous loop, giving the chair a skid base. A couple of cross bars separate the two sides of the chair and the seat is hung on the cross bars.

Set up a new drawing with the following parameters:

Name of Drawing: *Gstchr.dwg*
Units: *Architectural*
Drawing Limits: Lower Left at *0,0*
                 Upper Right at 10′,8′
Grid: Set grid spacing at 4″ × 4″.

Set up the following layers through **Data> Layer:**

Layer Name	Color	Linetype
0	White	Continuous
ARMATURE	White	Continuous
GUIDES	Green	Continuous
SEAT	White	Continuous

T3–6a Create the Arms for the Guest Chair

First, draw a 3D polyline loop running along the center of the arm and leg. Then draw a circle to be entered on the leg and perpendicular to it. The circle is then extruded along the loop, forming a solid tube to be one side of the chair. The tube is copied to the other side, and cross bars are then drawn to connect the sides.

Layer settings:

0	Off
ARMATURE	*On*
GUIDES	*Current*
SEAT	Off

1. An arbitrary, but convenient, position (5′,4′,0.375″) is selected as the center of the base of the right (as you face the chair) front leg.

Click on **View> Set UCS> 3 Point**.

Origin: *5′,4′,0.375″*

Point on +x-axis: *@0,4*

Point on +y-axis: *@0,0,4*

View> Named UCS

Rename the current UCS as *U1*.

Click on **View> 3D Viewpoint Presets> Plan view> Current UCS**.

2. Draw> Line

From point: *0,0*

To point: *@0,22* (P2)

To point: *@18,0* (P3)

To point: *@0,–22* (P4)

To point: *C* (for Close, to return to the first point).

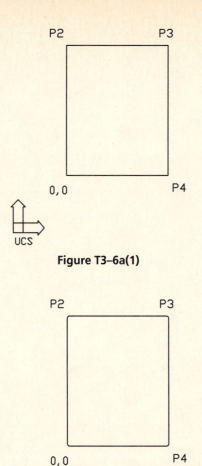

Figure T3–6a(1)

POLYLINE WITH FILLETED CORNERS

Figure T3–6a(2)

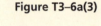

Figure T3–6a(3)

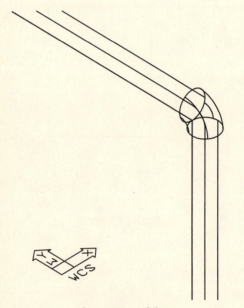

Figure T3–6a(4)

Construct> Fillet

Enter *R* (for Radius).

Enter *0.375"*. Press the RMB.

Press the RMB again, to repeat the Fillet command.

For objects to fillet, pick one of the vertical lines and the horizontal line connected to it. The intersection of these lines are filleted. Repeat filleting at each of the other three corners.

Modify> Edit Polyline

Pick one of the horizontal lines.

Answer *Yes* to make the line into a polyline.

Enter *J* (for Join).

Use a crossing window to select all the line segments on the screen. Be sure that the fillets are also included.

AutoCAD reports that the lines are now joined to become a continuous polyline loop.

3. Set **View> 3D Vpoint Presets> SW Isometric**. Set **View> Set UCS> World**. Make layer ARMATURE Current.

Draw> Circle> Center, Radius

Center: *5',4',22"*

Radius: *0.375"*

Zoom in on the circle.

Draw> Solids> Extrude

Select objects: Pick the circle.

Enter *P* (for Path). Pick the polyline loop as path.

The circle is extruded along the polyline loop through which the circle passes. The result is a solid tubular arm, legs, and skid base for the chair.

4. Create the armrest.

View is set at SW Isometric, zoom in on the upper horizontal member. UCS is set at WCS.

View> Set UCS> 3 points
Origin: *60,52,22.375″* (that is, 5′,4′4″,1′10.375″)
Point on +x axis: *@4,0*
Point on +y axis: *@0,0,4*

Draw> Line
From point: *0,1* (P1)
To point: *@0,0,–8*

Modify> Properties
Change the layer property of the last line to GUIDES.

Draw> Circle> Donut
Inside diameter: *0.8*
Outside diameter: *2.25*
Center: *0,0*. Press the RMB.

Draw> Solids> Extrude
Pick the donut.
For path, pick the line just drawn, at a point near the circle.

Turn layer GUIDES *Off*.

The donut is extruded along the path of the line to form a tube that serves as an armrest. The inside hole of the armrest is slightly larger than the arm itself, so that there will be no ambiguity as to the visibility of the armrest and the arm.

Set **View> UCS> World**.

Construct> Copy
Pick the arm and the armrest, and any point as base.
For displacement, enter *@–20,0*.

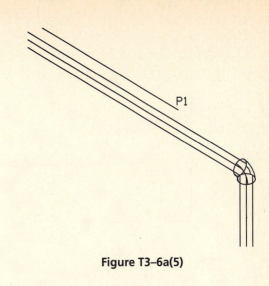

Figure T3–6a(5)

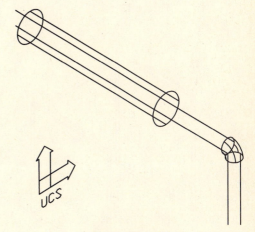

Figure T3–6a(6)

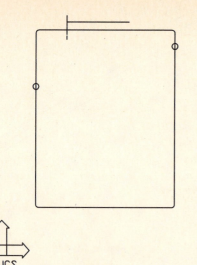

Figure T3–6a(7)

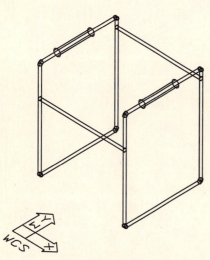

Figure T3-6a(8)

5. Now create the cross braces.
Make layer GUIDES Current.
Turn layer ARMATURE *Off*.

Set **View> Named UCS> U1**.

Set **View> 3D Vp Presets> Plan view> Current UCS**.

Draw> Circle> Center
Center: *0,15*
Radius: *0.375"*

Click on **Draw> Circle> Center** again.
Center: *18,20*
Radius: *0.375"*

Set **View> 3D Vp Presets> SE Isometric**.
Zoom in on the left circle.

Draw> Solids> Extrude
Pick the circle as object to extrude.
Height: *–20"*

Zoom in on the circle on the right.

Use **Draw> Solids> Extrude** to extrude the circle at a distance of *–20"*.

Modify> Properties
Change the layer property of both extruded circles to that of ARMATURE.

Make layer ARMATURE Current.
Turn layer GUIDES *Off*.

T3–6b   Create the Seat

Layer settings:

0	Off
ARMATURE	Off
GUIDES	*On*
SEAT	*Current*

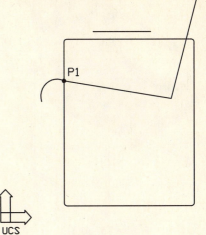

1. Set UCS at *U1*.
Set **View> 3D Vp Presets> Plan view> Current UCS**.
Toggle **F8** to turn Ortho *On*.

Draw> Line

From point: *0,16.5″* (P1)

To point: *@15<-9*

To point: *@18<75*

Figure T3–6b(1)

Draw> Arc> S,C,A

Start point: *'Endpoint* at P1

Center: *@–1,–2*

Angle: *135*

Click on **Draw> Arc> SCA** again.

Start point: *'Endpoint* at P2

Center: *@1.5,–1*

Angle: *–135*

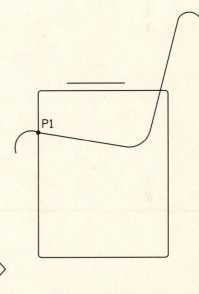

Construct> Fillet

Radius: *3*. Press the RMB twice.

Pick the lines near where they intersect.

The outline of the seat is complete, but there are still separate line entities. The next step will join them to-gether.

Figure T3–6b(2)

Figure T3–6b(3)

2. Modify> Edit Polyline

Pick one of the lines.

Answer *Yes* to make it a polyline.

Enter *J* (for Join).

Pick the straight lines, end arcs, and the fillet.

Enter *W* (for Width).

For width, enter *0.5″*

Click on **Modify> Properties**.

In the dialog box, set the Scale at *1*; Linetype at *Hidden2*; Thickness at *–18*.

If the linetype is not yet loaded, you will have to click on the **Data> Linetype> Load** box, and select the *Hidden2* linetype first, then go back into the Properties command to change the linetype of the polyline profile.

When you exit the **Properties** dialog box, the polyline profile of the chair seat will be extruded to become a solid with closely spaced lines across its surface. You may have to adjust the linetype scale to make the line display as a dashed line. Under **Options> Linetypes> Global Linetype Scale**, try a setting of 10. The seat should appear as if it is made of closely spaced slats.

Note: If you are plotting in paperspace, you have to readjust the Linetype Scale to make the seat display correctly in paperspace.

Click on **View> Set UCS> World**.

Modify> Move

Pick the seat and any base point.

Displacement: *@–1,0*

The seat is moved laterally to be centered on the armature.

Layer settings:

0	Off
ARMATURE	*On*
GUIDES	Off Freeze
SEAT	*Current*

1. Set **View> Set UCS> World**.

Click on **File> Export> Block**.

Name of drawing: *T3-chr.dwg*

Block name: Press the RMB

Insertion point: *0,0*

Objects to block: Pick all the visible objects with a crossing window.

Enter *Oops* to redisplay objects on the screen.

Save the current drawing: *Gstchr.dwg*.

Make a copy of it for use as a backup.

Use the exported block *T3-chr.dwg* for insertion into the bank building, when you set up perspective views in Chapter 5.

3D VISUALIZATION

ABOUT VISUALIZATION IN 3D

Architectural spaces should be conceived in volumetric terms in 3D, although most people begin their designs in 2D. They work through the beginning stages in orthographic projections before going on to consider their concepts in the third dimension. This is not necessarily a bad way to approach a design project, for architectural spatial concepts can be very complex. Diverse disciplines and professions are involved in just the formulation of a design concept. The human mind can best process information in small segments by going through organized steps. Working in flat 2D projections, such as plan views, and elevations is one way to concentrate the amount of information to be processed at a given stage in the design process.

However, an architectural space does not exist only in flat plan or elevation view. Sooner or later, you need to consider an architectural space in 3D, and the sooner the better. Do not fixate on the 2D. The trick is to know when that "sooner" stage has arrived. It has already arrived when you have even a few design elements and you need to consider what effect they may have on each other in the third dimension.

A bank teller counter, for example, is not just a fixture in plan view. There are a number of 3D factors involved. A customer stands in front and a cashier is behind the counter. There is interaction between them. Whether this interaction is direct and personal or through some high-security barrier affects the amount of space to allot for each teller station, the ceiling height of that area, and the tactile quality of surfaces and materials. The list goes on, and all of the attributes constitute a part of the total volumetric design concept of the building. And a building is, above all, a three-dimensional object.

To build any solid model, whether in reality or on the computer, you have to be able to see your creations in 3D. A computer can display in 3D as soon as enough parameters are given. In many ways, it actually can see better than the human eye. As alluded to earlier, one cannot see very complex forms totally, and human nature sometimes weeds out what it does not want to see. A computer does not lie; it shows all.

AutoCAD can display 3D models in wireframe or with hidden lines removed. It provides easy access to 3D views at predetermined viewpoints or through options where you can set the viewpoint. For realistic 3D views, you have to display your design in perspective views. AutoCAD provides this capability through the **3D Dynamic View** command.

This chapter discusses the display modes and details the steps to generate perspective views, using the bank interiors created in the tutorials.

VIEWING SOLID MODELS

Solid forms on the computer may be shown as wireframe drawings or as drawings with hidden lines removed. A wireframe drawing takes less time to display and regenerate, as it depicts solid objects by showing only their boundary outlines. Each side of a box, for example, is delineated by four lines. The area within the boundary formed by these lines is shown as a void, not a solid. That is, any object in the box and the outline of the other sides, can be seen. It is akin to making a box with thin copper wires, where the wires delineate the outlines of the edges of the box. Hence, the term wireframe.

Hidden-line-removed algorithms require more computational power and time, depending, of course, on the complexity of your design. Objects that are created as solids are shown with their faces opaque, hiding any objects lying behind them and, in turn, being hidden by objects in front. For realistic views and for checking on the accuracy of your drawing, however, you have to be able to display in a hidden-line mode.

AutoCAD allows you to display your design in the current drawing screen with hidden lines removed through the **Tools> Hide** command.

Once you have set up a view to your satisfaction, you can simply invoke the **Hide** command, then press the RMB. The screen will become blank while AutoCAD calculates the geometry involved. When it is done, the image will reappear with hidden lines removed. That is all there is to it.

System Variables. There are some system variables you can tweak. They affect the way AutoCAD displays solid objects. These are accessed through **Options> Sys Var**. Access the system variable by typing in its name.

Dispsilh   Controls whether or not a silhouette of a curved object is displayed. A setting of 0 means no silhouette, while a setting of 1 means a silhouette is displayed.

Facetres   Sets the value for the number of facets a solid object has on its curved surfaces. The initial value is set at 0.5; however, you have a range of 0.01 to 10. The higher the value, the smoother the appearance in Hide or Render. It also takes longer to generate.

Isolines   Sets the number of lines to represent each face of a solid object for visualization purposes. The initial value is 4. There is a range of values between 0 and 2047. The higher the value setting, the more solid the object appears, but the longer it takes to generate in Hide and Render.

See also 3Dface, Surftab1, Surftab2, Surfu, and Surfv.

DISPLAYING IN 3D VIEWPOINTS

In **View> 3D Viewpoint Presets**, you can obtain axonometric views such as plan, front left right, and back views. There are preset isometric views from the SW, SE, NW, and NE, looking toward the center of the drawing field.

The **View> 3D Viewpoint> Rotate** option allows you to set your own viewpoints via a compass and vertical angle indicator.

In **View> 3D Viewpoint>Tripod**, the figures of a tripod and a flattened globe allow you to dynamically choose a viewpoint.

View> 3D Viewpoint> Vector is an option that allows you to specify a viewpoint by typing in its coordinates.

See Chapter 3 for more details on 3D Viewpoints.

The 3D Viewpoint options create views that are based on a z-axis that remains vertical. While you can rotate around the z-axis or move up and down, or in and out from it, the views appear mechanical and not very realistic.

3D DYNAMIC VIEW

To generate realistic 3D perspective views, you have to use **View> 3D Dynamic View**, select *DVIEW* from the side menu, or enter *dview* through the keyboard.

While you may begin in any view, it is easier to specify various points if your drawing is set in plan view, zoomed to include the area you want included in the perspective.

Upon entering the DVIEW command, there are three choices you can make: (1) The most commonly used is to select objects, then use the options list. (2) You can select objects first, then pick points to set the direction and magnitude angles to create an orthographic 3D view. (3) Instead of picking objects, you may press the RMB to call up a special drawing of a prototype cottage with which you can set camera, target, and other criteria from the options list. Following is a more complete description of these choices:

1. On entering **3D Dynamic View**, you are prompted to select objects. At this stage, you only need to select enough objects so that a preview of the perspective will show the character of the view without all the objects showing. The number of objects affects the regeneration time while you are in DVIEW. After the various criteria are set up for a perspective view and you exit DVIEW, all the objects in your drawing will be regenerated in the perspective.

a. When you have selected objects, press the RMB. The following options list (abbreviated) is displayed on the Command Prompt Line:

CA/TA/D/PO/PA/Z/TW/CL/H/O/U/<eXit>:

Meanings of DVIEW options are explained here. In the next section, details will be given on how to set up naturalistic perspective views.

CAmera   Use this option to set the camera position. You are first prompted to set a camera to a target angle that is rotated up or down from the present setting. Then you are prompted for a rotation sideways from the camera to the target. These prompts are set through sliding scales on the screen. The sliders are quite sensitive, so move in small increments.

TArget   The target point is the point you (the camera) are looking at. With one end fixed on the camera, the first prompt is for a rotation up or down. The second prompt is used to set a new angle to the camera in a sideways motion.

Distance   This option allows you to set the target to camera distance. Changing the distance does not change the height of either the target or the camera. Therefore, if you shorten the distance, the angular relationship between target and camera will become more acute, while lengthening the distance flattens out the angle. Entering Distance also puts the image into perspective view. At this stage, you can refine the view by using any of the options, such as CA or TA.

POints   In this option, you first specify the camera location, then you are prompted to enter the target point. Do not forget to enter the height of the target and camera locations (z values.) See note below.

PAn   You can pan the camera, that is, slide the viewport, laterally or vertically by selecting a starting point and a second point.

Zoom   Without moving the camera, you can change the focal length of the camera lens by using the Zoom option. The default focal length is 50mm. You select a new lens setting by using the sliding scale or by entering on the keyboard.

TWist   You can twist the camera while pivoted on the target point. The dynamic movement of the image after you enter Twist is somewhat disorienting, due largely to the sensitivity of the sliding scales.

CLip   You can clip off extraneous objects that may be in the way of a clear view of the drawing. You can clip in front or in back of the target point by specifying Front or Back and a distance from the target.

Hide   You can put the current screen view into a hidden-line-removed image. With hidden lines removed, solid objects are displayed as solids with opaque surfaces. Use Hide to check on the accuracy of your drawings. An edge at the intersection of two objects may not be displayed. If you must have a visible edge, separate the objects by a small space.

Off   You can turn off a hiddens-line-removed image and return it to the wireframe mode.

Note: Once you have exited DVIEW, you can return a drawing to wireframe view by clicking on **View> Redraw**, or enter *Regen* on the keyboard.

Undo   Cancels the action of the last option.

<eXit>   Exits the DVIEW command.

Note that in this series of options in Dview, the running coordinates at the top of the Drawing Editor screen shows the coordinates of the cursor position, while the default <> brackets on the command line shows the current setting. If you pick a position with the mouse, you are entering the coordinates at the top. If you press Enter, you are entering the <default> value in the command line. Moreover, these coordinates only show x and y values, the z coordinate is assumed to be 0. With 3D views, you often need to add the height or z value. So use the x, y coordinates displayed for reference, but type in the desired x, y, and z coordinates.

b. If you select one of the options, you will be prompted for further input(s), then you will be returned to the options list.

2. Upon entering DVIEW, first select objects as noted above, then pick a point in your drawing with the pointing device. That point becomes the starting point from which you can move around the image, moving yourself (the camera) while focused on the target point. Then, specify the new camera position by:

a. Picking two points with the mouse, or

b. Entering two angles.

Pivoting on the target point, the starting point is rotated to the first angle coun terclockwise between 0 and 360. The second angle denotes the degree of magnitude and, therefore, how much closer or farther to set the viewpoint. A value of 0.5 would be half the current distance, while a value of 2 would set the new viewpoint at twice the distance.

If you are in plan view when you enter DVIEW, the plan will remain stationary, while 3D surfaces will change with the settings. If you are in a 3D view to start with, you will be manipulating in dynamic 3D space.

When you are done picking points, you are again returned to the options list, where you can choose to use any of them to refine the view or exit from the DVIEW command.

3. Upon entering DVIEW, instead of selecting objects, you can press Enter to invoke a special file that allows you to set target and camera positions around a sample model of a cottage. The model gives you a visual reference to set DVIEW points. You can enter coordinates for target and camera points or drag the cursor dynamically on the monitor screen and specify points with the mouse.

After picking a setting with the model cottage, press the RMB, and your drawing will be regenerated on the screen in the orientation you specified using the model cottage. You are returned to the options list, where you can choose to use any of them to set viewpoints, refine the view, or exit the command.

SETTING UP PERSPECTIVE VIEWS

Using the Points option in **View> 3D Dynamic View** is the best method to set up a drawing in perspective. This option allows you to specify camera and target points in a dynamic, interactive manner. But there are a number of caveats and criteria to consider.

1. Selecting objects.

Put your drawing in plan view and zoom in loosely on the area you want to include in your view. Have in mind, generally, where you want to set up a camera and what might be a focal point for the view.

Upon entering **View> 3D Dynamic View**, you are prompted to select objects. At this stage, selected objects are only for previewing while you are working in dynamic view. After all the parameters for a perspective view are set, the rest of the objects in your drawing will be regenerated unless you choose to have some of them clipped from the view. So select just enough objects to allow you to get a good sense of the space you want to see. Picking a lot of objects at this stage only slows down regeneration.

Use a crossing window to pick the major objects. In an interior view, you should include at least two or three walls that define the space.

2. After selecting objects, you are returned to the options list:

CA/TA/D/PO/PA/Z/TW/CL/H/O/U/<eXit>:

Enter *PO* to use the Points option.

a. In this option, the 1st point prompted for is the Target point.

By default, the target is set to the center of the viewing screen. Move the cursor to approximately the position you want to use as the focus of your 3D drawing. Round out the values of the x and y coordinates at the Status Bar at the top of the graphic screen. Determine a proper height to set the target point; this is the z coordinate. Enter the target point by *typing in* its x, y, z coordinates.

The target should be set at a height where you would normally look at that location. Vertically, do not select a target point exactly half way between the floor and ceiling, or the view may appear split in half. Do not select a target that is just off the floor, or you will get a view that is restricted to looking down on the space, without a broad view of its entirety. You may select a target that is higher than the camera, then you will get a view that looks up. This is especially true, if you have a multistory space.

b. The second (Points option) prompt asks for a Camera location.

Set the cursor at a point from which you are looking at the target. Follow the same procedure described above to determine the x, y, z coordinates for the camera point; that is, move the cursor to about where you want to stand and round out the coordinates shown in the Status Bar for the x and y positions. Choose a camera height that is approximately head high. For example, use a z value of 5′ to 6′6″, in a normal, standing view. Then enter the x, y, z values on the keyboard.

The line between the target and camera should not be perpendicular to the wa behind the target. This results in a one-point perspective view that is usually not very realistic. On the other hand, if the line between target and camera is too acute to the major wall, you will get a view that is unnaturally foreshortened with elements extremely exaggerated.

The best rule of thumb is to set a slightly off-centered target point and a camera position that is shifted no more than 15° to either side of the perpendicular.

3. On exiting the Points option, the drawing is put into a 3D orthographic view, where vertical elements are shown straight up and down and horizontal edges are displayed parallel horizontally without foreshortening.

And you are returned to the options list:

CA/TA/D/PO/PA/Z/TW/CL/H/O/U/<eXit>:

a. Enter *D* for the Distance option. The view changes into a three-point perspective view, which displays only those objects that were chosen at the start of the DVIEW command.

The Command Prompt line shows the distance as set by the target and camera locations in angled brackets: <value>. If you are satisfied with the perspective view in the screen, press Enter to accept the default distance. Your drawing will regenerate with all objects showing. However, you may wish to adjust the view by using the DVIEW options before pressing Enter.

There is a sliding scale across the top of the graphic screen. Put the cursor on the diamond-shaped icon and slide it laterally to increase or decrease the distance between camera and target points. As the heights of these points remain as set, the angle normal to the x-y plane will change as you alter the distance with the slider. The slider is quite sensitive, so move it in small increments. As you move the slider, the perspective view changes dynamically. When you are satisfied with the view, press the RMB (do not press Enter) to set the distance and exit to the DVIEW options list again.

4. Use any of the DVIEW options by typing in the capital letters, or press Enter to exit **3D Dynamic View** altogether.

Note: If you have objects that are in front of the target point, even if they are behind the camera point, or that you have clipped off, an impression of these objects may block your view when you invoke the Hide command or when you render the view. To overcome this, put the object(s) on a layer that is turned *off* and *frozen*. You may have to isolate these objects from others that are on the layer(s) that you do want to be visible by putting the unwanted objects on a temporary layer that can be turned off and frozen.

APPLIED PERSPECTIVE EXAMPLES

In this section, you can see how perspective views can be set up using the drawings created in the tutorials. Perspective views named with P1 prefixes are views of Tutorial 1, the customer waiting area. Those with P2 prefixes are of Tutorial 2, and so on.

Perspective View P1–1. Customer Waiting Area, View 1

The customer waiting area can be seen as a part of the two-story lobby space, and you can set up a view to look at the group of furnishings in the waiting area.

1. Open a copy of the *T1.dwg* file saved from the end of Tutorial 1. If necessary, set drawing to plan view by clicking **View> 3D Vp Presets> Plan view> World**.

Click on **View> Zoom> All**.

Insert copies of drawings *T1-chr.dwg*, *T1-tab.dwg*, and *T1-cab.dwg* into the customer waiting area. Use multiple copy to put a total of four chairs in the waiting area.

Put the lower exterior wall and column D2 onto a layer that is turned off and frozen.

2. Click on **View> 3D Dynamic View**.
Select objects: Use a crossing window to include all of the waiting area, rear wall, and the window wall.

This is a good view of the customer waiting area. Notice there are some ambiguities in the display of intersecting planes. All planes and surfaces will be displayed correctly in rendered views.

The list of options appears.
Enter *PO* (for Points).
The first prompt is TA. Enter *38',75',9'*.
The second prompt is CA. Enter *48',28',5'6*.

You are returned to the options list.
Enter *D* (for Distance).
For distance, enter *65'*.

You are again returned to the options list.
Enter *CL* (for Clip).
Enter *F* (for Front).
Enter *65'*.

On the monitor, you can see that objects more than 65' in front of the target point are clipped off.

3. When clipping is done, you are returned to the options list once more.
Enter *H* (for Hide).

The view will regenerate with hidden lines removed.

Exit the DVIEW command by entering *X* (for Exit).
All the objects that are not clipped off will be seen on the screen.

4. Click **View> Named View**.
In the **Named View** dialog box, click the New button.

Enter *P1–1*, then click the Save button.

File> Save the current drawing.

Perspective View P1–2. Customer Waiting Area, View 2

1. If you are continuing from the previous perspective view, return your drawing to the plan view, WCS, and zoom *All*.

If you are starting over, open a copy of the drawing *T1.dwg* saved from the end of Tutorial 1.

Insert copies of drawings *T1-chr.dwg*, *T1-tab.dwg*, and *T1-cab.dwg* into their respective places.

2. Click **View> 3D Dynamic View**.
Select all objects in the teller counter, the customer waiting area, the back wall, and the window wall.

From the DVIEW options list, enter *PO*.

Then enter the following values at the appropriate prompt:

TA: *34′,76′, 4′*
CA: *40′,55′,6′6*
D: *35′*
CL: *Front: 35′*

The large number of vertices in the polylines used to create the seat cushions causes the seats to appear black. Such surfaces will be displayed as smooth surfaces in AutoVision.

Enter *CL* again, then enter *B* (for Back).
You should enter a negative value to clip objects behind the target point. Try a value of *–7*.

Experiment with Distance, Pan, or Zoom to adjust the view.

3. Click **View> Named View**.
Name and save the view as *P1–2*.

File> Save the current drawing.

Perspective View P1–3. Customer Waiting Area, View 3

1. Continue from the previous exercise, or open a copy of *T1.dwg* saved from the end of Tutorial 1.

If necessary, insert copies of drawings *T1-chr.dwg*, *T1-tab.dwg*, and *T1-tab.dwg* into their respective places.

Put the lower exterior wall and column D2 onto a layer that is turned off and frozen.

2. Enter the following values at the appropriate prompts in **View> 3D Dynamic View> Points:**

TA: *34′,76′,9′6*
CA: *57′,29′,5′6*
D: *90′*
CL: *Front: 50′*

You are again returned to the options list.

Enter *Z* (for Zoom).
Enter *72* (mm)

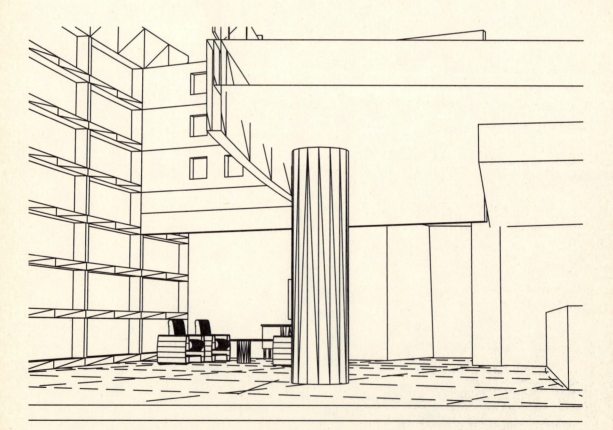

Shift the camera location to the left to avoid having the column lie squarely in the center of the view.

Experiment with different viewpoints by clipping distances, as well as Zoom, Pan, and Hide.

If you are still in a perspective view, but out of the DVIEW command, you can recall the DVIEW settings by clicking on **View> 3D Dynamic View** and selecting the objects visible on the screen with a crossing window. Enter *PO* to go into the Points option, then press the RMB to accept the defaults for target and camera points, as well as the distance setting. By accepting defaults, you are returned to the current settings.

3. Click **View> Named View**.
Name and save the view as *P1–3*.

File> Save the current drawing.

Perspective View P1–4. Customer Waiting Area, View 4

1. Continue from the previous exercise or open a copy of *T1.dwg* saved from the end of Tutorial 1.

If necessary, insert copies of drawings *T1-chr.dwg*, *T1-tab.dwg*, and *T1-cab.dwg* into their respective places.

2. Experiment with these settings of
View> 3D Dynamic View:

TA: *30′,70′,3′*
CA: *46′,32′,15′*
D: *42′*
CL> F: *20′*

This will be a view from the balcony. Try different settings of clipping front and back.

3. Click **View> Named View**.
Name and save the view as *P1–4*.

File> Save the current drawing.

A part of the wall next to the cabinet is cut off. Increasing the distance behind the back clipping plane will correct the view.

Perspective View P2–1. Conference Room, View 1

When setting up perspective views, the conference room presents a different set of problems. The room is quite narrow and small, so it is best to view the space by removing one of the walls. One scheme is to remove the northern exterior wall by freezing the layer containing the wall, so you will be looking down the depth of the room. Another may be to look through the double entry doors.

The first exercise in this section has you looking into the conference room through the window wall from the exterior.

1. Open a copy of the *T2.dwg* file saved from the end of Tutorial 2.

Click **View> Zoom> All**.

Insert copies of drawings *T2-cab.dwg*, *T2-tab.dwg*, and *T2-chr.dwg* into their respective places. Insert only one chair drawing, then copy it to the other places.

To make regeneration of the drawing faster, some elements of the upper part of the building were put on turned-off layers that were also frozen. This caused the ambiguous display of the upper part of this view. You can put some objects on thawed layers to adjust the realism of the view.

2. Click on **View> 3D Dynamic View**.
Select objects: Use a crossing window to include all of the conference room area, rear wall, and the window wall.

In the options list, enter *PO* (for Points).
Target point: *33',80',5'*
Camera point: *4',98',6'6*

You are returned to the options list.
Enter *D* (for Distance).
Enter *48'*
Now, you are in perspective mode.

If you press Enter on the keyboard, the <default value> will be accepted. You can use the slider to adjust the distance to about where you want the view to be, then click the LMB. The slider is very sensitive, so move it slowly. As you adjust the slider, the position of the cursor is reported on the status line at the top of the screen. When you have a satisfactory view, enter the distance according to the number reported on the status line, rounding it off to the nearest whole number.

3. Click **View> Named View**.
Name and save the current view as *P2–1*.

File> Save the current drawing.

Perspective View P2–2. Conference Room, View 2

This exercise generates a view of the conference room from the corridor, looking through the entry doors.

1. Continue from the previous exercise or open a copy of *T2.dwg* saved from the end of Tutorial 2.

If necessary, insert drawings *T2-cab.dwg*, *T2-tab.dwg*, and *T2-chr.dwg* into their respective places.

Turn off and freeze layer DPANE.

This close-up view was intended to show details of the conference table and chairs. However, the view is so close that not much spatial information was included. Try backingi up a bit with the Zoom option in the DVIEW command.

2. Click **View> 3D Dynamic View**.

Select objects: Use a crossing window to include all of the conference room area, rear wall, and the window wall.

In the list of options, enter *PO* (for Points).

TA: *22′,90′,4′6*

CA: *49′,79′,6′*

D: *31′*

Z: *40*

Some unwanted objects may hide your view unless you clip them off or freeze their layer(s).

3. When you are satisfied with the view, name and save it as *P2–2* under **View> Named View**.

File> Save the current drawing.

Perspective View P2–3. Conference Room, View 3

By freezing the layer on which the northern exterior wall resides, you can look into the conference room from the end without that wall blocking the view.

1. Continue from the previous exercise or open a copy of *T2.dwg* saved from the end of Tutorial 2.

If necessary, insert drawings *T2-cab.dwg, T2-tab.dwg,* and *T2-chr.dwg* into their respective places.

2. Click **Data> Layer**.
Turn off and freeze layers EXTWALL and DPANE.

In plan view, rotate the left (lower) door inwards 25°.

3. Click **View> 3D Dynamic View**.
Select objects: Use a crossing window to include all of the conference room area, rear wall, and the window wall.

Notice that the wall on the left and the floor slab were cut by the front clipping plane. It usually does not affect a view as long as the clipped objects are on or near the perimeter of the viewport where much of the view is not the main focus and will be faded out or cut off.

In the list of options, enter *PO* (for Points).

TA: *29′,80′,3′6*
CA: *34′,120′,6′*
D: *40′*

In the list of options, enter *CL* (for Clip).
Clip> Front: *16′*

4. Click **View> Named View**.
Name and save view as *P2–3*.

File> Save the current drawing.

Perspective View P2–4. Conference Room, View 4

This exercise generates a view of the conference room as if you are standing at the NW corner.

1. Continue from the previous exercise or open a copy of drawing *T2.dwg* from the end of Tutorial 2.

If necessary, insert drawings *T2-cab.dwg*, *T2-tab.dwg*, and *T2-chr.dwg* into their respective places.

2. Click **Data> Layer**.
Turn off and freeze layer EXTWALL

3. Click **View> 3D Dynamic View**.
Select objects: Use a crossing window to include all of the conference room area, rear wall, and the window wall.

In the list of options, enter *PO* (for Points).

You can assign a material to the object within the door frame. This object was created on the DPLANE layer, which was thawed and turned on in this view, causing the door to appear to have a solid material covering the frame.

TA: *33',80',4'*

CA: *23',100',6'6*

D: *41'*

CL> F: *24'*

PAN to left.

4. Click **View> Named View**.
Name and save this view as *P2–4*.

File> Save the current drawing.

Perspective View P3–1. Open Offices and Teller Counter, View 1

This exercise results in a view of the open office area from the vantage point of someone standing near the sit-down teller station.

1. Open a copy of drawing *T3.dwg* saved at the end of Tutorial 3.

Insert drawings *T3-cab.dwg*, *T3-chr.dwg*, *T3-wkn.dwg*, and *T3-xchr.dwg* into their respective places. Insert each drawing only once. Copy them to form other work station groupings and guest chairs.

2. Click **View> 3D Dynamic View**.
Select objects: Use a crossing window to include all of the conference room area, rear wall, and the window wall.

There is a lot of detail in the lower part of this view, but not much that is interesting on the top part. You can correct this by adding some large artwork on the back wall.

In the list of options, enter *PO* (for Points).

TA: *90′,27′,5′*
CA: *50′,54′,6′6*
D: *49′*
CL> F: *40′*

3. Click **View> Named View**.
Name and save the view as *P3–1*.

File> Save the current drawing.

Perspective view P3–2. Open Offices and Teller Counter, View 2

1. Continue from the previous exercise or open a copy of drawing *T3.dwg* saved at the end of Tutorial 3.

Insert *T3-chr.dwg* into the drawing, then copy it to make a total of two side chairs in front of the handicapped-accessible teller counter.

2. Click **View> 3D Dynamic View**.
Select objects: Use a crossing window to include all of the conference room area, rear wall, and the window wall.

In the list of options, enter *PO* (for Points).

TA: *65′,65′,5′*
CA: *40′,49′,6′*
D: *50′*
CL> F: *50′*

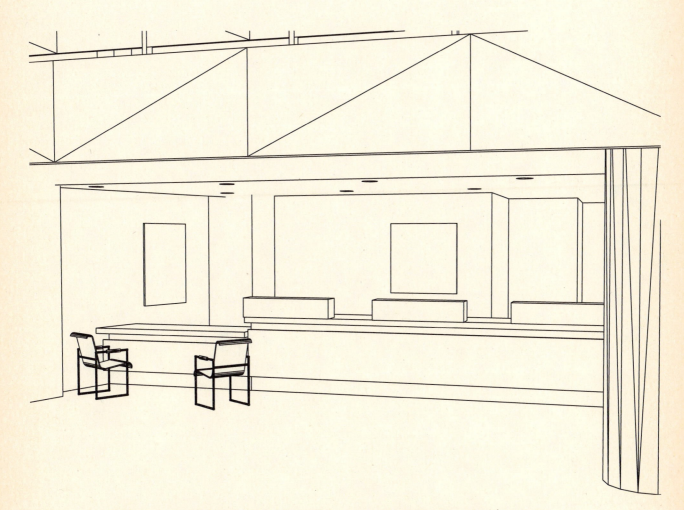

This is an interesting view of the teller counter area, but there is no indication that there is a two-story space where the viewer is standing.

If you want to see this view with hidden lines removed, turn off and freeze the layers that contain elements, such as the window wall, that are in line with the target point and camera point.

3. Click **View> Named View**.
Name and save the view as *P3–2*.

File> Save the current drawing.

Perspective View P3–3. Open Offices and Teller Counter, View 3

1. Continue from the previous exercise or open a copy of drawing *T3.dwg* saved at the end of Tutorial 3.

Insert drawings *T3-cab.dwg*, *T3-chr.dwg*, *T3-wkn.dwg*, and *T3-xchr.dwg* into their respective places, but insert only one copy of each drawing. Use copy and array to make other furniture pieces.

2. Click **View> 3D Dynamic View**.
Select objects: Use a crossing window to include all of the conference room area, rear wall, and the window wall.

In the list of options, enter *PO* (for Points).

TA: *56′,58′,4′*
CA: *100′,58′,5′*
D: *62′*
CL> F: *54′*

The generation of a hidden-lines-removed view from this angle takes some time due to the number and complexity of the 3D objects that are visible.

If you want to generate a hidden-line view, turn off and freeze the exterior wall that is in front of the viewer.

3. Click **View> Named View**.
Name and save the view as *P3–3*.

File> Save the current drawing.

Perspective View P3–4. Open Offices and Teller Counter, View 4

This exercise results in a view of the open office as seen from the side entrance.

1. Continue from the previous exercise or open a copy of drawing *T3.dwg* saved at the end of Tutorial 3.

Insert drawings *T3-cab.dwg*, *T3-chr.dwg*, *T3-wkn.dwg*, and *T3-xchr.dwg* into their respective places, but insert only one copy of each drawing. Use copy and array to make other furniture pieces.

2. Click **View> 3D Dynamic View**.
Select objects: Use a crossing window to include all of the conference room area, rear wall, and the window wall.

In the list of options, enter *PO* (for Points).

The corner of the teller counter hides too much of the office area from view.
Shift the camera to the right to get a better view.

TA: *74′,30′,4′*

CA: *32′,75′,6′6*

D: *74′*

CL> F: *74′*

If you want to generate a hidden-line view, turn off and freeze the exterior wall that is in front of the viewer.

3. Click **View> Named View**.
Name and save the view as *P3–4*.

File> Save the current drawing.

RENDERING WITH AUTOVISION

ABOUT RENDERING ARCHITECTURAL INTERIORS

A rendering of an architectural subject is a pictorial representation of the building or a part thereof. Architects normally show the exterior of a building, while an interior designer would most likely show its interior spaces. Typically, the view is in 3D, whether it is in some axonometric view or in perspective view. A perspective is either one-point or two-point, which is, in most cases, a more natural view. Usually, a rendering is used for formal presentations to clients, for public display, and/or for publicity.

There are no absolute standards for doing a rendering because, as in any art-form, the technique depends on the artist. Delineators or renderers of a building are often the designers of the building. And their skills in artistic expression vary with the individual. Just like architecture itself, certain trends and styles prevail for a time; they evolve and often reflect the society in which the designer lives.

Traditionally, watercolor has been the medium of choice for color renderings. Its subtle fluidity lends itself to expressing flowery details as well as flat surfaces. For those who prefer a harder medium, graphite and color pencils are often the media of choice. In recent times, the felt-tip marker, which combines flexibility with rigidity, has become very popular. Due to the fact that most markers are quick-drying, the user has to work rapidly. That saves time, which fits right into the tight schedule mentality of contemporary society.

Saving time, reducing tedious work, and making difficult tasks easily available to a wide segment of the population are, of course, the raisons d'être of computers and all the associated peripherals. There are numerous "paint" programs that can emulate drawing instruments from pencils to air brushes, markers to oil paints, and all kinds of surfaces, from canvas to fresco, with simulated textures and 3D shadows.

With the development of CAD for desktop computers, the capability to visualize one's design in solid 3D form has become commonplace. Even a rather basic, so-called "entry-level" desktop computer is powerful enough to generate pictures with realistic materials, user-defined lights, cast shadows, reflective surfaces, and so on, for the simulation of an interior space. Although the creation of a building in 3D can be time consuming, once created, the ability to look at the work from any angle, inside or out, and in color with realistic materials, is really quite amazing.

ESSENTIALS OF RENDERING WITH AUTOVISION

About AutoVision R2

Conserve System Resources.   Due to the need for conserving disk storage space and for faster regeneration, you should leave some of the lesser used entities on the CD-ROM, rather than installing them on your hard disk. Some of these entities are background and landscape image files that you do not often use. Read the *AutoVision User's Guide and Reference* to learn how to manage your system and its memory.

AutoCAD Drawings.   Read the *AutoVision User's Guide* carefully; it discusses rendering thoroughly. You should be aware of the differences in drawing clockwise and counterclockwise, as far as the "normalcy" of 3D surfaces is concerned. Other topics in Chapters 3, 4, and 5 of the *User's Guide* are also important.

AutoVision renders AutoCAD R13 drawings, in particular 3D solids and surfaces. If you have converted R12 AME solids, there may be problems, as R13 uses ACIS solids. The two systems are completely different.

AutoVision Installation and Access.   Check with your dealer or Autodesk to find out about installing AutoVision. You may be told to install the software in a directory other than what is written in the *User's Guide*. Once installed, AutoVision is an integral part of AutoCAD R13. It runs within AutoCAD. Its commands and features are found under **Tools> AutoVision** in the pull-down menu. At the first call of an AutoVision command after installation, or an abnormal termination, you are prompted to enter the Authorization Code. So you should first acquire this code from the Autodesk before attempting to use AutoVision. Then, have it handy for reentering later.

Rendering Attempts.   Rendering is best learned by trial and lots of errors. Remember to insert copies of drawing files, as abnormal termination may occur, perhaps even frequently. Once a file is corrupted, it is usually no longer usable for further rendering attempts.

Abnormal Termination.   After an abnormal termination of AutoVision, you may get a Page Fault message. AutoCAD will give up, and your drawing will be corrupted, even if you use the Recover option to reload the drawing. It is better to start over with a new copy of the drawing. This is the reason for advocating the use of copies of drawings to render. You will not lose your original drawing in case there are problems.

If you tried to load AutoVision, you may find that the Command Line returns a message that AutoVis or ARX will not load. Find and delete the *Autovis.pwd* file in the d:/AV/AVDOS directory. Restart AutoVision in the usual way. You will have to reenter the Authorization Code when you are so prompted.

Problems of this type are usually due to the lack of space for swap files. You should check that you have set the environment correctly in the Autoexec start-up file, and that swap files are set to a TEMP directory that has ample room. AutoVision requires a lot of space to swap files when it runs out of RAM. The amount of space may be 100MB or more, and it has to be contiguous space. You may have to organize your hard drive, remove unneeded files, clean up all temporary files, and run the Scandisk and Defragmentation programs under DOS to make enough contiguous free space for the renderer. Defragment with the Full Optimization option, and do it frequently. If you are not at a standalone computer, consult the network manager. See the configuration and installation instructions in both the AutoCAD and AutoVision manuals for further details.

Relevant AutoCAD Commands

As AutoVision works within AutoCAD, many regular AutoCAD commands are used in conjunction with the rendering software. You can, of course, create new objects or modify the geometry already created. Before you begin rendering, you can edit the drawing with the AutoCAD commands in the normal way. You can use various viewpoints to facilitate picking objects to which to assign AutoVision materials. At times, it may help to isolate objects by turning off surrounding layers.

Some other AutoCAD commands relating to the rendering process are:

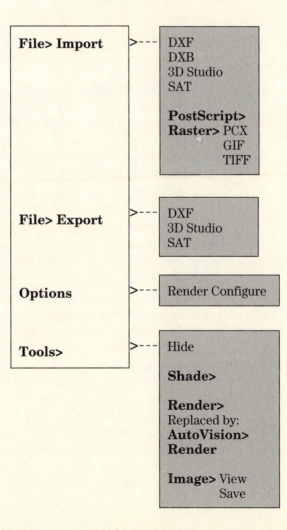

File> Import >---
DXF
DXB
3D Studio
SAT

PostScript>
Raster> PCX
GIF
TIFF

File> Export >---
DXF
3D Studio
SAT

Options >---
Render Configure

Tools> >---
Hide

Shade>

Render>
Replaced by:
AutoVision>
Render

Image> View
Save

AutoVision Commands

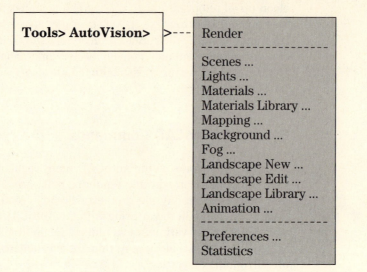

Tools> AutoVision> >---

Render

Scenes ...
Lights ...
Materials ...
Materials Library ...
Mapping ...
Background ...
Fog ...
Landscape New ...
Landscape Edit ...
Landscape Library ...
Animation ...

Preferences ...
Statistics

Tools> AutoVision> Render

In the **Render** dialog box, there are various controls you can set.

1. **Rendering Type**

    a. **AutoCAD Render.** This is the lowest quality renderer of the three types available. It renders with smooth shading, colors, and such surface characteristics as the degree of shine, but not shadows or bitmaps.

    b. **AutoVision.** This is the renderer to use in most cases. It renders with volumetric shadows, bitmaps, and shadow mapping.

    c. **AutoVis Raytrace.** Raytraced renderings are the most realistic, as the renderer supports reflection, refraction, and other features. It is also the most time-consuming and computing-resource hungry.

2. **Scene to Render.** The default scene to render is the *Current View*. If other scenes are already created, their names appear in this box. Highlight the one you want to render.

3. **Scene Palette.** AutoCAD uses a 256-color palette. Your rendering driver may use another color palette. It is necessary to resolve the differences by a process known as Palette Mapping. In this box, a pulldown list shows three options:

    a. **Best View/No Fold.** This is the option of choice because it gives views with the best color representation. However, colors in the rest of the display monitor may be affected, as the renderer uses its own palette and the AutoCAD palette for rendering, while the rest of the display uses only the AutoCAD colors.

    b. **Best Map/Fold.** In this option, renderings use the rendering palette and AutoCAD screen colors. (The palettes are "folded" into one another.) Rendered colors may be affected, but the monitor screen colors are not.

c. Fixed ACAD Map. Rendering and display use only the AutoCAD palette, resulting in no change between viewports and the rest of the display. As there may be differences between the two palettes, the rendered view may be affected by using the AutoCAD palette only.

4. **Destination**

   a. A rendering may be sent to the current AutoCAD **Viewport**, to a **File**, or to a preconfigured **Hardcopy** device such as a printer.

   b. Sub Sampling. This is used to tell AutoVision to render only a percentage of the total amount of pixels, thus making rendering faster. The resolution of the rendering will be affected; therefore, use this option for a quick check of your drawing. See Query for Selection and Crop Window later in this section for other preview options.

   c. The Current **Width, Height**, and **Colors**, in pixels and bits, are reflected in these data blocks.

   d. More Options. There are more destination file types available including GIF, X11, PBM, BMP, TGA, PCX, SUN, and FITS.

5. **Render Options.** Select an option by clicking on the white square next to the option name. An X appears in the square, indicating that it has been selected.

   a. Smooth Shading. This is used to soften the edges between faces in a rendering.

   b. Apply Materials. Click it on to have materials applied to surfaces and objects. To define materials, see **Tools> AutoVision> Materials**.

   c. Shadows. Click it on to have the AutoVision or AutoVis Raytrace render display shadows in the rendering.

   d. Smoothing Angle. Use this to set the viewpoint-to-object edge angle. At a larger angle, the edge will be visible in the rendering. At smaller angle, the edge will be smooth.

   e. More Options. There are more options in each of the three renderers. See the *AutoVision User's Guide and Reference*.

6. **Background.** This sets background colors and/or scene. See **Tools> AutoVision> Background**.

7. **Fog/Depth Cue.** You can regulate the degree of opacity of a white or black color screen that simulates depth or distance in a background scene. See **Tools> AutoVision> Fog**.

8. **Query for Selection.** This option allows you to pick some objects for a sample or preview rendering. If this option is selected by clicking on the white square next to the name, when you click the Render button, you will be prompted to select objects to render. Select some objects either individually or by a crossing window, then press Enter or click the RMB. AutoVision will render only the selected objects.

9. **Crop Window.** You can also select a portion of the viewport to render. Use a window to define the render area. Only that area will be rendered; the rest of the display will not be shown. If both the Query and Crop Window buttons are checked, you will first be prompted to specify a window, then you will be able to select objects within the window.

10. **Render.** After setting parameters, click this button to begin the rendering process. You may terminate a rendering by pressing Ctrl+C. After rendering, return to the AutoCAD screen by pressing any key.

Tools> AutoVision> Scene

In the **Scene** dialog box, you can adjust the following controls:

1. **Scene.** This is a list of scenes already created. The default is *None*. Highlight the one you want, then click the OK button.

2. **New.** To create a new scene, click on this button to access the **New Scene** dialog box.

   a. **New Scene.** In this dialog box, there are the following additional controls:

      i. **Scene Name.** Enter a name for the scene.

      ii. **Views.** This is a list of all scenes in the drawing. The current one is marked by *Name*.

      iii. **Lights.** This is a list of all lights already created in the drawing. You may select no lights, all lights, or any of the existing lights. Select a light by highlighting its name and deselect it by click off the highlight.

      iv. **OK.** Click this button to return to the **Scene** dialog box.

3. **Modify.** Click this button to access the **Modify Scene** dialog box. Use this to make changes in the selection of lights of an existing scene.

4. **Delete.** Do NOT use this to turn off a scene as this option will delete the scene from your drawing entirely.

5. **OK.** Click this button to exit the **Scene** dialog box.

Tools> AutoVision> Lights

In the **Lights** dialog box, you can define and modify lights and you can set up the Ambient Light in the rendering.

1. **Lights.** This is a list of all the lights already created. Highlight one and you can modify or delete it.

2. **Ambient Light.** You can set Intensity by entering a value or by using the slider. Similarly, set a Color by its Red, Green, or Blue tints or by means of the Color Wheel. Notice that the color is updated in the sample area as you change the color of the Ambient Light.

3. **New**

   a. Before you define a new light, be sure that the box next to the New button shows the type of light you want to create. If not, scroll down the list and highlight the correct type of light, then click on the New button. The types of lights available are Point Light, Spotlight, and Distant Light.

   b. The **New (Point or Spot) Light** dialog box. For Point Light and Spotlight, the dialog boxes are about the same except for the differences noted below.

      i. **Light Name.** Enter the name of the new light.

      ii. **Intensity.** Set intensity by entering a value or use the slider.

      iii. **Color.** Set the Color by its RGB values or by use of the Color Wheel. Note that the Color is updated in the sample area.

      iv. **Attenuation.** This refers to the way light fades as the distance increases between it and the surface of the object it strikes. The choices are None, Inverse Linear (the default), and Inverse Square. Click on one of the white squares to select.

    v. **Shadows.** Click Shadows on or off. Use the **Shadows Options** dialog box to select among volumetric or raytraced shadows, adjust shadow map size, and set shadow softness. In addition, you can have shadows mapped to only a selected set of objects in the rendering. See **Tools> AutoVision> Render> Rendering Type.**

    vi. **Modify.** Click this button and you are temporarily returned to the AutoCAD screen.

If you are modifying a **Point Light**, the prompt on the Command Line is for the location of the light. Enter x, y, z coordinates or visually place the light in the drawing. If you use the latter method, do not forget to check that the light is in its proper height.

If you are modifying a **Spotlight**, the first prompt is for the Target position. This is the position at which the spotlight is aimed. Then you are prompted for the position of the light itself.

Press Enter or the RMB to return to the **New (Point of Spot) Light** dialog box.

c. The Modify **Distant Light** dialog box.

    i. Enter the **Name** of the Distant Light you want to modify.

    ii. Enter values for the **Intensity, Color**, and **Shadows** in a similar manner as in Modify Point Light or Spotlight.

    iii. **Azimuth** refers to the compass direction of the drawing in plan view. The default Azimuth is set so that North (N) is at the 12 o'clock position. If it is not, check the **North Location** indicator in the main **Light** dialog box. You may set the Azimuth to be oriented to the building site or any other reference by entering a value in the **North Location** box. The N symbol will rotate to point in the direction of the current setting.

The direction of the Distant Light is indicated by the line from the edge of the Azimuth circle to its center. From this reference line, an Azimuth is set by entering a value from 0 to +180° (counterclockwise) or from 0 to –180° (clockwise).

Altitude refers to the vector, usually downwards, from the Distant Light to the center of the view.

You can also set a Distant Light to represent the sun by using the **Sun Angle Calculator**. See the *AutoVision User's Guide and Reference.*

Tools> AutoVision> Materials

In this dialog box, you can attach and modify material objects in the drawing.

1. Materials List. Under this list are all the materials already imported into the drawing, whether you are using them or not. The default is *Global*, which, if used, forces all objects in the drawing to take on the default AutoCAD materials and colors.

If there are no materials in this list, or if you want additional materials, click on the Materials Library button. See **Tools> AutoVision> Materials Library** below.

2. **Preview.** When a material is highlighted, you can click this button to get a view of what the material looks like. The material may be mapped onto a cube, a cylinder, or a sphere.

3. **Modify.** There are four dialog boxes associated with this option, because there are four material types: **Standard** and three others known as **Template Materials:** Marble, Granite, and Wood. The currently selected material determines which dialog box appears. You can also click the New button to access the list of material types.

   In the modify dialog boxes, you can set Attributes, Color, and various mapping options. See the *AutoVision User's Guide and Reference*.

4. **Duplicate.** You can save a customized material under a new name by using the Duplicate button.

5. **Attach.** With a material highlighted in the Materials List, click this button to attach the material to objects in the drawing. You are temporarily returned to the AutoCAD drawing screen. There you can click on the edge of objects to which to attach a material. When you are done, press Enter to return to the **Materials** dialog box.

6. **Detach.** This is the reverse of Attach. It is accessed and used in the same manner.

Tools> AutoVision> Materials Library

Use the **Materials Library** dialog box to load and transfer materials to Materials so they can be attached to the drawing.

1. **Materials List.** The default material listed is *Global*. If no material is attached to an object, when you render, the Global or characteristics defined by AutoCAD layers and ACI colors will be rendered.

   The Materials List shows all the materials already imported and ready to be selected for use. See the previous section on **Tools> AutoVision> Materials**.

   You may delete unattached materials by clicking the Purge button. And you can **Save** the current materials list as separate materials file.

   If there are no materials, or if you want to load another material, go to the Library List window.

2. **Library List.** The list shows the materials available loaded from the default materials library file: *Autovis.mli*. Highlight a material and you can press **Preview** to take a look at it. Press **Save** to save the list in a materials file of another name. Press **Open** to access other materials libraries.

3. **Import.** A highlighted material in the **Materials Library** may be moved to the Materials List by clicking on the Import button.

4. **Export.** A highlighted material in the Materials List may be moved to the **Materials Library** by clicking on the Export button.

5. **Delete.** Highlighted materials in the Materials List and **Materials Library** may be deleted with this button, even if the materials are attached to objects in the drawing.

Tools> AutoVision> Mapping

2D images in file formats BMP, GIF, JPEG, TGA, and TIFF can be projected or mapped onto surfaces of 3D objects to be rendered.

There are four types of maps: texture, reflection, opacity, and bump.

Mapping uses a U, V, and W coordinate system, so you can assign mapping coordinates to a surface independent of the x, y, and z coordinates in the drawing.

There are four types of projection: Planar, Cylindrical, Spherical, and Solid.

Each projection has its own dialog box where you can adjust coordinates, offset, scaling, and other attributes. See the *AutoVision User's Guide and Reference* for more comprehensive descriptions of mapping parameters and usage.

Tools> AutoVision> Background

The **Background** dialog box can also be accessed through **Tools> AutoVision> Render**.

1. **Background Types.** You can set up the background to show solid colors, gradient colors, or an image saved in one of the supported file formats.

   a. **Solid.** Click on this button to render the background in a single color. The Top Color button controls the color of a solid background. In this option, you can also use the current AutoCAD background color in the rendering. See **Colors** below.

   b. **Gradient.** A gradient background can have two or three colors. The colors may be sharply defined or diffused. See **Environment** below.

   c. **Image.** An image file stored in BMP, GIF, JPG, PCX, or TIF format can be used as a background. You may additionally set visual effects such as reflections in the background. See **Environment** below.

   d. **Merge.** You can use a GIF, TIFF, or TGA image as a background. First load the graphic file under **View> Image> View**. In the **Background** dialog box, click on the Merge button. Click on the Query for Selection box, and then pick objects to render.

2. **Colors.** Set up colors for the background using RGB values, ACI, or the Color Wheel. Soften adjoining colors by setting the middle color to bridge those of the top and the bottom colors, using the Color and the Height controls.

   a. **Top.** If you are using a solid background, set its color by activating this button.

   b. **Middle.** If you are using a two-color background, this color becomes the lower half. Set Height to 0 to use a two-color background.

   c. **Bottom.** In a three-color background, this is the lowest tier of color.

Tools> AutoVision> Fog

If you insert landscape objects or an outdoor scene into the background of a rendering, depth perception is enhanced by using the Fog/Depth Cue feature of AutoVision. The heavier the fog in the background, the more distant objects in the background appear to be.

In the **Fog/Depth Cue** dialog box, you can enter values or use the sliders to adjust the color of the apparent fog. There are fields in which you can enter values to set amount of fog in the near and far distance, as well as for the percentages of apparent fog in the background: 0 = no fog; 1 = total fog.

Tools> AutoVision> Landscape New

Keep in mind that inserting bitmap images can vastly increase the amount of time it takes to render the drawing. It may also demand system resources that are beyond the limits of this book. Therefore, use landscape objects judiciously.

The **Landscape New** dialog box is similar to the one in **Edit Landscape**.

1. **Library.** In this area, the name of the current library file is shown, followed by a list of the available landscape objects in a window box. Highlight an object to select it.
2. **Preview.** This is the standard Preview button. Click on it to see a preview of the current landscape object.
3. **Geometry.** You can set a preference for the way the landscape object will be displayed in the rendering.
   a. **Single Face.** Use this option if the object is, or may be seen as, flat or flattened. A sign on a wall comes to mind, but so does a tree in the far background or shrouded in fog.
   b. **Crossing Face.** This option gives a realistic 3D character, especially in raytraced shadows. However, it takes longer to render.
   c. **View Aligned.** An object in this option is oriented to the current view. If you are running an animation sequence, you would not want this option on a 3D object such as a tree because that tree will always look the same as you move the camera around the scene.
4. **Height.** Use the slider in this window or click on the top grip of a landscape object when you are in the AutoCAD graphic screen to change its height.
5. **Position.** This button puts you in the AutoCAD graphics screen and Drawing Editor. Use the normal AutoCAD commands to reposition and/or change the attributes of landscape objects. Use the top grip of a landscape object to change its height, the corner grips to change its scale, and the bottom grip to move the object.

Tools> AutoVision> Landscape Edit

The **Edit Landscape** command uses a dialog box that has the same controls as the one used under **Landscape New**.

Once entered, you are prompted to select an object, then you can edit the geometry parameters, change positions, and adjust the height of the object.

Tools> AutoVision> Landscape Library

In the **Landscape Library** dialog box there is a list of the available objects in the current library file. You can also modify, delete, or make it a new landscape object.

See the *AutoVision User's Guide and Reference* for details on using landscape objects.

Tools> AutoVision> Animate

In **Animate**, you have the capability to define a sequence of views to form a "movie" or a walk-through of your building. Essentially, **Animate** follows a film script and displays a series of still renderings in formats such as GIF or TGA. You can determine the number of views in the sequence, and you can base a sequence on a certain timeframe that may include sun angle calculations through the course of a day, a few days, or even a year.

However, **Animate** requires a great deal of memory space and computing power. It may well be outside of the context of this book. So if you really want to try out animation, consult the *AutoVision User's Guide and Reference* and the *Autodesk Animation Players* manuals.

Basic Rendering Process

The basic considerations and process for rendering are as follows:

A. Prior to Rendering

    1. LOAD DRAWINGS

       Load space drawing

       Insert furnishings

    2. CHECK VIEW

       Recall saved view or set perspective view

    3. MATERIALS

       Materials Library

       Specify materials

       Attach materials

    4. LIGHTS

       Create lights; adjust settings and positions

    5. CHECK LIGHTS

       Check specifications and positions

    6. SAVE DRAWING

B. Rendering Process for R1

    1. SET VIEW

       Check and correct view

    2. PREVIEW RENDERING

       Render partial view

    3. MODIFY

       Background

    4. RENDER

       Perform full rendering

    5. SAVE IMAGE

       Save rendering to output file

Tutorial R1. Customer Waiting Area

This rendering tutorial uses the perspective view *P1* from Chapter 5.

In this tutorial the following rendering features will be stressed:

Materials: Materials library
Check and change default settings
Basic materials assignment

Lights and lighting: Create distant light
Modify lights (attributes, location)
Adjust shadows

Display: Background: Merge image
Crop rendering window
Select objects for rendering

Render: Render type: AutoVision

Output: Save image

A. Prior to Rendering

1. LOAD DRAWINGS

a. Open a copy of drawing *T1. dwg.*
This drawing was saved at the end of Tutorial 1 and was used to set up perspective views in Chapter 5.
Name the copy as *T1-r.dwg.*

b. In plan view, click on **Draw> Insert> File**.
Insert drawings *T1-cab.dwg*, *T1-tab.dwg*, and *T1-chr.dwg*.

Use **Construct> Copy** and the Multiple option to make three more copies of the chair and place them as in the illustration.

2. CHECK VIEW

a. Check your drawing by clicking on **View> Named View> P1-1**.

b. If you did not save the view, Click **View> 3D Dynamic View** and set up a perspective view using the following points:

Use the Points option in 3D dynamic view.

Target point: *38′,75′,9′*

Camera point: *48′,28′,5′6*

Distance: *65′*

Clip> Front: *65′*

You may have to adjust the view by Clip, Distance, Pan, and/or another click of the Points option.

Be sure to put the lower left exterior wall and column D-2 on a turned off and frozen layer, otherwise their "shadow" will block the perspective view.

When you have a satisfactory view, be sure it is saved as **View> Named View> P1-1**.

3. MATERIALS

Before you can render, you should attach materials to the objects and place lights in the drawing. As you cannot perform some viewing and selection commands while your drawing is in perspective, you have to change the view to nonperspective. To better select objects for materials attachment, switch between plan and isometric views. You may have to turn layers on and off to isolate objects that are close to one another.

Note: The first time AutoVision is used after installation you have to enter the Authorization Code supplied by Autodesk. Keep this number handy. If you run into problems during rendering, you may have to enter it again. See the section on Abnormal termination in this chapter.

Click **Tools> AutoVision> Materials**.
The **Materials** dialog box appears.

In the Materials List box, *GLOBAL* should be present and highlighted. This means that any object not specifically assigned a material will have the default AutoCAD materials and layer colors.

If materials are already loaded, they will appear under the *GLOBAL* item. To attach a material, see the following Steps b and c.

If you want to modify the material or add more materials, see the following section.

Materials Library

If there are no materials, or if you need other materials, click the Materials Library button.

a. The dialog box is replaced by the **Materials Library** dialog box.

A list of materials already loaded appears on the left, and the available items in the **Materials Library** appear on the right. You select a material by highlighting its name in the library. You can see what it looks like by clicking on the Preview button.

If you click Import, that item is made a part of the Materials List on the left.

For rendering R1, import the following materials into the Materials List:

    BEIGE MATTE
    GRAY BLUE PAINT
    GRAY MARBLE
    LIGHT WOOD TILE
    WHITE PLASTIC 2S

When you have finished selecting and modifying materials from the Library, click on the OK button.

b. You are returned to the **Materials** dialog box.

    Highlight: BEIGE MATTE
    Click on Modify> and adjust Color:
        R = *0.90*
        G = *0.90*
        B = *0.79*

    Highlight: WHITE PLASTIC 2S
    Click on Modify> and adjust Color:
        R = *0.85*
        G = *0.92*
        B = *0.92*

Now, highlight a material, then click on Attach.

The dialog box disappears so you can use the AutoCAD graphics screen. Select an object to receive the chosen material by clicking on its edge. Select as many objects as you wish. You may have to reposition your viewpoint or zoom in and out to be able to pick on the edges of the objects. If you select a wrong object, enter *R* (for Remove), then pick the object to be removed from the selection set. Press the RMB when you are done selecting objects.

For this tutorial, materials are attached as follows:

Name of Material	Attach to
BEIGE MATTE	First and second floor walls, exterior walls, roof, and columns
GRAY BLUE PAINT	Window wall, rail and bulkhead, and chair seat
GRAY MARBLE	Painting above sideboard and floor slab
LIGHT WOOD TILE	Teller counter, sideboard and legs, and coffee table base
WHITE PLASTIC 2S	Upper, lower, and dropped ceilings; floor plane; chair body; sideboard top; coffee table top; and second floor window pane

When you have attached a material to all the objects on the list, press the RMB to return to the **Materials** dialog box.

Highlight another material and attach it to other objects in the drawing.

Notice you can also remove a material assignment by using the Detach button.

To keep it simple in this first rendering exercise, materials such as GRAY MARBLE will not be mapped onto the objects. See Rendering R3 for mapping instructions.

When all the objects have materials attached, click OK to exit the **Materials** command. You are returned to the Command Prompt.

4. LIGHTS

Rendering with many lights and complex shadows prolongs the process considerably. In the context of this book, where we are using rather basic equipment, it is prudent to attempt rendering a scene such as the current view by using only a distant light to simulate sunlight, and to use the Ambient light feature to create an overall lighting level for the interior of the building.

Click on **Tools> AutoVision> Lights**.

Distant Light

a. To define a distant light, highlight Distant Light in the **Lights** dialog box and click on the New button.

The other steps to follow for creating a new distant light are the same as those for creating a new point or spotlight.

For rendering R1, create one distant light.

Name: *D1*
Intensity: *0.60*
Color: R = *0.94*
        G = *0.90*
        B = *0.87*
Shadows: *On*
Azimuth: *−115* (from North = 0)
Altitude: 65

The azimuth angle is measured from the North Position (N) in the compass diagram in the Azimuth area. Clockwise directions are positive value angles, while negative values indicate counterclockwise directions.

You can use the Sun Angle Calculator to determine the direction of a distant light to simulate sunlight at a specified time of day and at a specific geographical location.

Azimuth and altitude values indicate the direction and height of a distant light, which emits straight, or nonconverging rays. A distant light's intensity and color affect the character of the light, as does its attenuation.

Ambient Light

b. Click OK to return to the **Lights** dialog box.

In the **Lights** dialog box, set Ambient Light so that the rendering shows a warm, late afternoon ambiance. Use the color and intensity controls to make changes.

For R1, set Ambient Light as follows:

Intensity: *0.60*
Color: R = *0.92*
        G = *0.89*
        B = *0.77*

Point Light

c. Make sure Point Light is showing in the **Lights** dialog box; click the New button.

In the **New Point Light** dialog box, set:

Light Name: *P1*
Intensity: *350*
Color: R = *0.91*
        G = *0.88*
        B = *0.81*
Shadow: *On*
Modify> Light location: *40',59',23'*
Click OK to return to the **Lights** dialog box.

Spot Light

d. With Spot Light highlighted, click on New.

In the **New Spot Light** dialog box, set:

Light Name: *S1*
Intensity: *340*
Color: R = *0.90*
         G = *0.92*
         B = *0.89*
Hot Spot: *30*
Falloff: *75*
Shadow: *Off*
Modify: Target location: *31',76',3'*
          Light location: *37',74',9'6*

Click OK to return to the **Lights** dialog box.

e. Click the OK button in the **Lights** dialog box, and you exit the Lights command to be returned to the AutoCAD graphic screen.

5. CHECK LIGHTS

Check the drawing to see that the lights are properly positioned and at the correct heights. Do this in plan view, WCS, and in **View> 3D Viewport Presets> Front**, to get a frontal view to check that there are no light symbols at any incorrect elevations.

6. SAVE DRAWING

Now that all the physical attributes have been specified, save your drawing. Then use Save As and another drawing name (such as, *T1-r1.dwg*), so that you will use the second drawing to render.

B. Rendering Process for R1

Rendering is a trial-and-error effort. Many things can happen during rendering that can cause an abnormal termination of the AutoCAD session. This is especially true if you are using rendering for the first time, or if you are rendering a particular drawing for the first time. Mistakes may have been made in drawing AutoCAD objects. Upon entering rendering, AutoVision goes through the AutoCAD geometry. If there are problems with the drawing, they may be detected at this stage. After updating the geometry, AutoVision calculates rendering parameters such as shadows. Since we are talking about using basic computer equipment, there may be insufficient space to swap files. For more information, see Abnormal Termination earlier in this chapter.

1. SET VIEW

Click on **View> Named View**.
Restore the view: *P1-1*

2. PREVIEW RENDER

Click on **Tools> AutoVision> Render**.

Now that you have defined some of the parameters, run a partial rendering to see what some of the objects in the drawing look like. It is more than likely that adjustments have to be made to the materials, lights, and other factors.

Some of the rendering parameters can be left set at default values for this first rendering trial. But be sure that the **Apply Materials** box is checked or the renderer will render with default AutoCAD materials and colors.

Render Parameters

In the **Render** dialog box, make sure of the following settings:

>   Rendering Type: *AutoVision*
>   Scene to Render: *Current Viewport*
>   Screen Palette: *Best Map/No Fold*
>
>   Rendering Options: Checked with X
>   **X**   Smooth Shading
>   **X**   Apply Materials
>   **X**   Shadows
>   Smoothing Angle: *45*
>
>   Destination: *Viewport*
>   Sub Sampling: *1:1 (Best)*
>
>   **X**   Query For Selection
>   **X**   Crop Window

Preview Rendering

When all the parameters are set, press Render.

a. The dialog box will disappear and you are asked to select points to open a window. For the first point, select a lower left corner; then select an upper right corner to include an area in the center of the view.

After setting the window, you are prompted to pick objects to be rendered. You can use a crossing window that covers the area defined in the step above to select objects to render. You can also individually pick objects to render.

After AutoVision calculates the geometry involved in hiding surfaces and the shadow volumes, the portions of the selected objects that lie within the window will be rendered. The status of the display is reported on the Command Prompt Line. Rendering is displayed one horizontal line at a time.

You may terminate a rendering by entering Ctrl+C.

b. After a rendering has been displayed, examine it closely and make notes about changes you may want to make. You can return to the graphic screen by typing *Regen*.

This trial rendering indicates that the spotlights are set to shine too brightly on the picture wall. Increase the difference between the Hot Spot and Falloff setting of the spotlights.

3. MODIFY RENDERING

You can modify the materials, lights, and/or any of the other parameters.

Background

In this rendering, a solid background will be used. To do this, click on **Tools> AutoVision> Background**, or select Background in the **Render** dialog box.

Click on the Solid button at the top of the **Background** dialog box. Use Color Controls to set:

> R = *0.96*
> G = *0.93*
> B = *0.96*

Check the color in the Top box or in Preview.
Click the OK button to exit **Background**.

Lights

> Light: D1. Modify the following:
>> Azimuth: *–150*
>> Altitude: *50*
>> Intensity: *95*

> Light: P1. Modify the following:
>> Intensity to: *120*

> Light S1. Modify the following:
>> Intensity: *100*
>> Color: R = *0.94*
>> Falloff: *80*
>> Shadow: *Off*

New Light

Add new lights:

> New Point Light Name: *P2*
> Intensity: *100*
> Color: R = *0.99*
>> G = *0.94*
>> B = *0.87*
> Shadow: *Off*
> Modify> Light location: *49',55',10'6*
> Click OK to return to the **Lights** dialog box.

New Point Light Name: *P3*

Intensity: *100*

Color: R = *1.00*

          G = *0.90*

          B = *0.86*

Shadow: *Off*

Modify> Light location: *55',36',10'6*

Click OK to return to the **Lights** dialog box.

New Spot Light Name: *S2.*

Intensity: *85*

Color: R = *0.95*

          G = *0.87*

          B = *0.78*

Hot Spot: *32*

Falloff: *88*

Shadow: *Off*

Modify: Target location: *45',88'*

          Light location: *46',94',10'6*

Click OK to return to the **Lights** dialog box.

4. RENDER

1. Click on **Tools> AutoVision> Render**.

   After you have modified the rendering parameters, you are ready to generate a full rendering.

a. In the **Render** dialog box, make sure of the following settings:

   Rendering Type: *AutoVision*

   Scene to Render: *Current Viewport*

   Screen Palette: *Best Map/No Fold*

   Rendering Options: Checked with X

   X   Smooth Shading

   X   Apply Materials

   X   Shadows

   Smoothing Angle: *45*

   Destination: *Viewport*

   Sub Sampling: *1:1 (Best)*

   Query For Selection (not checked).

   Crop Window (not checked).

b. Click on the Render button.
   AutoCAD will render the full screen image.

5. SAVE IMAGE

When the rendering is done, you can save the image. In this tutorial, save the view in a GIF file.

> In **Tools> Image> Save**.
>
> Name your file.
>
> Click on the GIF button.
>
> Click the OK button.

Your rendering is saved in the CompuServ GIF format.

Review of Rendering Process for R1

A. Prior to Rendering R2

1. LOAD DRAWINGS. *T1.dwg, T1-cab.dwg, T1-tab.dwg, T1-chr.dwg.*
2. CHECK VIEW. View: *P1-1*
3. MATERIALS. Materials Library, specify and attach materials.
4. LIGHTS. Create and place: Distant, Point, and Spot Lights.
5. CHECK LIGHTS.
6. SAVE DRAWING. SaveAs: T1-r1.dwg.

B. Rendering Process for R1

1. SET VIEW. View: *P1-1*
2. PREVIEW RENDERING. Rendering parameters.
3. MODIFY. Background, lights; add new lights.
4. RENDER. Final rendering parameters.
5. SAVE IMAGE. GIF file.

Using the Marble material without Mapping on the floor creates a carpet-like effect.

Tutorial R2. Conference Room

This rendering tutorial uses the perspective view *P2-3* from Chapter 5.

Some of the rendering features stressed in the previous tutorial will be used in this tutorial. In addition, this tutorial uses the following features.

Lights and lighting: Point lights, Spot lights
Display: Scenes
                                   Background Image display
                                   Fog/Depth Cue
Render   AutoVision renderer

A. Prior to Rendering R2

1. LOAD DRAWINGS

a. Open drawing *T2. dwg*.

Note: This should be a copy of the original drawing. If you do not have a copy, make one and then use the copy for rendering.

While in plan view, open the lower door by rotating it 35° into the room. Freeze and turn off layers 3DEXTWALL and DPANE.

2. CHECK VIEW

a. Check your drawing by clicking on **View> Named View**. Restore the view *P2-3*, saved from Chapter 5.

b. If you did not save the view, Click **View> 3D Dynamic View**, and set up a perspective view using the following points:

Use the Points option in **3D Dynamic View**.

Target point: *29',80',3'6"*

Camera point: *34',120',6'*

Enter *D* (for Distance) to put view in perspective mode.

Distance: *40'*

Clip> Front: *18'*

You may have to adjust the view by Clip, Distance, Pan, and/or another click of the Points option. When you have a satisfactory view, be sure it is saved as **View> Named View> *P2-3***.

c. Prior to being able to render realistically, you have to attach materials and place lights in the drawing. Switch between nonperspective viewpoints while selecting objects. Use AutoCAD commands such as Move and Copy to place lights.

To begin, set view to SE Isometric.

Note: The use of rendering parameters already described in the previous tutorial will not be repeated. Only new uses are detailed here.

3. IMPORT FILES

At plan view, click on **Draw> Insert> File**.

Insert drawing *T2-cab.dwg*.

Insertion point: *0,0*

Repeat Import to insert *T2-chr.dwg* and *T2-tab.dwg*. Insert only one chair, then copy and rotate the others into place. There are five conference chairs in this scene.

4. MATERIALS LIBRARY

Tools> AutoVision> Materials Library

a. In the **Library List** box, highlight the following materials one at a time, click Import to load each into the Materials List.

    BEIGE MATTE
    CHROME GIFMAP
    GRAY BLUE PAINT
    GRAY MARBLE
    GRAY MATTE
    WHITE PLASTIC 2S
    WOOD - WHITE ASH

For now, just leave the selected materials in their default attributes. Later you can modify them by changing their colors and so on.

b. Click the OK button to exit **Materials Library**.

5. MATERIALS

Tools> AutoVision> Materials

The names of the materials you just imported should appear under the Materials List.

Highlight one and click the Attach button. On the AutoCAD graphic screen, pick the object(s) as listed in the following chart:

Material	Attach to
BEIGE MATTE	Left and far walls and ceiling
CHROME GIFMAP	Chair and table, bases only
GRAY BLUE PAINT	Entry doors, except pulls, and chair cushions
GRAY MARBLE	Floor slab and table top
GRAY MATTE	Window wall and chair body
WHITE PLASTIC 2S	Ceiling panels and marker board in cabinet
WOOD - WHITE ASH	Door pulls and cabinets

6. LIGHTS

Tools> AutoVision> Lights

a. In the **Lights** dialog box, set the following:

Ambient color: R = *0.95*

G = *0.86*

B = *0.77*

Intensity: *0.40*

Distant Light

b. Highlight **Distant Light** in the light type box and click the New button.

In the **New Distant Light** dialog box, enter values as in the following list, leaving other parameters set at default values.

Name of distant light: *D1*

Intensity: *0.75*

Color: R = *0.97*

G = *0.88*

B = *0.79*

Shadow: *On*

Azimuth: *–53*

Altitude: *50*

Spot Lights

c. Highlight **Spot Light** in the light type box and click the New button.

In the **New Spot Light** dialog box, enter values as in the following list, leaving other parameters set at default values.

Name of spot light: *S1*

Intensity: *170*

Color: R = *0.94*

G = *0.88*

B = *0.86*

Hot Spot: *45*

Falloff: *65*

Shadow: *Off*

Modify: Target point: *30′9,86′,0*

Light location: *33′,81′,9′9″*

Name of spot light: *S2*

Intensity: *170*

Color: R = *0.94*

            G = *0.88*

            B = *0.86*

Hot Spot: *30*

Falloff: *65*

Shadow: *On*

Modify: Target point: *29′8,87′,0*

           Light location: *26′8,81′,9′*

Name of spot light: *S3*

Intensity: *130*

Color: R = *0.94*

            G = *0.88*

            B = *0.86*

Hot Spot: *30*

Falloff: *50*

Shadow: *On*

Modify: Target point: *31′8,80′,0*

           Light location: *30′,81′,9′9*

Name of spot light: *S4*

Intensity: *160*

Color: R = *0.85*

            G = *0.87*

            B = *0.86*

Hot Spot: *25*

Falloff: *75*

Shadow: *On*

Modify: Target point: *27′9,91′,0*

           Light location: *25′,96′,9′*

Name of spot light: *S5*

Intensity: *170*

Color: R = *0.86*

            G = *0.80*

            B = *0.81*

Hot Spot: *44*

Falloff: *120*

Shadow: *Off*

Modify: Target point: *33′,88′6,0*

           Light location: *35′,96′,9′9*

7. CHECK LIGHTS

Use the regular AutoCAD Drawing Editor to check the positions of the lights already specified. If any of them are out of place, use Copy, Move, and Erase to place the lights in their proper places. Note that lights S1 and S5 have their shadows turned *Off*.

8. SCENE

a. When you are satisfied with the drawing, click **Tools> AutoVision> Scene**.

> Name in the **New Scene** box: *R2-S1*
> In the Views list, highlight: *P2-3*
>
> Highlight lights: *D1*, *S1*, *S3*, and *S5*.
> Click the OK button.

b. You can create other scenes in which you turn lights on/off. Here is how to do it:

> Click on **Tools> Render> Scene**.
> Name in **New Scene** box: *R2-S2*
> In the View list, highlight: *P2-3*
> In the Lights list, highlight: *D1*, *S2*, and *S4*
>
> This scene will not be rendered in this book, but you can try it on your own.
> When you render, be sure the Scene you want is highlighted in the **Scene to Render** box.

c. Click the OK button and you are returned to the **Scenes** dialog box.
> Check to see that *R2-S1* appears in the **Scene to Render** box.
> Click OK to return to the Command Prompt.

B. Rendering Process for R2

Now that the drawing has been given materials and lights for rendering, save the current drawing.

Then click **File> Save As**.
Name the drawing to save as *T2-rnd.dwg*

The current drawing is saved under the new name. Use this copy to render. If you are unsuccessful in rendering, you should abandon this copy of the drawing. Reload *T2.dwg* and start over.

1. SET VIEW

Switch to the previously named perspective view.

View> Named View.
Restore view: *P2-3*

2. PREVIEW RENDER

Click on **Tools> AutoVision> Render**.

Render Parameters

In the **Render** dialog box, make sure of the following settings:

>Rendering Type: *AutoVision*
>Scene to Render: *R2-S1*
>Screen Palette: *Best Map/No Fold*
>
>Rendering Options: Checked with X
>**X**   Smooth Shading
>**X**   Apply Materials
>**X**   Shadows
>Smoothing Angle: *45*
>
>Destination: *Viewport*
>Sub Sampling: *1:1 (Best)*
>**X**   Query For Selection
>   Crop Window (not checked)

Preview Rendering

When all the parameters are set, press Render.

a. The dialog box will disappear and you are asked to select objects for a preview rendering. Note that with this method, lighting and shadows may not be the same as in a full rendering, since some of the lights may not be included in the selection set.

b. AutoVision will first organize the geometry in the drawing, then it will calculate shadows. The rendering will generate one line at a time. If you do not like the way the rendering is coming out, or if you can see that it will be a bad picture, you can stop the rendering by entering Ctrl+C.

When it is done, examine the partial rendering. Enter *Regen* to return to the AutoCAD graphics screen and the Drawing Editor.

3. MODIFY RENDERING

You may modify materials, lights, and/or any of the other parameters.

Background

Use **Tools> AutoVision> Background**.

Click on the Image button, then click on the Find File button at the bottom of the dialog box.

This rendering was created by using the Select Objects rather than the Crop Window option, hence only some objects are rendered. However, enough of the picture has emerged for you to check on the settings for lights, materials, and other elements.

Scroll down the list of drives and directories until you find AV\AVDOS\SAM-PLES\BIGLAKE.TGA. Highlight it and click the OK button.

Note: This scene of a lake with trees and mountains will be displayed only during rendering.

Fog/Depth Cue

Click on **Tools> AutoVision> Fog**.

Set color to a pale white by setting:

R = *0.93*

G = *0.93*

B = *0.88*

Set Near Distance: *0*

Far Distance: *0.85*

Near Fog Percentage: *0*

Far Fog Percentage: *0.35*

Click on the Enable Fog and Apply Background buttons.

4. RENDER

1. Now you are ready to generate a full rendering.

Restore named view to *P2-3*.

Click on **Tools> AutoVision> Render**.

a. In the **Render** dialog box, make sure of the following settings:

Rendering Type: *AutoVision*

Scene to Render: *R2-S1*

Screen Palette: *Best Map/No Fold*

Rendering Options: Checked with X

X Smooth Shading

X Apply Materials

X Shadows

Smoothing Angle: *45*

Destination: *Viewport*

Sub Sampling: *1:1 (Best)*

Query For Selection (not checked)

Crop Window (not checked)

b. Click on the Render button.

Rendering takes time.

Gaps between the suspended ceiling panels cause strange shafts of light and shadows to appear in this view. To eliminate the spill of light, create vertical edges between the layers of ceiling panels.

5. SAVE IMAGE

You can save the rendering in a number of formats.

In **Tools> Image> Save**.
Name your file.
Click on the GIF button.
Press the OK button.

Your rendering is saved in the CompuServe GIF format. You can specify the drive to which you want the file to be saved, and you can also save it in TIFF and TGA formats.

Tutorial R3. Open Offices and Teller Counter Area

This rendering tutorial uses the perspective view *P3-2* from Chapter 5.

This tutorial will continue to use some of the features already used in previous rendering tutorials. It will introduce the following features:

Materials:	Transparency
	Landscape materials
	Mapping images
Lights and lighting:	New lighting attributes
	Shadow mapping
Display:	Image-saving formats
Render:	AutoVision Raytrace renderer

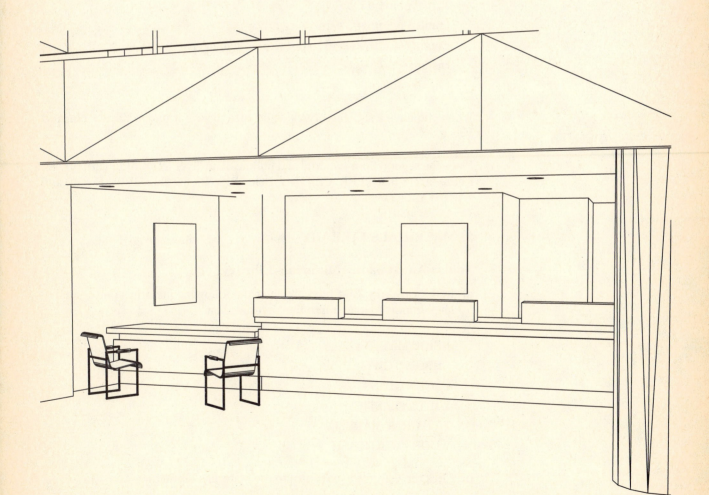

A. Prior to Rendering R3

1. LOAD DRAWINGS

a. Open drawing *T3. dwg*.

Note: This should be a copy of the original drawing. If you do not have a copy, make one and then use the copy for rendering. Use a distinct name for the copy, such as *T3-r.dwg*.

For the sake of containing the size of the rendering file, insert the minimum amount of furniture in this scene. Insert *T3-chr.dwg* and copy it to make up two guest chairs at the handicapped-accessible teller counter.

2. CHECK VIEW

a. Check your drawing by clicking on **View> Named View**; restore view *P3-2*.

b. If you did not save the view, Click **View> 3D Dynamic View**, and set up a perspective view using the following points:

    Use the Points option in 3D dynamic view.
    Target point: *65',65',5'*
    Camera point: *40',49',6'*
    Enter *D* (for Distance) to put view in perspective mode
    Distance: *50''*
    Clip> Front: *50'*

When you have a satisfactory view, be sure to save it under **View> Named View**, *P3-2*.

Place the second floor handrail and bulkhead on layer INTWALL. Turn off and freeze layers 3DUPPER, CEILING, COLGRID, EXTWALL, GRID, ROOF, and WINDWALL.

3. MATERIALS LIBRARY

Tools> AutoVision> Materials Library

a. In the **Library List** box, highlight the following materials one at a time; click Import to load it into the Materials List.

    BEIGE MATTE
    CHROME GIFMAP
    GREEN GLASS
    WHITE PLASTIC
    TILE GRAY MARBLE
    WOOD - WHITE ASH

b. Click the OK button to return to the Materials Library.

Highlight: GREEN GLASS and click on Modify.

In the **Modify Materials** dialog box:

Set Color: R = *0.72*

G = *0.76*

B = *0.69*

Click on the Transparency button.

Click OK to exit Materials Library.

4. MATERIALS

Tools> AutoVision> Materials

Under the Materials List, the names of the materials you just imported should appear.

Highlight one and click the Attach button. On the AutoCAD graphic screen, pick the object(s) as listed in the following chart:

Material	*Attach to*
BEIGE MATTE	Interior and back walls; teller counter (except front panels); and window wall.
CHROME GIFMAP	Chair armature.
GREEN GLASS	Teller counter front panels only.
WHITE PLASTIC	Ceiling objects, columns, and chair seats.
TILE GRAY MARBLE	Floor
WOOD - WHITE ASH	Teller counter (except front panel)

5. LIGHTS

In this rendering, the lighting level will be quite mellow and low.

Click on **Tools> AutoVision> Lights**.

In the **Lights** dialog box, set the following:

Ambient Light

Ambient Light:

Intensity: *0.15*

Color: R = *0.92*

G = *0.92*

B = *0.80*

Point Lights

a. With **Point Light** highlighted, click the New button.

In the **New Point Light** dialog box, enter values as in the following list, leaving other parameters set at default values.

> Name of point light: *P1*
> Intensity: *100*
> Color: R = *0.93*
>   G = *0.86*
>   B = *0.83*
> Shadow: *Off*
> Modify> Light location: *61'9,63',9'6*

> Name of point light: *P2*
> Intensity: *100*
> Color: R = *0.91*
>   G = *0.79*
>   B = *0.67*
> Shadow: *Off*
> Modify> Light location: *65'3",50'9",9'*

> Name of point light: *P3*
> Intensity: *250*
> Color: R = *0.92*
>   G = *0.82*
>   B = *0.75*
> Shadow: *Off*
> Modify> Light location: *48',50',10'6*

> Click: OK to return to the **Lights** dialog box.

> **Note:** If the names of any of these lights already exist, use different names.

Spot Lights

b. Highlight **Spot Light** in the light type box and click the New button.

In the **New Spot Light** dialog box, enter values as in the following list, leaving other parameters set at default values.

> Name of spot light: *S1*
> Intensity: *100*
> Color: R = *0.81*
>   G = *0.76*
>   B = *0.72*

Hot Spot: *30*

Falloff: *85*

Shadow: *Off*

Modify: Target point: *56',71'6",3'*

  Light location: *60',69',9'6"*

Name of spot light: *S2*

Intensity: *225*

Color; R = *0.77*

  G = *0.82*

  B = *0.87*

Hot Spot: *44*

Falloff: *90*

Shadow: *Off*

Modify: Target point: *67',61'9,3'*

  Light location: *63'6",56'9",9'6"*

Name of spot light: *S3*

Intensity: *120*

Color: R = *0.91*

  G = *0.83*

  B = *0.75*

Hot Spot: *45*

Falloff: *75*

Shadow: *On*

Modify: Target point: *58',54'6",0*

  Light location: *57'8",52',9'*

Name of spot light: *S4*

Intensity: *225*

Color: R = *0.87*

  G = *0.89*

  B = *0.83*

Hot Spot: *15*

Falloff: *80*

Shadow: *Off*

Modify: Target point: *51',66',0*

  Light location: *52'3", 70', 9'6"*

6. CHECK LIGHTS

In regular AutoCAD Drawing Editor, check the positions of the lights. If any of them are out of place, use **Modify> Move** to place the lights in their proper places.

A quick check shows that the spotlight on the picture is too strong.

B. Rendering Process for R3

Now that the drawing has been given materials and lights for rendering, switch back to the previously saved perspective view.

1. SET VIEW

View> Named View> *P3-2.*

2. PREVIEW RENDER

Click on **Tools> AutoVision> Render**.

Render Parameters

In the **Render** dialog box, make sure of the following settings:

> Rendering Type: *AutoVision Raytrace*
> Scene to Render: *Current Viewport*
> Screen Palette: *Best Map/No Fold*
>
> Rendering Options: Checked with X
> **X**   Smooth Shading
> **X**   Apply Materials
> **X**   Shadows
> Smoothing Angle: *45*
>
> Destination: *Viewport*
> Sub Sampling: 1:1 (Best)
>
> **X**   Query For Selection
> **X**   Crop Window

Preview Rendering

When all the parameters are set, press Render.

a. Use a window to define the area you want rendered, then individually pick objects to be rendered.

b. After rendering, examine the partial rendering. Enter *Regen* to return to the AutoCAD graphics screen and the Drawing Editor.

Another check shows that the ambient light over the back counter is low, while the spotlight on the back wall is too strong.

3. MODIFY RENDERING

You may then modify the materials, lights, and/or any of the other parameters.

Materials

> Click on **Tools> AutoVision> Materials**.
> Highlight BEIGE MATTE.
> Change its Color to: R = *0.85*
>   G = *0.73*
>   B = *0.62*.

Lights

Click on **Tools> AutoVision> Lights**.
In the **Lights** dialog box, change the Intensity of the Ambient Light to *0.35*.

Landscape

Click on **Tools> AutoVision> Landscape New**.

The **New Landscape** dialog box is similar to that of the **Materials** dialog box. You can designate a landscape object from the Landscape Library and insert it into your drawing. For this tutorial, select WANDERING YEW. Its height defaults at 20 (in the current drawing units, that is 20″.) Change it to *80*, and insert it next to column C-2. Do this plan view, WCS.

Opacity File

Each Landscape Object must have a corresponding Opacity File. The name of this file is usually similar to the object file, but prefixed or suffixed by the letter "O." Enter the name of an object's opacity file in the Opacity File field.

4. TRIAL RENDER

1. Click on **Tools> AutoVision> Render**.

a. In the **Render** dialog box, set the following:

> Rendering Type: *AutoVision*
> Scene to Render: *Current View*
> Screen Palette: *Best Map/No Fold*
>
> Rendering Options: Checked with X
> **X**   Smooth Shading
> **X**   Apply Materials
> **X**   Shadows
> Smoothing Angle: *45*

Destination: *Viewport*

Sub Sampling: *1:1 (Best)*

Query For Selection (not checked)

Crop Window (not checked)

b. Click on the Render button.

Rendering takes time. This one took 1.5 hours using a 486DX2-66 computer with 20MB RAM.

This view shows that the overall ambient light is too low. It also shows that a planter is needed under the plant, and that the images mapped onto the picture frames should be properly aligned.

5. REFINEMENT

a. In the **Lights** dialog box, set the Intensity of the Ambient Light to *0.50*.

b. In plan view, WCS, add a solid cylinder with a 12″ radius and 24″ height. Be sure that the entire cylinder is placed away from the Wandering Yew landscape object, toward the teller counter.

Mapping

c. Click on **Tools> AutoVision> Mapping**.

Select object: Pick the painting at the end of the handicapped-accessible teller counter.

> Leave Projection set at Planar.
> Click on Adjust Coordinates.
> Click the button next to WCS, XZ plane.
> Click OK to exit the command.

Invoke the mapping command again and select the painting at the back wall. Set its coordinate orientation to WCS, YZ plane.

d. If your system is equipped with a CD-ROM drive and you have the AutoVision Sampler CD, insert it into the drive.

Images as Materials to Be Mapped

Set view to **View> 3D Viewport Presets> SW Isometric** and zoom in on the teller counter area.

Tools> AutoVision> Materials
Click on the New button.
Name: *Dash*
Click on the **Find File** dialog box.

Click on the CD-ROM drive and highlight the file under AutoVision Map/ *Dash.tga*.

Click the OK button to return to the **Materials** dialog box.

Now Click Attach and pick the painting at the end of the handicapped-accessible teller counter. The picture called Dash is now attached to the painting.

Similarly, attach the file AutoVision/*Ape.tga* to the painting on the back wall.

Note: You can copy the above files into your computer if you do not have CD-ROM capability.

New Landscape Object

Set view to **View> 3D Viewport Presets> Plan View, World**.

Click on **Tools> AutoVision> Landscape New**.
In the **Find File** box scroll the CD-ROM to SCHREIBER> WOMAN02.TGA. Enter that into the New Object field.

In the CD-ROM, find the file \OPACITY\A_WOMAN02.TGA. Click on or enter that name in the Opacity File field.

Set the height at 65″.

Position the object behind the teller counter next to the handicapped-accessible desk.

Click OK to exit the **New Landscape** dialog box.

Modify Landscape Object with Grips

In SW Isometric view, zoom in on the new object. Click on **Options> Grips**. Check On to enable.

Click the LMB on the new landscape object symbol. Grips appear on the triangular symbol. Click the LMB again on the left base corner grip of the symbol. Now an options list is displayed on the Command Prompt Line, and Scale is set as the default. Enter @–12,0 (@x,y coordinates). This action causes the object to be scaled out in all directions.

In AutoVision Landscape objects, the top grip is used for changing heights, while the middle base grip is used to change positions and rotation (if the view is set to be oriented to the Viewport). The corner grips on the triangular symbol are used for scaling.

Use the middle base grip to move the symbol some 24″ in the negative Z direction. You may feel that this particular image of a woman needs other modifications in order to be rendered correctly.

6. FINAL RENDERING

After you have made the necessary adjustments to the rendering parameters, you are ready to generate a final rendering.

1. Click on **Tools> AutoVision> Render**.
a. In the **Render** dialog box, make sure of the following settings:

Rendering Type: *AutoVision*
Scene to Render: *Current View*
Screen Palette: *Best Map/No Fold*

Rendering Options: Checked with X
X Smooth Shading
X Apply Materials

X Shadows

Smoothing Angle: *45*

Destination: *Viewport*

Sub Sampling: *1:1 (Best)*

Query For Selection (not checked)

Crop Window (not checked)

b. Click on the Render button.

Some of the AutoCAD image files, such as the one of the woman behind the counter in this rendering, are not very detailed.

7. SAVE IMAGE

You can save the rendering in a number of formats.

> In **Tools> Image> Save**.
> Name your file.
> Click on the GIF button.
> Press the OK button.

Your rendering is saved in the CompuServe GIF format. You can also save it in TIFF and TGA formats; however, a GIF file is usually smaller, and there are many versions of TIFF readers, raising the possibility of problems in reading this version of TIFF files.

OUTPUT AND SUMMARY

ABOUT OUTPUT AND OUTPUT DEVICES

Now that you have created CAD objects and rendered them, what can you do to preserve the drawings and images? Much depends on the nature of your working environment and the audience for your work. In the tutorials, you have already seen how images can be saved in electronic format. They may be displayed by using various graphic file viewers, such as VGASHOW that is on the R13 CD-ROM disk. Electronic images and line drawings saved as *.plt* files may also be printed out in black and white, or in color on laser printers.

Line drawings saved as *.dwg* files are often plotted on plotters, which come in different sizes and plot with various media. AutoCAD supports many types of printers and plotters. See the *AutoCAD Release 13 Installation Guide* for a list of supported devices.

The Extended Output section of this chapter describes details on setting up drawings and working with viewports in modelspace and in paperspace.

If you are in school, you probably do not have to worry about setting up output devices. Those are already installed in your institution and, hopefully, running properly. If you are working in a design firm, there may be output devices in house and, again hopefully, have enough power to let you generate drawings and renderings. You should consult your instructor or the system manager if you have any problems with printing or plotting.

In any case, you need to know some things about output formats and output devices.

OUTPUT WORK TO THE DISPLAY MONITOR

The basic method to show the results of your work is to have the drawings and renderings displayed on the computer terminal at which you work. You can configure AutoCAD to draw and render on a single screen, or you can input data on one screen and display the graphics on another. See the *AutoCAD Release 13 Installation Guide* for detailed information on single- and dual-screen setup.

The type of graphics driver and the resolution and color capabilities of the monitor are key considerations when you are dealing with graphics display. Even though the context of this book makes it necessary to consider basic equipment, it is much more satisfying to be able to see your renderings in full color and with fine picture definition. So, if you have any choice at all, opt for a graphics display system that gives you the best picture.

The features that relate to output of pictures on the monitor are found in the Tools category.

Tools> Image> Save

Rendered images may be saved and viewed under this command. Files may be preserved in GIF, TGA, or TIF file formats. Of these, the TIF or TIFF format is perhaps the least favored for the simple reason that there are a lot of versions of TIFF encoding software out there, making it very possible that your *tif* file may not be readable by others, or that you cannot read someone else's file. On the Command Prompt, Saveimg is the command to enter to save or make an image. To view a file, enter Replay on the Command Prompt.

Tools> Slide> Save

AutoCAD saves the current view in ASCII form, which can then be recalled by the **Tools> Slide> View** command. Slide files cannot be plotted, nor can objects in them be edited. The commands can also be accessed on the Command Prompt by the Mslide (to make slide) and Vslide (to view a slide) commands.

Options> Sys Var

Some system variables affect the way objects, particularly 3D objects,, are displayed on the monitor. See the *AutoCAD Command Reference*, *User's Guide*, and the *Installation* manuals for information on the following system variables.

Facetres	Ltscale
Maxactvp	Plinegen
Pfacemax	Riaspect
Ribackg	Riedge
Rigamut	Rigrey
Rithresh	Shadedge
Splframe	Surftab1
Surftab2	Surfu
Surfv	Viewmode

You can save drawing and rendered images to a file, which can then be displayed or used in other applications. Some of the commonly used commands relating to output to files are listed here as they appear in the pulldown menus.

Output to a Plot File

The setting up of prints or plots in the **Plot Configuration** dialog box will be discussed in the following section. Here only the Plot to File option will be mentioned.

Click on **File> Print** to display the **Plot Configuration** dialog box. After setting the other plotting parameters, such as Device, Paper size, and so on, click on the Plot to File box. A name/drive list box comes up in which you can specify the name of the plot file and the drive where you want to save the file. The default file extension is *.plt*. This type of file can then be printed out on printers and plotters.

File> Export> PostScript

You can save drawings in Adobe Encapsulated PostScript or EPS format and then use them in applications that can incorporate such files. Remember, though, this file format can result in very large files. Compacting a file into binary form may not make a file small enough to fit on a high-density diskette. You may have to resort to a removable storage device to transport the drawing to another computer.

File> Export> DXF

The Drawing Exchange File (*.dxf*) in ASCII and its companion *.dxb* format in binary form are files that can be read by other CAD software, display utilities, or as Object Linking and Embedding (OLE) in Windows applications.

When you click on this option, you are returned to the AutoCAD graphics screen where you can select objects to be saved to the file. You are then asked if you want to save the entities as objects (DXF format) or in binary (DXB format); in each case, you can specify the degree of fineness or precision in which to save the drawing. The finer the setting, of course, the larger the file, but *.dxf* and *.dxb* files are generally smaller than the original *.dwg* files.

File> Export> 3DS

AutoCAD objects and renderings can be exported to be read by the 3D Studio programs. In the dialog box of this command, you have to define smoothing, welding, and division method prior to exporting to 3DS.

File> Export> SAT

3D objects are exported in *.sat* ASCII files in ASCII format.

File> Export> STL

AutoCAD objects are made ready for use by stereolithography software for extrusion of scaled models of, typically, machine parts and industrial products.

OUTPUT TO PRINT OR PLOT

One of the most often used forms of hardcopy output is a print or a plot of the drawing. Traditionally, copies of drawings are made by a wet chemical bath process, as in blueprints, or some dry chemical process on light-sensitive paper. The electronic age brought on plotters and printers. While plotters tend to use ink pens that draw lines on paper much like a human drafter, printers use electrostatic and/or laser technology to reproduce drawings done on the computer. There are raster plotters, but most plotters plot vector or line drawings. Printers, on the other hand, can generate grayscale pictures as well as full-color, near-photographic images. The major limitation in printers is that they produce small, letter-size copies. There are some large-format printers, but they run into the tens of thousands of dollars. Plotters can be rather expensive too, but more of them can handle construction drawings for the architectural design professions.

Plot Configuration Dialog Box

Clicking on **File> Print** brings up the **Plot Configuration** dialog box.

1. **Device and Default Information.** The name of the current device is shown at the upper left-hand corner. Click on the Device button to display a list of previously configured output devices. Highlight a name to select another device.

   To load a plotter or printer, exit the Print command and go through the menu in **Options> Configure**. See the *AutoCAD Installation and Configuration Manual* for detailed information.

2. **Paper Size and Orientation.** You may select Inches or Millimeters as the basis for plotting units. And you can use standard-sized paper or user-defined sizes for plots and prints.

3. **Pen Parameters.** Pen point sizes and colors may be assigned by layer or universally in this area of the **Plot Configuration** dialog box. Using different pens and colors is possible, of course, only if the plotter is capable of doing so.

4. **Scale, Rotate and Origin.** At the upper left-hand corner of this area, either MM or Inches is displayed as the default measurement unit. If Inches is the standard unit, then Plot Inches = Drawing Units is shown. In the box under each label, you can enter the units. Think of it as your normal scale notation. For example: $\frac{1}{4}'' = 1'$ or $\frac{1}{8}'' = 1'$. Note that the Drawing Unit defaults to display $1''$, so be sure to overwrite it to the correct notation.

   You can simply plot to fit the paper by clicking on the Scale to Fit box.

5. **Additional Parameters.** In this area, you can set the plot to plot the Display, Extents, Limits, View, or Window. The latter two are only available if you are plotting from modelspace.

You can specify the plot to Hide Lines, Adjust Area Fill. Click Plot to File and you can specify the name of a plot file (with a *.plt* extension), which can be saved on a disk for later plotting.

6. **Preview.** You may elect to see your plot partially or in full. Click on either of the choices and then click Preview to see the plot.

7. **OK.** Click this button to exit the **Plot Configuration** dialog box and return to the AutoCAD command prompt. You have to press Enter to plot or Stop to ready your plotter.

There is a large variety of printers and plotters on the market. Make sure your devices are set up properly before attempting to send a drawing to plot or print.

Printing in Modelspace

In AutoCAD, there is modelspace and paperspace. Generally, you work with a 2D or 3D model in modelspace, but print or plot what is displayed on the monitor in paperspace. In modelspace, you work with creating and manipulating the model or data base, while in paperspace, you set up the format and information that is aligned with a output print or plot. The terms *print* and *plot* are used interchangeably in this chapter.

Print: Scale to Fit

If you do not need to do a sheet layout (if you do not have a title block or a border around your drawing, for example), then you do not have to use paperspace. You can send your drawing out to print in modelspace. This is often the case when you have, say, a 3D view of a building that you want printed out at no particular scale, just to fit the printout paper. The process of setting up such a print is as follows.

First, be sure that your printer or plotter can handle the size of paper to fit a scaled output of your drawing. If not, you will have to change the scale of your drawing (specify "Scale to Fit" in the **Plot Configuration** dialog box) or get a new printer. Second, set the view to plot at Display. You may also set view to Extents, or Limits.

Text is usually drawn in plan view, however, so if you are printing a 3D view of your creation, any text will be shown aligned with the floor plane. If you want the text to be aligned with the printed sheet, then you should put the text and plot in paperspace. More details on this aspect are in the following section.

If you have text in your drawing, be sure to set the height(s) to be scaled to the output print. That is, if you want a block of text to be, say, ½″ high on the final paper, and you are printing in a scale of ¼″ = 1′–0″, then you should set the text height at 24″, since 2′ at ½″ scale plots out to be ½″ high.

Printing in Scale in Modelspace

To print a drawing in scale without a paperspace sheet layout, do the following:

Use **View> Zoom> Window** to display all the objects you want to plot, or click **View> Zoom> All** to display the entire drawing.

Click on **File> Print**.

In the **Plot Configuration** dialog box, type in *25 = 12* in the appropriate fields. This example assumes that you are using a ¼″ = 1′–0″ scale. Other scales are entered similarly. Notice that you can mix decimal and fraction notations when entering distance values. You do not have to use the (″) mark either, as AutoCAD assumes the basic unit to be an inch, since you have specified Architectural in **Data> Units**. But if you mean to specify 1′ instead of 12(″), be sure that the Scale field on the right displays 1′, because it defaults to 1″.

Displaying with Zoom X/XP

To display a drawing so that it will print in scale, highlight DISPLAY/ZOOM on the side menu.

Select objects by specifying a window to include all the objects you want to be in the print.

A list of options for Zoom appears on the Command Prompt line. Use the default <X/XP> option by typing in *1/48XP* (for ¼″ = 1′–0″ scale). This is equivalent to saying that you want every plotted inch to represent 48 drawing inches, or 4 feet of distance drawn.

Printing in Paperspace

One advantage of using paperspace is that you can set a sheet containing master information such as a border, project title, company name and logo, and other title block information. For items such as sheet number, notations, and drawing titles that pertain to a specific sheet, create a layer for each one of these sheets.

Creating Layers in Paperspace

Click on **Data> Layer**.
Create a new layer in a distinct color and name it LABEL, or some other name appropriate to its context. Make the new layer Current.

Click on **View> Paperspace**.
The monitor screen becomes blank, the paperspace icon comes on, and a "P" is displayed new to the layer information on the status bar at the top of the monitor screen.

Click **Data> Drawing Limits**.
Leave the lower left corner set at 0,0.
Upper right corner: 36 × 24
(In this example, a 36″ wide by 24″ high paper is used. Note that measurements are entered in *actual* values in paperspace.)

Now, click **View> Zoom> All**.

While the LABEL layer is current, you can draw any or all the information you want on the sheet. Remember, you are drawing in actual size.

So, to draw a border for the sheet in this example, with a ½″ margin all around, click on:

Draw> Polygon> Rectangle
First corner: *0.5,0.5*
Other corner: *@35,23*

Print at Actual Scale

You may print just the sheet alone. Set the plot scale to: 1 = 1.

Creating Viewports

A sheet laid out in paperspace is opaque. You can draw on it, but you cannot enter into your building or model. To do that, you need to open one or more viewports. Viewports are like holes in the sheet of paper through which you can see the building or whatever you have been creating. You can then use the **View> Floating Modelspace** option to get into the "hole" and manipulate your creation in modelspace.

Here is how to make **viewports**.

If you have made a sheet in paperspace as outlined in the previous section, and you want to use its sheet layout, make it current and set view to Zoom: All.

If you have not made a sheet in paperspace, you should follow the instructions in the previous section. Even if you have no need for a title page, you can still display your model on the sheet in paperspace.

Create Viewports

Make a new layer called VIEW in a color to make it easier to identify and set it as the current layer.

Click on **View> Floating Viewports**.
Highlight and click 1 Viewport.
There are other options that you can try out on your own.

Once you have selected an option, you are prompted to define the area within the sheet of paper in which you want the viewport(s) to appear. Use a normal method to define a window on the paper.

Print Objects with Hidden Lines Removed

In **View> Floating Viewports**, click on **Hideplot**.
When prompted to select objects, click on the frame of the viewport that contains the solid objects you want to be plotted with hidden lines removed.

Editing and Displaying Viewports

Edit Viewports

In paperspace, you can edit a viewport (not your drawings) by moving, copying, scaling, or erasing the viewport altogether.

Not Displaying Viewport Frames

When you turn off the VIEW layer, the views of the drawing remain, but the edges, or the frames, of the viewports will not be seen and your plots will not show hard edges around the views of your drawing.

Not Displaying Objects and Viewports

Turning off layers will cause the frames of viewports to not display, but the objects within the viewports are still visible. There are occasions when you want to turn off the visibility of these objects and open other viewports.

An example of this may be when you have a title page that is common to all the sheets in your set of drawings, and you have a number of sheets with different viewport layouts that show various views of the building.

Make the master (paperspace) sheet the current layer. Leave layers with viewports on.

Click on **View> Floating Viewports> Viewports Off**.
Select the viewports you want turned off.

In this scenario, the objects in the turned-off viewports will not be displayed, but the frames of the viewports are still visible. To turn those off, go to **Data> Layer** and turn off and freeze the layers of the viewport frames.

An alternate method is to use **Construct> Block**.
Block or Write-block (Wblock) the individual viewports that you do not want displayed. Use an Insertion point of 0,0. Blocking causes the viewports to disappear from the screen. You can redisplay the viewports by inserting the blocks into place.

Controlling Visibility of Selected Objects within Viewports

By freezing and thawing layers within viewports, you can set the visibility of selected objects. To do this, the objects whose visibility you want to control must be on discrete layer(s), so that turning off and freezing their layers will not affect the visibility of other objects in your drawing.

Click **View> Floating Model Space**.

Click on the **Data> Layers** dialog box.
Highlight the name of the layer containing the object(s).
Click the button FRZ in the Cur VP line.
This causes any object(s) in the highlighted layer and in the current layer to not display or plot. Clicking the THW button reverses the process.

More File Formats

Other outputs include those that are available only on the Windows platform. They are the Microsoft Windows Matafile (*.wmf*) and bitmap (*.bmp*) file formats.

Image Manipulation

For these and the other digital files mentioned earlier, numerous graphics software programs can be used to manipulate the stored images. The software used to edit, enhance, clip, or imbed images has become very much a part of the visual communication industry.

Animation software, including Autodesk's 3D Studio, can take you beyond still renderings into full-motion graphics and virtual reality.

Alternate devices allow you to encode drawings and renderings onto laser and CD-ROM disks. Recording devices such as digital cameras are now relatively easy to access.

If such services, equipment, or knowledgeable personnel are not in house, there are commercial firms that create and preserve images via the computer. Exactly what you should acquire or use depends on what you want to do with your drawings and renderings.

SUMMARY

Learning So Far

Having gone through the text of this book, you should have a better overall understanding of the functions and structure of AutoCAD, at least in versions R13c1 to R13c4. If you have followed the tutorials, you have gained some insight into manipulating and visualizing in 3D space.

What More Is There in Software?

You could migrate to R13 for Windows 95 or Windows NT. This will give you more functions and flexibility: more portability, compatibility, and multitasking with other Windows applications.

However, some aspects of R13 for Windows are the topic of criticism by some users. Its menu icons and layout are not as easy to grasp as the more logical order of the pulldown menus. Some icons are graphically esoteric and not arranged to be accessible intuitively. Tool bars are awkward to access and they easily clutter up the graphics screen, leaving little room for seeing the drawing.

Yet, to take full advantage of R13's intrinsic power, 32-bit processing, and its object-oriented technology, you have to leave DOS. You could go to UNIX or

Windows 95, but more and more software developers are using Windows NT. All these operating systems are supported in R13c4.

Hardware Enhancements

This book is about what you can learn about CAD on a basic computer. All the drawings and tutorials were done on an IBM Value Point PC with an Intel 486DX2-66 CPU. There are 20 MB of RAM, and two 200 MB hard drives. Each disk has about 130 MB of free space. R13 is loaded on one drive, while file swapping and rendering are done on the other. There is a 15″ SVGA monitor displaying 256 colors at 1048×780 resolution, with no added graphics accelerator.

This computer is sufficiently fast for drawing files of less than 1.5 MB. Beyond that, regeneration and file-saving time start to increase. Some renderings took two to three hours to complete, which may be unacceptable to those who are jaded by faster computers.

As with most high-performance CAD programs, sufficient RAM and hard disk space are the most necessary features on any hardware platform. Having an advanced graphics accelerator and upgrading the monitor would be secondarily important to enhancing performance.

A year after starting this manuscript based on using the then entry-level 486xx computers, those with the Pentium class of CPUs are rapidly becoming the standard. Having 32 MB of RAM and at least 1 GB or larger hard disk space would be a nice stand-alone computing environment for modeling and rendering architectural interiors.

CAD and Design

As mentioned at the outset of this book, design is not an exact science. It is an open-ended creative activity. As the exercises and tutorials in this book exemplify, design and designed objects are always open to further experimentation and refinement.

Learning, too, is an open-ended process. Having learned something about AutoCAD R13, you can see that there is a lot more to its use than what is shown in the book. This is also true of the process of visualization. Having learned the steps to set up perspectives and renderings, you can create other views. Those shown here are not the definitive or the ultimate ones. There are many shortcomings.

Considering the leaps and bounds in advancements of the past two decades, development in computing software and hardware seems also to be an open-ended process. Hence, you should not wait for the ultimate computing environment to come along before getting involved with CAD. It will never arrive. Instead, you can start at a basic level and still be able to create sophisticated designs.

Software and hardware are but tools. They do not create; you do. It is important to consider how you and the computer think and how you can work together in designing architectural spaces.

INDEX

Floating Model Space. *See* Model Space
Floating Viewport. *See* Viewport
Fog, (Depth Cue), 292, 293, 297–8
Follow, 78, 79
From, 6, 15, 69, 70, 155
Front, 57, 59

G

GEOMCAL. *See* Calculator
GIF (gif), 293, 296, 297, 312, 322, 336, 338
Global Linetype Scale, 78, 80, 338
Glossary, 86
Grid, 25, 69, 71
   See also Designing
   See also Drawing Aids
Grips, 14, 78, 79
Group, 69
Group Objects, 69, 72
Group Selection, 69, 72

H

HATCH, 27, 41
HtachEd. *See* Edit Hatch
HELP menu commands, 85–6
hidden lines removed display, 259–60
HIDE
   View> 3D Dynamic View>, 262
   Tools>, 80, 82, 83, 260, 291
Hideplot, 343

I

Icon, 78, 79
IconOrigin, 78, 79
Image, 82, 84, 291
   See also Background (AutoVision)
Import, 66, 64
Implied Boundary, 52
In, 57, 58
Inquiry, 69, 72–73
Insert, 26, 34
Insertion, Assist>Object Snap>, 69, 70
INTERFERENCE, 27, 39, 40
INTERSECTION
   Assist>Object Snap>, 15, 16, 69, 70
   Construct> command, 40, 43, 46
Isoline, 260

J

JPG (JPEG), 297
Justification, 30, 76

K

keyboard
   commands, 42, 56
   inputting. 14, 16–7

L

Landscape
   Edit, 292, 298
   Library, 293, 298
   New, 292, 298
lapse time for saving drawings, 81
Last, 69
LAYER, 74, 75
   in paper space, 342
Left
   View>3D Viewpoint Presets>, 57, 59
   View>Pan>, 57
   View>Zoom>, 57
LENGTHEN, 28, 48, 51
Library List. *See* Materials Library
Lights, 292, 294–5
Limits, 57, 58
   See also Drawing Limits
LINE, 26, 28
Linetype, 74, 75
Linetype Generation, 78, 80
Linetypes, 78, 80
List, 69, 72, 78, 81
List File dialog box. *See* Utilities
LMB (Left Mouse Button), 6, 14, 28
Load, Data> Shape File>, 76
Locate Point, 69, 73
Log Files, 78, 81
LTSCALE. *See* Global Linetype Scale

M

Management, 64, 68
Mapping, 292, 296–7
   coordinate system, 297
Map Types, 297
Mass Properties, 69, 73
MATERIALS
   attaching, 296
   detaching, 296
   modifying, 296
   Tools>AutoVision>, 293, 295–6
Materials Library, 296
Materials List, 296
MAXACTVP, 338
MEASURE, 26, 33, 34, 80
Menu Access (Pull-Down Menus), 86

XREF. *See* External Reference
X/XP, scale factor, 61, 342